ANATOMY OF 55 MORE SONGS

Also by Marc Myers

Rock Concert

Anatomy of a Song

Why Jazz Happened

ANATOMY OF 55 MORE SONGS

The Oral History of Top Hits That Changed Rock, Pop and Soul

MARC MYERS

Grove Press

New York

All photos printed throughout the text courtesy of Getty Images, with the following exceptions:
Chapter 14 (Joffrey Ballet): Courtesy of New York City Center. Chapter 26 (Redbone):
Shutterstock. Chapter 35 (Steely Dan): Henry Diltz. Chapter 36 (The Cars, Ric Ocasek):
Scott Weiner. Chapter 38 (Earth, Wind & Fire): Courtesy of Allee Willis. Chapter 53
(Keith Richards): Lynn Goldsmith. Chapter 55 (Sheryl Crow): Interfoto via Alamy.

FIRST EDITION

Published simultaneously in Canada
Printed in Canada

This book was set in 10-pt. Palatino by Alpha Design & Composition of Pittsfield, NH.

First Grove Atlantic hardcover edition: December 2022

Library of Congress Cataloging-in-Publication data is available for this title.

ISBN 978-0-8021-6020-1
eISBN 978-0-8021-6021-8

Grove Press
an imprint of Grove Atlantic
154 West 14th Street
New York, NY 10011
Distributed by Publishers Group West

groveatlantic.com

22 23 24 25 26   10 9 8 7 6 5 4 3 2 1

To Alyse,
Olivia, and Dylan

CONTENTS

INTRODUCTION

On a blazing hot afternoon in August of 2016, I was at the California Mid-State Fair for the *Wall Street Journal* to interview Brian Wilson and Al Jardine for my "Anatomy of a Song" column on "Good Vibrations" that appears in this book. Backstage, hours before they went on that evening, I sat with Brian on a maroon leather sofa. The temperature outside was well over 100, but the trailer we were in was in the 70s. As we caught up, I could hear an easy listening album playing lightly on a digital player next to him. I soon recognized the music. It was *The Beach Boys Song Book: Romantic Instrumentals by the Hollyridge Strings*.

The orchestral, easy listening album from 1964 was recorded by Capitol to leverage the Beach Boys' early pop success and reach the more mellow adult market. After "The Warmth of the Sun" finished, I asked Brian why he was listening to it. "To relax," he said. "The Hollyridge Strings help me relax. You know, before the show." Then I asked what he thought of the instrumental arrangements of his Beach Boys songs. "They're good. Nice and easy. It takes me back."

Brian's preconcert audio therapy made sense. Neuroscience-based studies show that songs from decades ago have the power to relax us, stir

1

up nostalgic feelings, and unconsciously rekindle memories we associate with those recordings. The reason we like to listen to pop songs from our past is that they are instantly familiar, we already know the words and music, and they transport us back to a time when our lives seemed less complicated. Whether life really was simpler is another matter. Most of us like to think so. What is true is that hits first heard during our adolescence or in college remind us of our younger selves and lower our stress levels. These days, I've found that many of us want to know how the songs that defined us were conceived, written, and recorded.

I began writing about the art of songwriting in 2011, when the *Wall Street Journal* arts editors and I launched the "Anatomy of a Song" column. My initial forty-five columns for the *WSJ* between 2011 and early 2016 appeared in the first volume of this book—*Anatomy of a Song: The Oral History of 45 Iconic Hits That Changed Rock, R&B and Pop*. Over the next five years, I wrote another sixty columns. Fifty-four of them are included here plus one written exclusively for this volume: Arthur Brown's 1968 hit "Fire," which launched shock rock and paved the way for artists such as Alice Cooper, Kiss, Iggy Pop, and Twisted Sister.

This book, like the first volume, tells two stories. Since the columns are arranged chronologically based on their release date, the newly written column introductions set the stage by shedding light on the genre of each song, the importance of the artist or band that recorded the hit and how well the song did on *Billboard*'s charts. Collectively, these introductions form a time line of rock's evolution, from pop rock in 1964 to heartland rock in 1996. The second story told is about each song's birth and development in the words of the lyricists, composers, producers, musicians, recording engineers, and others who played key roles in the writing and recording.

As with my last *Anatomy of a Song* book, the songs I chose for this volume date back at least twenty-five years. I have long felt that for a song to be truly iconic, it must be groundbreaking, influential, or have other qualities that enable the recording to remain exciting and meaningful today. Like many prominent halls of fame in sports and entertainment, a specified period of time must pass before induction can take place. Time allows a song's initial perceived accomplishments to settle in and be measured against our revised thoughts, new standards, and new works. Only then can we determine how a song has held up artistically and whether it is a true classic or was just a passing fad that excited us back then but no longer has the juice it once did. Twenty-five years is a good, solid duration for an accurate assessment.

A word on my reporting, writing, and editing process for these columns. Before interviewing sources for each "Anatomy of a Song," I did a sizable amount of research. This was necessary not only for obvious journalistic reasons but also because I always want to nudge sources beyond everything else that has been written previously about the song. Sometimes what emerges from such nudging are deeply buried emotions. In other cases, I'm able to pull loose forgotten writing and recording details. Armed with knowledge, I can plan interview strategy and know when and where to push for more information to enrich the song's story arc.

Once I've written up the interviews, I edit the result into a chronological narrative. I take steps to have the story unfold as a cinematic visual. In other words, I edited these columns as if they were movie screenplays. My goal was to create a narrative that lets you see in your mind what took place and imagine the subject is in the room telling the story directly to you. I also want you to hear the cadence of sources' voices—how they talk and how they put things. Then I tackle the fact-checking, verifying that every single piece of information is 100 percent accurate. I take this last step seriously. Music history is important and needs to be free of errors.

Over the past ten years, I have often been asked how I chose the songs to profile or why I picked one hit by an artist or band over another. It's a process guided largely by feel and what I call the "oh wow" factor. The songs I ultimately pitched to my editors had a few criteria in common. First, I looked for hits that were iconic but not tired. In other words, songs the reader will know but haven't been worn out, which would exhaust their appeal. Second, I looked for songs that played a significant role in influencing the direction of pop in general or the subcategory the artist or band was pioneering. And third, I favored songs with aspects that long puzzled readers. I liked to use the interviews to resolve them for readers. For example, who is singing, "Be quiet, big boys don't cry" in 10cc's "I'm Not in Love"? Why was "ba-dee-ya" used so prominently in the lyrics of Earth, Wind & Fire's "September"? And was Jackson Browne's "Doctor My Eyes" a metaphor or was it about a real-life trip to the ophthalmologist?

Once I had a green light from my editors, I then had to convince artists to be interviewed, which wasn't as easy as it sounds. Many artists don't like looking back at earlier recordings, no matter how successful those hits were or how sizable their royalties today. Instead, they prefer talking about what they're doing now or next. Getting them to agree is about timing and passion. Each column in this book has its own story of how I wrestled it to the ground. That's for another book.

For me, "Anatomy of a Song" has been more than a column. I was on a mission. These are the songs of my life just as they are the songs of yours or your parents. I've been driven by a love of music history and a passion for capturing as many stories behind important pop songs as possible. But not just the stories. I also wanted these stories to be told in the voices of those who imagined the songs. I wanted to convey what they were going through at the time and how they took creative ideas and turned them into records that found their way into our collections and hearts.

As for Brian Wilson, his life has been spent capturing the music he hears in his head and finding ways in the studio to make it connect with you. So Brian listening to easy listening versions of his own songs wasn't really as strange as it seems. His motive was to achieve a desired frame of mind before his concert. And isn't that why we all listen to these songs? This book will tell you how 55 hit songs were conceived and created and will help explain why you love them so much.

Dionne Warwick and Burt Bacharach in London in 1964.

1: Walk On By

DIONNE WARWICK

Released: April 1964

In the early 1960s, singles released by Motown began peaking high up on *Billboard*'s R&B and pop charts. The accomplishment was remarkable for the time, since most records by many Black artists tended to perform best only on the R&B chart. Motown clearly had figured out a formula for appealing to record buyers beyond its core Black market. Other record labels such as Scepter took notice. Founded by Florence Greenberg in New York in 1959, Scepter followed Motown's lead, signing songwriters and artists with the express purpose of releasing urban-market songs that would become mass-market hits. One of Scepter's top songwriting teams at the time was lyricist Hal David and composer Burt Bacharach.

David and Bacharach wrote "Walk On By" in 1963 for singer Dionne Warwick, whom they had just signed to their music publishing company. Interestingly, Warwick's husky, trained voice and mature delivery appealed to both Black and white young adults. At the time, the song was unusual for its sophisticated chord changes, orchestration, and lyrics written from the perspective of a woman who had been jilted by her boyfriend. Most Top 40 pop songs then were about falling in love not coping with the emotional fallout of a breakup.

After "Walk On By" was released in 1964, the single reached No. 1 on the R&B chart and No. 6 on *Billboard*'s pop chart. The song also was a turning point for Bacharach, whose music would continue to be marked by his dramatic melodies, unusual time signatures, and catchy instrumental arrangements. The single was inducted into the Grammy Hall of Fame in 1998.

Burt Bacharach
(composer)

In 1963, lyricist Hal David and I were focused on Dionne Warwick. We had signed her a year earlier to our publishing company to record our songs, and we were signed to Scepter Records. We were trying to write songs that would click with the urban market. Dionne had a singular voice that was perfect for us—young, earthy, edgy, and confident. The first three singles we wrote for her were "Don't Make Me Over" in '62 and "This Empty Place" and "Make the Music Play" in early '63. All three charted, but they weren't big pop hits. We needed to do better.

Hal and I began writing "Walk On By" in mid-'63 in our office at New York's Brill Building. I sat at our terrible upright piano, and Hal sat at a small desk with a pad and pen. Hal had just three lyric lines. They would become the song's opener: "If you see me walking down the street/And I start to cry, each time we meet/Walk on by."

I came up with a melody line and we evolved from there. Hal wrote the verses that day, and I added the music. "Walk On By" had an unusual structure, musically. Unlike most pop songs, I used quite a few minor chords in the verses. Hal's lyrics also were different for us and for most songs back then. Instead of a woman singing about falling in love, she endures the pain of being rejected and tells the guy who dumped her to keep moving when she runs into him on the street. It's about a woman's vulnerability, pride, and self-worth.

But Hal and I never thought about the psychology of the lyrics at the time. We were just trying to write songs that would click with the urban market. Hal was going against the lovestruck trend in music then, and his verses for this song focused on the heartbreak: "Make believe/

That you don't see the tears/Just let me grieve/In private, 'cause each time I see you/I break down and cry."

The chorus—repeating "walk on by"—creates a break before the verses continue, imploring the guy to keep going and not worry about her if she seems down: "I just can't get over losing you/And so if I seem, broken and blue/Walk on by, walk on by/Foolish pride, that's all that I have left/So let me hide/The tears and the sadness you gave me/When you said goodbye."

The lyric came from Hal's superiority as a wordsmith. I just wanted notes that sounded fresh against them. I wasn't trying to get the arrangement to match the lyrics' meaning. Once I had the basics written out, I made a tape of me playing piano and singing Hal's lyrics. I took it home to my apartment on 63rd Street near Third Avenue to work on. Next, Dionne came to the Brill Building to hear what I had come up with.

Dionne Warwick
(singer)

I liked the song as Burt played and sang it for me. I was in my early twenties, so we all had fights with boyfriends and told them to get lost. I knew right away I was singing a special lyric. I'm sure Hal had overheard a woman say "walk on by" to someone someplace. He told me many of his phrases came from the environment.

Bacharach

I envisioned the orchestration as I wrote out the chords and melody. Two very important elements distanced the song from being normal and were indelible. When Dionne sings "walk on by" in the verse, I wanted her to be answered not by background singers but by two flügelhorns echoing those words. The flügelhorn is fleshy and sensual. Two trumpets would have been too hard and piercing. By having the two flügelhorns play in unison, the notes would be slightly uneven around the edges and sound human.

To ensure they delivered soulfully, I wrote words on the flügelhorn parts, like "Just look in my eyes, dear." This let the flügelhorn players visualize and feel the drama I wanted in their notes. I also wanted two pianos. I had one piano play in the verses but two in the chorus. There, I had them both play accented eighth notes that formed a chord. It added a feeling of impatience. At Bell Sound Studios, we recorded two songs that day—"Walk On By" and "Anyone Who Had a Heart." "Walk On By" came first.

Artie Butler
(pianist)

When I arrived, Burt had two concert grands with the keyboards positioned at a right angle. Paul Griffin, a terrific studio pianist and a friend, was the second pianist. Burt played us what he wanted. The music was unique and complicated—harmonically and rhythmically. It was intelligent and beautiful, with sophisticated twists and turns in the melody. Burt wanted our souls in there.

Bacharach

In the intro and the verses, the sharp "shicks" you hear were created on the electric guitar by Bill Suyker. It gave the song a rhythmic, Brazilian *baião* feel that was subliminal and suspenseful. Russ Savakus was on bass, Gary Chester on drums. Before we started recording, I got them around the piano and sang each part so they knew how I wanted them to sound. Then Dionne went into the glass vocal booth and we recorded between nine and eleven takes.

Warwick

It was more like fifteen. Burt marches to his own drummer. He kept pushing for one more take, just one more that was a little better. Singing background was my sister Dee Dee, my cousin Myrna Utley, and Sylvia Shemwell. They were background singers known as the Sweet Inspirations. On top of that gospel sound, Burt wanted an airy choir. So he brought in Linda November, Valerie Simpson, Maeretha Stewart, and Elyse Brittan.

Bacharach

I wanted the deeper church voices in the core and the lighter, angelic sound to broaden the harmony on top, almost like vocal strings. I had the two groups sing an octave apart. For the strings in the second half, I used nine violins, two violas, and two cellos. But after the first or second take, I knew I had to rework the strings at the end. The part was too busy. Instead, I had them play a single note. My goal was to make all of the different elements in "Walk On By" seamless. I didn't want the listener to notice. I wanted the shifts to sound and feel totally natural.

Warwick

Scepter released "Anyone Who Had a Heart" first, in January '64. It went to No. 8. Then they released "Walk On By" in April—on the B-side. Can you imagine? My vocal on Burt and Hal's "Any Old Time of Day" was the A-side. Both were great, but "Walk On By" had the drama. Fortunately, Murray the K, the influential New York DJ, liked "Walk On By" better. He kept playing it until Scepter called to protest. So he had his listeners vote by phone. "Walk On By" won, and most DJs around the country followed his lead. It went to No. 6.

Bacharach

"Walk On By" was a turning point in my musical voyage. Looking back, the success of its sound freed me to develop irregular time signatures and instrumentation on all my songs moving forward. For the first time, I had given myself permission to use two flügelhorns and two pianos. That led me to use five pianos on "What's New Pussycat?" in 1965 with Tom Jones and a pair of flügelhorns with Dionne on "I Say a Little Prayer" in '67.

After the success of "Walk On By," I never had to worry about a record company second-guessing me. I was no longer at their mercy. I was free to explore a new approach without thinking twice about it.

11

Martha and the Vandellas, from left, Martha Reeves, Betty Kelly, and Rosalind Ashford at New York's Apollo Theater in 1964.

2: Dancing in the Street
MARTHA AND THE VANDELLAS
Released: July 1964

When singer Martha Reeves was hired at Motown's Hitsville office in Detroit in 1962 as a receptionist, she quickly became invaluable. That summer, Reeves and her vocal group, the Del-Phis, caught a break when Marvin Gaye needed backup singers on "Stubborn Kind of Fellow." The vocal group became the Vandellas and recorded their first hit, "Come and Get These Memories," in late 1962. "Heat Wave" would be their next big hit in 1963 when it reached No. 4 on *Billboard*'s pop chart.

In July 1964, Martha and the Vandellas released "Dancing in the Street." The single was unlike anything Motown had ever produced. It was funkier—with grinding horns, a throbbing bass line, and explosive drum shots on the second and fourth beats. It had enormous energy, and the song's raucous message, about people coming together and dancing in the street, resonated with Black and white audiences. Written by Ivy Jo Hunter, William "Mickey" Stevenson, and Marvin Gaye, "Dancing in the Street" became a civil rights anthem of unity several years later.

"Dancing in the Street" reached No. 2 on the *Billboard* pop chart and became the group's biggest seller. Many cover versions followed by artists ranging from the Mamas & the Papas and the Grateful Dead to a duet by David Bowie and Mick Jagger. The song was inducted into the Grammy Hall of Fame in 1999.

Ivy Jo Hunter
(cowriter)

In early 1964, I had just joined Motown as a songwriter. I knew how to create chords and rhythms on the piano but I wasn't accomplished enough yet to play them together with melodies. One day I was upstairs at Motown's Hitsville studio in Detroit in a little room with an upright piano. I was there trying to write a song—not anything specific for any particular artist. Just a song.

I often started songs by playing a bass line on the keyboard. As I played this one, I stuck to a single note, rocking my pinky and thumb back and forth an octave apart. I came up with this pulsating figure, starting with the higher note. Then I came up with a melody and chords, using the bass line's notes at the bottom of each chord. But I couldn't play all of it together, so I went to find Paul Riser to see if he could help.

Paul Riser
(arranger)

When Ivy came by, we talked through what he wanted and what I thought would help. Then I wrote it out. My job was to enhance and expand his ideas to help him achieve his dream for the song. When we were set, I sat down in the arranging department and created a skeleton chord sheet for the Funk Brothers—Motown's house rhythm section. If you gave them the basics of what you wanted, they would invent something extraordinary.

When I had Ivy's ideas down on paper, we brought the rhythm section into the studio: Earl Van Dyke on keyboards, guitarist Robert White, bassist James Jamerson, and drummer Freddie Waits. Ivy and I talked them through each of the parts. The drums and bass were most important, since they always set the feel for a Motown song.

Hunter

The goal was to come away with a rhythm track on tape that I could listen to while coming up with lyrics. The Funk Brothers ran through the music as Paul had written it and then did their thing and locked it in the pocket. Wow, they always came up with something great. When we were done, I took the tape over to [producer] Mickey Stevenson's house on Sturtevant Street. He had a rehearsal room there in his attic. I sat on the floor with my yellow pad and wrote melancholy lyrics, which is how I envisioned the music. Fortunately, Marvin [Gaye] was at Mickey's house.

William "Mickey" Stevenson
   (cowriter-producer)

Marvin and I always worked on songs together at my place. Marvin and I needed a song that day for singer Kim Weston. Kim and I were living together then before marrying in 1967. The song Ivy was working on seemed perfect for her, but Marvin had a different idea about the song's feel.

Hunter

As I wrote the lyrics, I'd sing them to the rhythm track. The music was different from what Motown had produced up until that point. Most Motown songs were based on the Charleston. This song was more like a freight train with a heavy backbeat. Marvin heard me singing to the music and came over. He thought my melancholy lyrics were off. Mickey agreed. Marvin said the rhythm track sounded more upbeat, like people "dancing in the street," which he also thought should be the song's title. As soon as Marvin said that, I knew he was right. You don't argue with the truth unless you're an idiot.

About a half hour later, I finished the new lyrics. I opened with "Callin' out around the world/Are you ready for a brand new beat?/

Summer's here and the time is right/For dancing in the street." Marvin added three cities to a verse—"Philadelphia P-A, Baltimore and D.C., now," since he knew the Motown Revue tour stops.

Stevenson

I first met Martha Reeves in 1962 at Detroit's 20 Grand club. Martha was singing there as Martha LaVaille. After her last song, I walked up to her and handed her my business card. She had talent and belonged at Hitsville. A week or so later, Martha came by Hitsville to audition, but we only held auditions on Thursdays. Meanwhile my phone was ringing off the hook, and I had to go to a meeting with Motown founder Berry Gordy. When I returned hours later, Martha had taken over the office—answering my phone, taking neat messages, handling musicians' questions, and so on. I asked if she would stay and she did.

Over the next two years, she recorded six singles as Martha and the Vandellas with Rosalind Ashford and Annette Beard. These included hits like "Come and Get These Memories" and "Heat Wave." When Annette left the Vandellas in early '64, Betty Kelly replaced her. One night in the spring of '64, Ivy, Marvin, and I were working late at the studio on Ivy's song, "Dancing in the Street." We had a rhythm track and lyrics, but we needed a vocal demo so I could play it for Kim. Marvin took a shot, but it wasn't quite right. By then, Martha had wandered down to Motown's basement studio.

Martha Reeves
(lead singer)

The first time I heard "Dancing in the Street," I was in the doorway of Studio A watching Marvin sing it. I admired him, since the Vandellas and I had sung background on Marvin's first three hits. When he spotted me, he suggested that Mickey and Ivy give me a shot. I asked the guys if I could sing it the way I felt it in my heart. They said, "Sure, go ahead." I went into the studio and put on the headphones. I sang the song with push, as if singing it to our entire neighborhood from my family's porch in Detroit. At the end, through the control-room glass, I could see Ivy, Mickey, and Marvin congratulating each other.

But Lawrence Horn, the engineer, had forgotten to turn on the recording machine. The guys asked me to sing it again. On the second take—the one you hear on the record—there was fire in my voice. I wasn't happy about having to do it twice, since my first take was perfect. While I sang, I thought about Riopelle Street, where I grew up on Detroit's East Side. We had street-dance parties there all the time. I loved the East Side. When I came up with the Vandellas' name, I combined Van—for Van Dyke Street, the East Side's main boulevard—and the first name of singer Della Reese, whose voice I admired.

Stevenson

When Martha finished singing the second take, Ivy said, "Did you hear that?" Marvin said he did. So did I. It was the sound of a hit. But I was in big trouble. The song was supposed to be for Kim, and Martha had just aced it. I headed home at around 3:30 a.m. with an acetate of Martha's demo. At the house, I woke up Kim. I told her I had a demo I wanted her to hear. Half-asleep, Kim listened and said she wasn't crazy about it. I told her not to worry, that I'd find her another song. The next day I told Paul I wanted a dense wall-of-sound arrangement behind Martha's vocal, like what Phil Spector was doing in L.A. with groups like the Ronettes.

Riser

The conviction in Martha's voice told me what was needed—a tight horn arrangement. I liked the music of classical composer Richard Wagner, especially his famous opening for "Ride of the Valkyries." I had that feel in mind for the six horns on the introduction, like a clarion call. I also overdubbed two more guitarists—Eddie "Chank" Willis, who hit a hard "chank" sound on the second and fourth beats, and Joe Messina, who played jazzy fills to enhance what we had.

Stevenson

When Paul was finished, I overdubbed some percussion, including the claves [two short wooden sticks] on the offbeats and a tambourine hit hard by Jack Ashford with a drumstick on the second and fourth beats to add snap. Paul arranged the background vocals that were over-dubbed by Ivy and the Vandellas. To make the tambourine sound even bigger, I fed the track through our echo chamber, which was a hole in the bathroom wall. By rerecording the tambourine track bouncing off that tile wall, we got a bigger dance beat.

Reeves

In August 1966, two years after the song came out, the Vandellas and I were on Dick Clark's new TV show, *Where the Action Is*. Dick had moved to Los Angeles by then, and parts of the show were taped out-doors. For the taping, Roz, Betty, and I went to the Roostertail supper club in Detroit. We had performed there many times before. Dick Clark's producer wanted us to climb a ladder to the flat roof. A phonograph inside played "Dancing in the Street" through outdoor speakers, allow-ing us to lip-sync and dance. The clip is on YouTube. The Detroit River is in the background and a lawn party is going on below.

Roz and Betty were a bit scared up there, and I gave it all I had to keep from getting blown off that roof by the wind. Crazy, but that's just how it was.

Donovan and Linda Lawrence at their wedding in Windsor, England, in 1970.

3: Sunshine Superman
DONOVAN
Released: July 1966

The first psychedelic hit to top *Billboard*'s pop chart was "Sunshine Superman," by Scottish singer-songwriter Donovan Leitch. Written as a valentine to Linda Lawrence, his love interest at the time, the song was recorded in December 1965. That year, a growing number of U.S. and U.K. pop musicians had begun to experiment with LSD, which was legal then.

Many of these artists believed that the psychotropic drug freed them from inhibitions and allowed them to take greater creative risks. Pop-rock songs that reflected the hallucinogenic feel of an acid trip soon followed in 1966. Among them were the Beatles' "Yellow Submarine," "Good Day Sunshine," and "I'm Only Sleeping"; the Beach Boys' "I Just Wasn't Made for These Times" and "Good Vibrations"; and the Rolling Stones' "Paint It Black" and "Lady Jane."

After "Sunshine Superman" was released in the United States, it reached No. 1 on the *Billboard* pop chart in September 1966. If the LSD influence in "Sunshine Superman" wasn't clear enough, the single's reverse side, "The Trip," surely was. "Sunshine Superman" also is notable for the overdubbed guitar solo by Jimmy Page, who was a

London studio musician at the time before moving on to found Led Zeppelin in 1968.

Donovan
(singer, guitarist, and composer)

I first met Linda Lawrence in March 1965 in the green room of *Ready Steady Go!*, the British pop TV show. Linda was a friend of one of the cohosts. She had an art-school vibe and, after a brief conversation, I asked her to dance to a soul record playing. As we jazz danced, I fell in love. In the weeks that followed, Linda and I spent time together. She told me she had recently separated from Brian Jones of the Rolling Stones. She said while they never married, they had a one-year-old son named Julian.

After their split, Linda lived quietly at home, building her modeling portfolio. In the spring of '65, she moved to Los Angeles to find work. Brian wasn't providing financial support, and Linda wanted to start fresh. She left Julian with her mother until she was settled. That summer, my song "Catch the Wind" became a hit in the U.S., and I wound up in L.A. to promote it. I visited Linda, and we spent many weeks together. I asked her to marry me, but she said she needed time and wanted to remain in California.

I was miserable but undeterred. Back in London, in the early fall of '65, I lived above the flat of my manager, Ashley Kozak. Missing Linda, I began to write "Sunshine Superman." In the flat's main room, I sat cross-legged on a tatami mat and played the cherry-red Gibson J-45 I had bought in L.A. As I wrote the words and music, it became an optimistic heartbreak song. Like many of my songs, it expressed hopeful melancholy.

The second line, "Could've tripped out easy a-but I've, a-changed my ways," has nothing to do with an acid trip. It means I could have allowed my thoughts to slip into depression, but I didn't. I had, of course, tried LSD by then in London. Acid was legal and it was easily available. When I wrote "Sunshine Superman," I probably had smoked a bit of herb. To take the edge off my long days promoting records, Gyp Mills, my closest friend and flatmate, and I often began the day with a joint.

"Sunshine" was indeed slang for LSD, but the reference was actually about the sun coming through my flat's window. "Superman" had nothing to do with the superhero or physical power. It's a reference to the book *Thus Spoke Zarathustra*, by Friedrich Nietzsche, who wrote about the evolution of consciousness to reach a higher superman state. "Everybody's hustlin' just to have a little scene" was about the attention that fame attracts and people who want to be part of that.

"Superman or Green Lantern ain't got a-nothin' on me" refers to my childhood obsession with comic books in Glasgow, Scotland. I had become fascinated by the Green Lantern and loved the emerald stone in his ring—a symbol of the Inner Light in all of us. "When you've made your mind up forever to be mine" was simply a prediction that, in time, Linda and I would once again be together.

In late 1965, my U.K. manager introduced me to Allen Klein, who advised the Rolling Stones and would later manage the Beatles. Klein introduced me to Mickie Most, a hugely talented English record producer who wanted to work on my upcoming third album. Mickie first asked me to sing a selection of my new songs. Right away, he chose "Sunshine Superman." It would be the first song we'd record at Abbey Road Studios in December '65.

Mickie asked me what sort of instrumentation I imagined. I said, "harpsichord, Latin drums, acoustic bass ..." Mickie cut me off and said we needed an arranger. He hired John Cameron. My guitar playing always included bass lines, melody lines, and rhythm-guitar grooves. John listened to what I was doing and expanded the parts for the band.

John Cameron
(arranger and keyboardist)

At Abbey Road, I had the song begin with Tony Carr's conga, Spike Heatley on acoustic bass, and John Paul Jones on electric bass. That set a jazzy, suspenseful mood. Then my harpsichord and Eric Ford's meowing guitar line came next, giving the song both a heritage and contemporary feel. When Don's voice and acoustic guitar join in, the song clearly is folk. It's a fascinating instrumental texture and style progression. Jimmy Page was brought in later to add the rock guitar solo. From the start,

Don wanted a light, trippy backdrop—something quite different then. But the psychedelic sound we created was an accident, really. I had never taken LSD, so I had no idea how an acid trip would translate into music. We were just shooting for a mystical feel.

Donovan

With Jimmy's guitar and John on electric bass, I had half of the future Led Zeppelin on the session. The album version of the song ran 4:42 but was cut down to 3:14 for the single. At the end of the longer version, you can just barely hear me say, "Hello John, hello Paul." I had met the Beatles by then. When the album was completed in May 1966, a legal battle began. I had become the first artist signed to Clive Davis's Epic Records in the States. Pye Records, my label in the U.K., sued, which meant that the "Sunshine Superman" single and album were held up. Legal matters were eventually resolved.

Originally, when we recorded "Sunshine Superman," it had a sub-title—"For John and Paul." But we dropped it. When the album was temporarily delayed in '66, Mickie begged me not to play "Sunshine Superman" for Paul [McCartney]. Mickie knew we had an innovative album, and he was afraid Paul would like it and be inspired. I played the album for Paul anyway. "Sunshine Superman" was a pioneering work that for the first time presented a fusion of Celtic, jazz, folk, rock, and Indian music as well as poetry. Paul liked it.

As the court case dragged on in early '66, Gyp and I decided to take a break. We went to Paros, a secluded island in Greece. One day in September, a call came for me at the village's only taverna. It was Ashley, my U.K. manager. "Get to Athens as soon as you can," he said. "There are two first-class plane tickets to London waiting for you. 'Sunshine Superman' is No. 1 in the States and in the Top 5 all over the world." From London, I flew to New York to promote the album and then on to L.A., where I first heard it on KRLA in a rented Ford Mustang. Linda, of course, was on my mind. I knew she would realize the song was about us. Five other songs on the album also were written for her.

By 1970, I had recorded six more albums and had toured to support them. I was exhausted, so I decided to retreat to the woods of

Hertfordshire, England, where I had a little cottage that I rented out when I was away on tour. One day, not long after I returned, I was sleeping upstairs when I heard a car pull up. As I came down the stairs, the front door opened and Lorey, a friend of mine, breezed in. With her was Linda, who had assumed I was away and was considering renting the place. Linda and I were both in awe.

I gave Linda a hug. Then I grabbed my guitar and we walked into the woods to a field, where we sat down. I sang her a song I was writing. A cow came along and licked her on the face and walked off. We laughed. Soon after, Linda and I moved in together with Julian, and we married on October 2, 1970. Linda and I have been together ever since.

Linda Lawrence
(Donovan's wife)

The first time I met Don on *Ready Steady Go!*, I felt something deep. But I had a young son then and I was only seventeen and a half. I needed time after Brian [Jones] and I split up. Don courted me all that summer in London and asked me to marry him when he was in L.A. I wasn't ready. Don was heartbroken, but I did love him. When I first arrived in L.A., I had cashed in my return ticket and rented an apartment on the Sunset Strip. Then my London modeling portfolio was stolen and so were the lovely lace and velvet clothes Don had bought me. I couldn't land modeling work easily, so I supported myself by making clothes and cutting hair.

One day in 1966, I was home with my best friend, Cathy, when "Sunshine Superman" came on the radio. At the end, Cathy just looked at me. "Oh my God," she said. "He still loves you."

Brian Wilson, left, and Al Jardine with the Beach Boys, rear, in 1966.

4: Good Vibrations
THE BEACH BOYS
Released: October 1966

Using the recording studio as a lab to weave musical fragments and instrumental textures into a fully realized pop song began with the Beach Boys' "Good Vibrations." Predating the Beatles' recording of their *Sgt. Pepper* album by a year, the song was produced by Brian Wilson over the course of seven months in 1966 at an estimated cost of more than $400,000 in today's dollars—a record at the time for a single.

Despite the towering expense, the euphoric psychedelic-pop love song with densely layered instrumentals and flower power vocal harmonies pioneered new standards for recording and experimentation. At first considered for inclusion on the Beach Boys' *Pet Sounds* and then expected on the ill-fated but never-completed Beach Boys' *Smile* album, the song cowritten by Brian Wilson and Mike Love was initially released as a single in October 1966.

Internal bickering among the Beach Boys and legal clashes between the band and Capitol had caused *Smile*'s delivery deadline to be extended into 1967. Then Wilson and Van Dyke Parks, Wilson's collaborator on many of *Smile*'s songs, had a falling out. "Good Vibrations" would wind up on the Beach Boys' *Smiley Smile* album in September 1967. The song quickly became a summer anthem and was inducted into the Grammy Hall of Fame in 1994. It remains a transformative work that changed how pop music was recorded, elevating the value of emotive mood pieces and experimental studio techniques.

Brian Wilson
(Beach Boys singer, producer, and composer)

When I was fourteen, a neighbor's dog barked at my mom. I couldn't figure out why. My mom said, "Brian, sometimes dogs pick up vibrations from people. If they feel threatened, they bark." About nine years later, in 1965, I was at home at my piano in L.A. after smoking a joint. I wrote a chord pattern for a song based on what my mom had said about vibrations.

Mike Love
(Beach Boys singer and lyricist)

At the end of 1964, Brian no longer wanted to tour with the Beach Boys. The stress of the planes, airports, and screaming fans at concerts was too much for him. So when the band went on tour in '65, Brian stayed in L.A. and wrote, arranged, and produced songs for us. We added our vocals when we returned from the road.

Wilson

When rehearsals began for "Good Vibrations" at Western Recorders [in February 1966], I used many of the same great studio musicians I had been recording with for several years. Most had worked with [producer] Phil Spector. I watched Phil work at Gold Star Studios in the early '60s and was blown away. Phil was a master. He combined guitars and pianos to create brand-new sounds. That's what I wanted to do on "Good Vibrations"—but much bigger and better.

Hal Blaine
(studio drummer)

We did more than twenty instrumental sessions for "Good Vibrations." At some, we'd record just four bars. Other sessions went on all day. The musicians got Brian's genius. He'd come in with musical parts written out, and we'd play them as written. Then he'd sit with us to explain the feel he wanted and listen to suggestions. He knew exactly where that song was going.

Don Randi
(studio keyboardist)

There were no vocals when I recorded on "Good Vibrations." Occasionally, I'd hear Brian in the control room singing falsetto over the monitor speaker as we played. I guess he was test-driving what we were doing. At one point, Brian wanted me to hold down a bass pedal on the Hammond organ for a long, drawn-out tone. There were screens in front of me to isolate the organ's sound, so Brian and I couldn't see each other. I just heard him over the studio's monitor speaker. He asked me to do this over and over again. Finally, I leaned over and grabbed a pillow. I set it on the pedal, rested my head, and conked out for about a minute. I woke up when Brian came on the speaker and said, "Don, that was great, thanks."

Wilson

Combining a cello and Electro-Theremin on the song's chorus was my brother Carl's idea. When I put the two instruments together in the studio early on, we wound up with this cool vibrating sound, like a humming sonic wave [he illustrates the wave with his hand].

Al Jardine
(Beach Boys singer and guitarist)

At the time, we were recording a lot of material for *Pet Sounds*. But Brian wanted to hold "Good Vibrations" for *Smile*, our next scheduled album. We begged Brian to put "Good Vibrations" on *Pet Sounds*, due for release in May. But Brian felt the song was too far-out for the album. Capitol was reluctant to release *Pet Sounds* without a hit single, so they inserted "Sloop John B," our cover of the Kingston Trio's "Wreck of the John B." This gave Brian the entire summer of '66 to work on "Good Vibrations."

Wilson

Eventually, I needed lyrics for the song. I was writing with Tony Asher then, who I had met months earlier.

Tony Asher
(initial lyricist)

I first met Brian in the fall of '65, at Western Recorders, when I was working for the Carson/Roberts ad agency. I already knew who he was. Brian was funny. When I told him I wrote jingles, he said, "I'd love to do some jingles, man." He asked if I also wrote song lyrics. I said for him I'd give it a try. Soon after, he called and asked me to come over to his house. When I arrived, we talked for an hour. Then he got a demo of the music he had been working on for the Beach Boys' next album, *Pet Sounds*. We started tinkering with a song.

Wilson

That afternoon, we had "God Only Knows" written in a half hour. Tony was amazing. Over the coming months, Tony wrote the lyrics to most of the songs on *Pet Sounds*.

Asher

At some point, Brian asked me to write lyrics for a song called "Good Vibes." He had a tape of the music, and I took it home. I felt that "vibes" was a cheap word and trivialized the song. I suggested "vibrations." My lyrics to the first verse and chorus were: "She's already working on my brain/I only looked in her eyes/But I picked up something I just can't explain/I pick up good, good, good, good vibrations, yeah." But it wasn't quite gelling, and we set it aside.

Wilson

Tony's original lyrics were good. The reason I asked Mike [Love] for lyrics had nothing to do with Tony's. I just wanted to see what Mike had. In the end, I liked Mike's better. They were more poetic for a song about good vibrations, you know? And "excitations" was very off the wall [he laughs].

Love

Brian called me sometime in the summer of '66. He said that the instrumental tracks for "Good Vibrations" were ready, and he wanted to see what I could come up with for lyrics. He never mentioned that Tony had written a set or that he wasn't satisfied with them or why. All I knew is that the song was called "Good Vibrations." While playing an acetate of the music at home, my ear went to the song's walking jazz bass line, and I came up with lyrics for the chorus [Love talk-sings]: "I'm pickin' up good vibrations/She's giving me excitations." I knew "excitations" wasn't a real word when I jotted it down. It just sounded like "excitement" and "vibrations" squeezed together.

By then, the drug culture had emerged with hippies and flower power. All of this created an image of a girl in a field of flowers, bathed in sunlight, who was into peace and love. That's what was on my mind when Suzanne, my wife then, and I drove to the studio [on August 24] in my yellow Jaguar XKE to record the vocal tracks with the guys. I still hadn't written the song's verses. I should have worked on them sooner, but I was the prince of procrastination then.

Suzanne and I had been visiting her parents in the San Fernando Valley. The drive to the studio was about a half hour. Before we drove off, I listened to the composite instrumental acetate one more time on the mini 45-rpm turntable installed under my car's dashboard. Then I turned it off. Otherwise, I would have been distracted while driving. On our way to L.A., I dictated lyrics to Suzanne. In the spirit of a flower power poem, I said, "I, I love the colorful clothes she wears/And the way the sunlight plays upon her hair." The double "I" was purposeful. The first "I" is there to grab your attention. It's almost like an ecstatic sigh—"Ahhh."

The rest of the first verse was "I hear the sound of a gentle word/ On the wind that lifts her perfume through the air." At first, I wanted to use "incense" instead of "perfume," but I thought that would be a little much for middle America.

The second verse I wrote went like this: "Close my eyes, she's somehow closer now/Softly smile, I know she must be kind/When I look in her eyes/She goes with me to a blossom world we find."

At the studio, I copied over Suzanne's notes and wrote out the lyrics for Carl, Dennis, Brian, Al, Bruce [Johnston], and myself. Brian arranged the vocals. The only change Brian made to my lyrics was dropping the words "we find" from the end of my second verse. He did this to let the bass and drums come pounding through. I thought it was weird at first, but I came to appreciate the missing lyrics, since it made the rest seem like a haiku.

Wilson

Listening back to the vocals, the song needed a downshift—a ballad section for contrast. So Mike [Love] and I sang a duet that I added as a bridge to the final chorus. It was pure and ethereal, in the style of Stephen Foster's Americana songs. [He sings] "Gotta keep those lovin' good vibrations a happenin' with her." Dennis played the organ chords, and Tommy Morgan played the harmonica solo.

Tommy Morgan
(studio harmonicist)

Brian let me do what I felt was right there for the solo. I played high on my chromatic harmonica and bent the notes. It created this unusual sound that he liked.

Love

On a later session [September 21], Brian decided Carl should record the lead vocal, since it was in his range. His mellifluous voice had this soft beauty.

Jardine

Brian was wise to have Carl sing lead on the recording. Carl was going to sing lead on the song on tour. We recorded Carl at Columbia, one of the only studios in town with an eight-track recorder. Most of the others had only four-track recorders.

Wilson

Producing "Good Vibrations" took a long time because I didn't want to copy anybody, you know? I wanted the song to sound totally original. The night I heard everything together [September 21] was one of the highlights of my life. The guys kept saying it was going to be a No. 1 hit. I said, "I know, I know."

The 5th Dimension, from left, Marilyn McCoo, Lamont McLemore, Billy Davis Jr, Ron Townson and Florence LaRue in 1970.

5: Up, Up and Away
THE 5TH DIMENSION
Released: May 1967

With the onset of darker psychedelic pop by the Beatles, the Beach Boys, the Rolling Stones, the Yardbirds, and other bands in the mid-1960s, a more harmonic and sunnier form of pop emerged on a parallel track. Songs such as the Mamas & the Papas' "California Dreamin'," the Association's "Cherish," and the Mindbenders' "A Groovy Kind of Love" climbed into the Top 10 of *Billboard*'s pop chart in 1966. This genre would later be called sunshine pop.

In 1965, Jimmy Webb wrote the words and music for "Up, Up and Away" while attending San Bernardino Valley College and struggling to make ends meet. Originally composed by Webb as a theme for a teen-movie concept that he and a local DJ cooked up while in a hot-air balloon, the song was recorded by the 5th Dimension in 1967 for their first album. It became one of many breezy hits for the vocal group.

Coproduced by Webb, "Up, Up and Away" reached No. 7 on the *Billboard* pop chart in 1967, won six Grammys, and was inducted into the Grammy Hall of Fame in 2003. The song's success solidified

Webb's reputation as a major songwriter and launched the career of the 5th Dimension, who were signed to Johnny Rivers's Soul City record label.

Jimmy Webb
(pianist, composer, and lyricist)

I was going through a frustrating period in 1965. Living in San Bernardino, California, I was failing badly in my junior college music program. Most of my spare time was spent in Hollywood trying to break into the music business. My heart wasn't in my studies. To make matters worse, I was almost eighteen with no viable means of support. My family had moved back to Oklahoma, and I was rooming with identical twins. All of us ate the same pizza and went to the all-you-can-eat bar at King Buffet twice a week.

In Hollywood, I was hustling as a freelance songwriter and starting to write part-time for Motown. During this time, I was friends with a popular radio DJ, William F. Williams, who was on KMEN-AM in San Bernardino. One day Willie came by campus to hear me play some of my songs. Then he drove us out to this hot dog stand where KMEN was broadcasting a promo for the place. If you knew what time it was, you got a free hot dog. Something that simple. At the stand, KMEN had a hot-air balloon in an adjacent lot. As part of the promo, it went up about a hundred feet with the station's letters on the side. The balloon was tethered to the ground.

As we walked toward the balloon, Willie said, "Would you like to ride in my beautiful balloon?" I was an aviation nut. My greatest joy growing up was building model planes with my father. We jumped in the basket, they fired up the balloon, and we slowly began to rise. The ascent was an epiphany. It was a beautiful day, and the sun splashed across the balloon's surface. Looking up inside, the bright colors seemed like a cathedral's stained glass window.

Seeing those colors was uplifting. Up there, Willie and I joked with each other. He said, "We ought to make one of those teen beach movies, but in the desert about ballooning." Willie went off on this stream-of-consciousness description of the movie. It could be about these kids in

Palm Springs who love ballooning and fall in love. It all sounded good to me. I said I'd write the music.

The next day, I drove to Valley College and went down to the basement practice rooms. Because of me, all the practice rooms had signs that said: NO SONGWRITING. Composing is a process and an annoyance for music majors practicing. In one of the rooms, I ignored the sign and started cranking away. I wrote a song for the balloon movie in about forty minutes. I used a line from *Superman* for the title and chorus line. On the radio, when I was a kid, Superman would say "Up! Up! And Away!" just before he flew off.

As I wrote the lyrics, I thought about the balloon's colors, the breeze, and Willie's movie idea. But I also wrote with a cinematic quality so listeners would visualize the story. The key was to hook the listener in the first line. I remembered what Willie had said to me: "Would you like to ride in my beautiful balloon?" It's a question that begs for an answer. Hearing it, the listener would think, "Huh, a ride in a balloon?" The lyrics that followed would have to feed the listener's curiosity: "We could float among the stars together, you and I/For we can fly, we can fly."

After the chorus, I worked out a nice bridge that became typical of my music. A bridge offers a musical variation of what you've already heard and builds anticipation for the next verse: "Suspended under the twilight canopy/We'll search the clouds for a star to guide us/If by some chance you find yourself loving me/We'll find a cloud to hide us/We'll keep the moon beside us." The song needed that bridge. My short verses didn't add up to a full-length song. The bridge also let me modulate from the key of G major to C, which was uplifting.

As for the song's introduction, I based the music's feel on the Association's opener for their 1966 hit "Along Comes Mary." When I finished the words and music, I went back to Willie and played it for him. I said, "Let's make the movie." Willie looked at me sheepishly. He hadn't given a film treatment much thought.

By 1966, I was working as a songwriter for singer Johnny Rivers. He had just signed a new group, the 5th Dimension, to his Soul City record label. I wrote five of the eleven songs they wound up recording on their first album. One was "Up, Up and Away." I coproduced and put together a rhythm section. We recorded a scratch rhythm track at Western Recorders. I played piano and brought in bassist Joe Osborn, guitarist Tommy Tedesco, and drummer Hal Blaine.

Then came the vocals. I played piano and rehearsed the 5th Dimension for a few days before we went into the studio. We invented a vocal harmony arrangement that worked beautifully.

Marilyn McCoo
(5th Dimension vocalist)

The first time we heard the song, Jimmy played it for us in a rehearsal space. I remember feeling happy. The melody was so beautiful. The question was how to arrange our voices so they fit the times. Jimmy made suggestions and we worked out the lead and harmony.

Billy Davis Jr.
(5th Dimension vocalist)

For the bridge, Jimmy suggested having Marilyn and Florence LaRue sing first and the guys respond before we joined together. But the chord voicings were more complex than they sound, especially the high notes. The goal was to feel the song as we sang, so it sounded as if we were up in the sky at the mercy of the wind.

Webb

When it was time to record at Sound Recorders in February '67, we ran through it for the studio musicians. They picked up what we had done and made it sound better. Once the vocal and rhythm tracks were recorded, arranger Marty Paich scored the brass and strings for the jazzy introduction and throughout. Because we had recorded the vocals before the orchestration, Marty was able to write his arrangement around the 5th Dimension's voices instead of intruding on them. He did that very carefully. We also worked hard on the record's fade at the end. As the music's volume began to trail off, the orchestra had to chase the vocals and sound as if they were all drifting away into the clouds.

When the single was released in May, Willie came in and I played him the record on the big speakers. We talked about the movie idea.

I still kick myself for not trying to realize it. Before Willie left, he said with a laugh, "Don't say I never did anything for you."

"Up, Up and Away" was even a hit on the influential KOMA-AM in Oklahoma City, near where my family lived. But that was short-lived. The station's program director thought it was about getting high and banned DJs from playing it. My father, a Baptist minister and a former Marine, got in his pickup truck and drove over to the radio station. He said, "I know my son, and that song isn't about drugs. It's about a balloon. Look at the album cover." Ultimately, he held a "prayer meeting" there and got the record back on the air.

In 1969, Dad officiated at the marriage of Florence and the group's manager, Marc Gordon. It took place above the parking lot at L.A.'s Century Plaza Hotel—in a hot-air balloon.

The Youngbloods, clockwise from top, Jerry Corbitt, Jesse Colin Young, Lowell Levinger and Joe Bauer in 1968.

6: Get Together
THE YOUNGBLOODS
Released: July 1967
Reissued: June 1969

In the early 1960s, there were two rival folk scenes on the East Coast—one in New York and the other in Cambridge, Massachusetts. Older, established artists were in New York along with up-and-coming players hoping to follow in their footsteps. They performed at a bevy of clubs and coffeehouses in Greenwich Village and in Washington Square Park. In Cambridge, promising young folk artists tended to be more experimental and eclectic in their influences. Many came out of the New England university experience and had traveled abroad, where they were exposed to different forms of ethnic music. In Cambridge, these musicians played at clubs like the Ballad Room, Golden Vanity, and Café 47. While New York players adhered to common political themes in songs, Cambridge artists preferred differences and exotic musical elements such as flamenco and bluegrass.

In 1965, singer-guitarist Jesse Colin Young and singer–bluegrass musician Jerry Corbitt met in Cambridge and began performing as a duo. Soon, multi-instrumentalist Lowell "Banana" Levinger joined, and the trio added drummer Joe Bauer. After moving to Greenwich Village in 1966, they began performing a song called "Let's Get Together," written by Chet Powers, whose stage name was Dino Valenti. The Youngbloods soon were signed by RCA.

The trio released "Get Together" on their first, eponymous album in January 1967. They performed in San Francisco several times that year, and "Get Together" became a flower power anthem during the city's Summer of Love. But the single only reached No. 62 on *Billboard*'s pop chart. Two years later, after San Francisco's counterculture expanded into a nationwide movement as hippies returned home and influenced friends, the single was reissued. This time, the song about peace and love peaked at No. 5 in 1969.

Jesse Colin Young
(Youngbloods lead singer and bassist)

I didn't know Chet Powers. He wrote the song "Let's Get Together" in Los Angeles in 1963. The title was later shortened. Between 1964 and early '65, the song was covered by the Kingston Trio, Hamilton Camp, the Mitchell Trio, and We Five. I never heard any of those versions. Back then, before the Internet, unless a song was on the radio or a friend had the record, you never knew about it. Early in '65, after the release of my second solo album, *Young Blood*, I toured the Cambridge clubs several times. At one of them, I met Jerry Corbitt, a ragtime guitar picker from Georgia.

Lowell "Banana" Levinger
(Youngbloods multi-instrumentalist)

In early '65, Jesse and Jerry were booked into a Toronto club and decided to form a folk-rock band—with drums and electric guitars and bass. They brought along Joe Bauer, a jazz drummer from Memphis who lived nearby in Cambridge, and a bassist friend of ours. The quartet called themselves Jesse Colin Young and the Jerry Corbitt Three. When they returned to Cambridge from Toronto, they landed a gig at Gerde's Folk City in New York. Jerry suggested they add me. The bass player had moved on, which left the group with three guitarists. As a result, the group's name no longer worked. We decided on the Youngbloods, since Jesse's most recent album was called Young Blood.

Young

Since we had one guitarist too many, I switched to the bass and bought a cherry-red Guild Starfire model. If Paul McCartney could sing and play bass, I'd give it a go. Down in New York in the summer of '65, the Youngbloods became the house band at the Cafe Au Go Go on Bleecker Street. We were paid just $20 a night, but the manager let us rehearse at the club.

One day that fall, I went to the club to see if the space was available for the band to rehearse. Down the first flight of stairs, I heard music and assumed it was an open mike session. At the bottom, inside the club, folk singer Buzzy Linhart was onstage rehearsing a song: "Love is but a song we sing/fear's the way we die/You can make the mountains ring/ or make the angels cry/Though the bird is on the wing/And you may not know why/Come on people now/Smile on your brother/Everybody get together/Try to love one another right now."

It was the first time I'd heard the song. I had an awakening. After Buzzy finished, I ran backstage to ask him about it. Buzzy said, "Dino wrote it." I had no idea who Dino was. Buzzy jotted down the lyrics, and I scribbled the chord changes. I went home and practiced the song on my guitar. Then I told the band about it.

Levinger

Buzzy performed the song during his sets at the Cafe Au Go Go. He used a raga-rock style, with an Indian drone behind his vocal. His ballad tempo and raga feel caught us emotionally.

Young

Over the next six months, we performed the song during our sets and developed an arrangement. In the spring of '66, we signed with RCA. By then, I was playing electric bass on "Get Together" as the song's lead instrument. Jerry and Banana's guitars framed my bass and lead vocal. Later that year, we went into RCA's studio on East 24th Street to record our first album, *The Youngbloods*.

Levinger

On the intro, I played the obbligato lines on my electric Guild M-75 Bluesbird. When Jesse began to sing, I played the fills and answered Jesse's vocal lines on my guitar.

Young

Banana's guitar gave the song a mystical, Indian feel. That was his exceptional bluegrass background. He added ninths so that chords yearned for resolution. The ninth tells the listener the song isn't finished yet, that there's more.

Levinger

In the middle of the song, I played a guitar solo. I stuck to the melody line but with appoggiatura—or ornamentation. My solo was inspired by Buzzy's raga version, which had a psychedelic flavor. I also added classical filigrees around the notes. But Jesse's vocal was really something. His singing voice was so warm and relaxed and persuasive. It sold the song.

Young

I recorded my lead vocal, with Banana singing beautiful middle harmony notes on the chorus and Jerry singing on the bottom notes. We loved the Beatles back then. Their songwriting and success proved that pop didn't have to be moronic and that folk musicians could use electric instruments and even drums. On the song's final measures, Joe struck the drums on all four beats to give the song greater urgency as it built toward a crescendo. Instead of a fade-out, we used a vocal harmony: "I said come on people now/Smile on your brother/Everybody get together/Try to love one another right now/Right now/Right now." Our voices held that last "now" as we played a series of uplifting final chords, sort of like the outro to the Beatles' "Eight Days a Week."

"Get Together" was so tightly arranged, no one at RCA dared edit down our album version for the single. The recording was pure and a self-contained art piece. Its sacred nature was apparent. But we had a problem. Soon after our album came out in January '67, we started our tour at New York discotheques. "Get Together" didn't go over too well. Brotherhood and harmony weren't priorities for young adults in miniskirts and suits and ties dancing freestyle to go-go records.

By June, our tour reached San Francisco. On June 15, 1967, we played the Avalon Ballroom and were stunned. The place was jammed with kids who just stood and listened. Until then, Banana was the only person I knew who had really long hair. Looking out at the audience at the Avalon, everyone was in jeans and colorful shirts. They all looked like Banana.

That July, "Get Together" became huge on FM radio in San Francisco. The song had clicked there during the Summer of Love, when thousands of hippies poured into the city. We played several runs at the Avalon in July and again in September and November. But "Get Together" peaked at only No. 62 on Billboard's pop chart. Remember, most TV sets were still black-and-white, and magazines' color coverage of the Summer of Love and the hippie scene was slow to roll out.

Two years later, in '69, after many in San Francisco had run out of money and headed home, the hippie movement spread throughout the country. During the week of February 17, 1969, the National Conference of Christians and Jews put out a series of public service ads on TV and radio. The ads promoted National Brotherhood Week, celebrating religious differences and tolerance. The ads used our record "Get Together" as background music. We had no idea. When Augie Blume, RCA's national promotion manager, heard the ads, he pushed RCA to reissue our earlier single. RCA executives were hesitant. Augie said, "You do it or I'm leaving." They reissued it. When the single reappeared in June 1969, it went to No. 5. Most people in the peace movement heard it as an antiwar song.

In San Francisco during the summer of '67, everyone in the Haight-Ashbury District smiled at you—the girls and the guys. It was cosmic and unifying. Everyone there wanted to learn to love one another. By '69, hippies throughout the country advocated for this and our song became a big summer hit. I don't know why we weren't at Woodstock. I have no idea if the Youngbloods were invited. Or if the promoters tried to reach us and couldn't. Or, if they did, who passed on the opportunity. Back then, we would have considered Woodstock just another one of the country's many mud festivals, and we played a lot of them. Little did we know that around 400,000 people would show up at Woodstock and that a massively popular documentary would be released a year later.

Now, of course, I wish we had been there. "Get Together" was reissued just months earlier and helped pave the way for Woodstock's spirit of unity, peace, and love. That weekend, Richie Havens opened at Woodstock and performed "Get Together." By the end of the festival, the counterculture had become the mass culture of a generation.

The Band's Robbie Robertson at his hotel before a concert in 1969.

7. The Weight
THE BAND
Released: August 1968

In the late summer of 1965, Bob Dylan needed a backup band. He was planning a national "electric" tour following his controversial appearance on electric guitar at the Newport Folk Festival. After hearing the Hawks perform in Toronto, Dylan asked members Levon Helm and Robbie Robertson to join his band. But they balked, insisting that their entire group be hired. Dylan gave in. But after his tour, in July 1966, Dylan was seriously injured in a motorcycle accident near Woodstock, New York, which forced him to take time off to heal.

Dylan rented a house painted salmon pink in West Saugerties, New York, where the Hawks rehearsed with him in the basement. The result was a series of personal recordings that Dylan would release in 1975 as *The Basement Tapes*. By late 1967, Dylan's backup ensemble decided to go out on their own as the Band. Original songs were written, including "The Weight." The enigmatic song about a traveler, the characters he meets, and the burdens they lay on him first appeared on the group's 1968 album *Music from Big Pink*.

Released in August 1968, "The Weight" only reached No. 63 on *Billboard*'s pop chart. Nevertheless, the folk-rock journey song with biblical overtones was covered by dozens of artists including Aretha Franklin, Jackie DeShannon, the Staple Singers, and the Grateful Dead, ushering in the roots-rock movement.

Robbie Robertson
(The Band guitarist, singer, and songwriter)

I wrote "The Weight" in late 1967 at a house I was renting in Woodstock, New York. All of us in the Band had been living up there while playing with Bob Dylan and recording what would become *The Basement Tapes*. We played at a house in nearby West Saugerties that we called Big Pink. Prior to moving to Woodstock, I lived at the Chelsea Hotel in New York. One day, poet Gregory Corso, who was staying there, urged me to check out the Gotham Book Mart on West 47th Street. The bookshop was a dusty, funky place owned by Fanny Steloff that sold used and new books. After looking around, I found that the store also stocked movie scripts.

I loved film and had long wondered how plot elements in a film fit together. These scripts were like blueprints. The script that punched me between the eyes was Ingmar Bergman's screenplay for his 1957 movie *The Seventh Seal*. Luis Buñuel's scripts for *Nazarín* and *Viridiana*, which examine the impossibility of sainthood, also captivated me. Up in Woodstock in '67, images from all these scripts were stirring around in my head. The Band was just finishing up with Bob, and we had already written enough material for an album we would call *Music from Big Pink*. But I wanted one more song as a fallback, just in case.

Our drummer and singer, Levon Helm, had just returned after spending nearly two years away from the music business. I wanted to write a song that Levon could sing better than anyone in the world. One night in Woodstock, upstairs in my house in a workspace next to my bedroom, I picked up my 1951 Martin D-28 acoustic guitar to write a song. I turned the guitar around and looked in the sound hole. There, I saw a label that said "Nazareth, Pennsylvania," the town where Martin was based. For some reason, seeing the word "Nazareth" unlocked a lot of stuff in my head from *Nazarín* and those film scripts.

Once I had a few chords written, I sang, "Pulled into Nazareth, was feelin' about half past dead." I didn't have any grand story planned. I don't even know where the melody came from or the chord structure. As for the words, I just knew I wanted characters to unload their burdens on the song's main character in each verse. The main guy in my song starts by asking the first person he sees in Nazareth about a place to stay the night, a biblical concept.

The chorus I came up with was "Take a load off Fanny"—not Annie, as many people think. I'm not sure I had the Gotham's owner in mind when I used "Fanny." But her name was certainly buried back there in my imagination. "Fanny" just felt rhythmic. "Take a load off and put it right on me" also was pure Buñuel. Once you lend a hand and assume someone else's burden, you're involved. "Carmen and the devil walkin' side by side" is from *The Seventh Seal* and the chess game with Death.

As the song's words came to me, I wrote them on my portable typewriter. I got used to typing lyrics from Bob [Dylan]. I never saw him write anything with a pen or pencil. He'd make little corrections on his typed pages, but everything he wrote initially went through his typewriter. There was no magic to this process. It was just that Bob knew how to type. He had taken typing in school.

"Crazy Chester" was based on someone I saw in Fayetteville, Arkansas, when I was sixteen. There was this guy in a wheelchair who was kind of nuts. He'd roll into the town square, and when girls went by, he'd call out: "Hoocha, baby, hoocha." It was like a tic. Chester was stuck in my head. The only major change I made in the entire song was the name of Chester's dog. Originally, I named the dog "Hamlet," after [bassist] Rick Danko's dog at Big Pink. I changed it to "Jack" because Hamlet didn't sing right.

When the Band got together to rehearse at Big Pink in late '67, I had a basic chord structure, a melody, and words. I taught them to everybody. At some point during rehearsals, I stumbled across Levon adjusting his drumheads and the sounds they made. I had him loosen the heads so when he hit them, the sound would slide to another tonality. The only tricky part came at the end of each chorus, when I wanted the guys to

sing "and, and, and—you put the load, you put the load right on me."
The harmony parts took a few minutes for everyone to feel.

We recorded "The Weight" in early 1968 at New York's A&R Studios. We set up in a circle. We couldn't record in isolation booths with headphones. We needed to look at each other to lock in. We were used to sitting around playing together in Big Pink's living room and basement and hearing everybody at once. Our engineer, Don Hahn, warned us we'd sound terrible in a circle, since our instruments and voices would bleed into each other's microphones.

[Producer] John Simon asked if the studio had mikes that would pick up only what was in front of them. Don suggested the Electro-Voice RE15. It was a directional mike that wouldn't pick up anything around you. They put RE15s on just about every instrument, and the result sounded really good. I decided to open the song with my Martin D-28, playing these Curtis Mayfield–like licks before the band came in. But the Martin D-28 can be a little boomy, so we moved my mike behind the guitar to give it an old, nasally sound.

In the studio, my decision to have Rick Danko step forward to sing the Crazy Chester verse came out of nowhere. It just seemed like a refreshing change to have a new character voice enter the narration. I sang it for Rick so he'd know what I was thinking, and he got it. At the end of the verse, Levon jumped back in with a "yeah!" and sang the last verse—"Catch a Cannonball now, to take me down the line"—with Rick singing background on certain words, which picked things up to another level.

We always wanted to have the song end abruptly on an unexpected chord. It created suspense and felt fresh. In some ways, the ending was cinematic, like those movies that end in a freeze-frame. The listener is forced to hear the final chord that isn't played.

At the Woodstock festival in August 1969, we performed on Sunday, the last full day, at 10:00 p.m. I'd never seen anything like it. There were nearly a half-million people out there in the dark rootin' and tootin'. They wanted excitement. Our set was more subdued. When we played "The Weight" toward the end, you could feel a beautiful somber mood come over the place. It felt like we'd caused the audience to feel nostalgic for a period they never actually experienced.

I've lost track of how many cover versions of the song there are. The funny thing is nobody knows what the song is about. So why other artists would bother to record it has always mystified me. My favorite version was the one the Staple Singers recorded for Stax in '68 soon after *Music from Big Pink* came out. The way their voices came together, it was like a train in the distance.

Before we performed with the Staple Singers for *The Last Waltz* documentary in '76, Pops Staples asked me, "Robbie, what's this song actually about?" I said, "Pops, you know as well as I do." He looked at me, laughed, and said, "Go down Moses."

As we performed, Pops sang by sliding to the notes on his guitar, and his daughters' voices slid right behind his. That was beautiful. It was like doing God's work. And maybe that's what motivated the song in the first place.

Arthur Brown on the U.K.'s *Top of the Pops* TV show in 1968.

8: Fire
THE CRAZY WORLD OF ARTHUR BROWN
Released: September 1968

Before Alice Cooper, Kiss, the Plasmatics, and other shock-rock artists and groups, there was Arthur Brown. Performance art had always been a European specialty, dating back to the start of the twentieth century. Dadaism and other art movements often used performance art to subversively chide conformity in the arts and the rigidity of society and political systems. Performance art worked its way into rock in the mid-1960s, particularly in the U.K., as British art and music schools evolved in close proximity to each other and students mingled and formed groups. Starting in 1966, Arthur Brown added costumes, makeup, and even crowns set ablaze during his performances while in Paris.

To stand out, Brown believed that he needed to engage the eye as well as the ear. He was the first rock artist to add macabre, Gothic theater to his rock performances. He cowrote "Fire" with members of his group, the Crazy World of Arthur Brown, and his upstairs neighbors. His first performance of "Fire" took place in early 1967 at London's Marquee Club before moving to the UFO Club. Then the group recorded its first album in 1968 in London.

After "Fire" was released as a single from the album in the United States, it reached No. 2 on the *Billboard* pop chart. Abroad, the single was No. 1 in the U.K. and Canada and in the Top 10 in European markets. A performance by Brown on Britain's *Top of the Pops* TV show in July 1968, complete with a flaming crown, can be seen on YouTube.

Arthur Brown
(The Crazy World of Arthur Brown lead singer and cowriter)

When I was little, I was fascinated by fire. I loved lighting matches and seeing them burn. One time my brother and I set fire to my grandfather's hair to see if it would burn. It did! Fires in the fireplace were especially captivating—the reddish-orange flames with the white and blue in the center. The concept behind the song "Fire" came early. When I was fifteen, I wrote a dramatic poem about fire that I eventually used for "Fanfare—Fire Poem," the spoken piece that precedes "Fire" on my first album. I also was very much into the Greek gods and goddesses while growing up in Whitby, England.

Both of my parents were a bit eccentric. Dad had been a Royal Air Force bomber during World War II and fancied ESP and mystical thinking. When I was twelve, my mum took me to see evangelical preacher Billy Graham when he visited England. He seemed to be as much about theater as he was about the Lord's work. After high school, I began King's College in London in 1960. I studied law but quit after a year. I had little interest. I wound up at the University of Reading. The avant-garde theater and art-music scenes were just emerging and overwhelmingly appealing.

At Reading, I formed my first band in 1963. At first, it was a modern jazz quartet. During our performance in Southampton, I heard strange noises coming from another part of the building. After our final notes, I went door to door backstage until I found one that opened. There, I saw around 1,300 people watching the blues-rock band Manfred Mann. My jazz quartet immediately became an R&B band. I sang lead. During my final year at Reading, I joined SW5, a mod band from Putney. It quickly became the Arthur Brown Union and took up residence at Jimmy James's Plughole Club.

In 1965, I decided to record "You Don't Know" for a college fund-raiser. It was a funky-jazzy take on a blues song that Peggy Lee recorded in 1958 for the B-side of her "Fever" single. I recorded it in London backed by the Black Diamonds at Marquee Studios. After the single came out, I felt pretty proud. I played it for dozens of managers and agents in London. They loved my voice but hated the song. So I set music aside and planned to return to Reading and work in a local shoe shop.

But before leaving London, I went out on the town one last time. I wound up at Le Kilt, a discotheque near Soho Square. I ordered a drink at the bar. When it arrived, the man sitting next to me placed his hand over mine. The guy was Philip Woods, the recording engineer on my recording of "You Don't Know." Philip said, "I know you, old boy. How'd you like to start a rock empire in Paris? We'd have to be there in ten days." I was game, but I didn't have a band at the time. So we formed one and named it the Arthur Brown Set. We went over to Paris in the fall of 1965 and remained there through much of 1966.

Phil was right about our reception. About two weeks after we arrived, our band was playing three sets a night, seven days a week at L'Ange Rouge in Montmartre. The club changed who I was as an artist. The crowds were far-out and let me carve a slot for myself as a performer. It was a wild scene. Instead of standing still at the microphone, the way I had been performing as a serious singer, I began to move around. I lost my inhibitions there and turned our sets into art pieces. We did a lot of improvising, and I found I could hold a scream for several bars. Onstage, we'd put on skits to the music we were playing. The audiences went wild.

I lived at Hôtel André Gill in Montmartre. There were lots of wild parties there. One morning I opened my door and found a crown with twelve candles in it. Someone leaving a party the night before must have dropped it. I loved the crown and began wearing it with candles lit in my act. Eventually the crown wore out and we fashioned an aluminum pie dish containing petrol that was held on to my head with a leather strap. Once lit, I found I could wear that pie tin crown for four minutes, max.

After one of our sets, a woman came back to our dressing room with her son, who was about seven. The kid looked up at me and said, "You should black out some of your teeth." The next day I bought some black crayons. People really liked that, too. By the summer of '66, long lines waiting to get into L'Ange Rouge were blocking the doors of neighboring mob-run strip clubs. L'Ange Rouge was shut down, so we moved on to a club in Torremolinos, on Spain's Costa del Sol.

One night before we left, I had drinks with Greg, our saxophonist. He asked what I was going to do next. I said start a new band called the World of Arthur Brown. He said, "That's a bit tame, isn't it?" I replied, "How about the Crazy World of Arthur Brown, then?" It worked. When I returned to London from Spain, I stayed at a bohemian boardinghouse in West Kensington. That's where I met organist Vince Crane, who lived upstairs. We decided to form a band, but we needed a drummer. We looked through the classifieds in the *Melody Maker* music tabloid.

We saw that a drummer named Drachen Theaker was looking for work. We set up an audition, and he got the job. At this time, a new art-rock scene began popping up around Notting Hill. I wanted to develop original songs and expand my poetry for song lyrics. I also wanted to develop the visual with costumes. At our gigs, I wanted us to take the music and performances to a new level. At some point soon after I moved into the bohemian rooming house, I sat down with Vince to write songs. On the floor above Vince's flat were two guys—Peter Ker and Mike Finesilver—working with an Iranian singer.

Vince played organ and ran a bass line on the organ's foot bars. I came up with the song's overall concept and the line "I am the God of Hellfire" and some of the lyrics. I involved Mike and Peter and used bits of lyrics from their tune "Baby You're a Long Way Behind." The first verse I came up with got to the point pretty quickly. "I am the god of hellfire, and I bring you/Fire, I'll take you to burn/Fire, I'll take you to learn/I'll see you burn." They came up with "You've been living like a little girl/In the middle of your little world." I came up with the rest. Drachen played a big part in developing the song's underlining rhythmic feel, and Vince created the orchestral arrangement.

We first performed "Fire" at the Marquee Club on Oxford Street in London. By early 1967, we were playing at a range of clubs. Some of our gigs were more successful than others. Our opening was a cover of the

Move's "Night of Fear." I'd come out with my pie pan and petrol and set it ablaze. It was quite an opening number. At the end of March '67, we started playing at London's newly opened UFO Club on Tottenham Court Road, which held an all-nighter every Friday. I swung onto the stage on a long rope wearing an orange robe. I had makeup on, and I'd sing and dance to the music. Audiences went wild.

We started to make it, theatrically. We realized that UFO audiences liked the audio-visual experience. If we just got up and sang songs like "Fire" in normal clothes, it wouldn't have made much sense. We were on to something. Even the Beatles, Tom Jones, and Pete Townshend came to see us perform. Once I began appearing in my orange robe, audiences wanted to see it with pagan symbols, so we added them. I painted my body and face. Onstage, I'd do a death dance under the strobe lights. I wore a black waistcoat jacket and trousers. There also was smoke. Soon we moved "Fire," one of our most popular numbers, to the end, so it was our showstopper.

In early 1968, we were invited to record an album by the Who's manager and producer, Kit Lambert, who owned Track Records. Pete Townshend liked us and had introduced us to him. I didn't think of it as a concept album, exactly, but as a string of poetry songs featuring the God of Hellfire. Kit warned me against developing the "Fire" theme over two sides of an LP. He felt it would be overkill and wouldn't sell. Eventually we came to an understanding. We'd do it over a single side.

We recorded our album from February to April of 1968. The demos were done at the Who's Ramport Studios. Then we recorded at different studios all over London. It was just the three of us recording. If you listen carefully to the end of "Fire," you'll hear a rising sequence that bleeds into the song's outro. There's a loud thumping sound. At the time, Kit asked Drachen what he thought they should do about it. Drachen suggested Kit run the tape of his bass drum backward, record the odd result, and overdub it onto the master. So he did. That's the thrashing sound you hear during the crescendo.

But Kit had a bigger problem. Atlantic Records in America had agreed to put out the album there, but they didn't like Drachen's style of drumming. They felt it was too jazzy and too busy and lacked a big solid beat. So British horn players were hired by Kit to add riffs to fill out the chorus and reinforce the beat. Horns also were used on the outro. They were arranged by Vince and then overdubbed.

There were many incarnations of the fire helmet over the years. The winged one that's in the 1968 *Top of the Pops* video was designed by me, artist Mike Reynolds, and a couple of techno wizards. Of course, there were mishaps. Perhaps the biggest was catching fire on a night where the stage also caught fire, sending up flames and smoke.

My two sons have old versions of the helmet, and my brother has plants growing out of the one from *Top of the Pops*. Interestingly, the plants seem to be thriving.

John Fogerty performing with Creedence Clearwater Revival in New York in 1970.

9: Bad Moon Rising
CREEDENCE CLEARWATER REVIVAL
Released: April 1969

In the mid-1960s, better artists, with the help of a new generation of producers, began to take creative control of their albums. The first wave of British rock bands tapped into American blues and included the Rolling Stones, Cream, Led Zeppelin, and Savoy Brown. In response, sophisticated American rock artists in the late 1960s turned to bluegrass, mountain music, rockabilly, and honky-tonk for inspiration. Among them was Creedence Clearwater Revival, formed in 1968 by John Fogerty.

The group's first song to chart was a cover of "Suzy Q," originally cowritten and recorded by Dale Hawkins and released in 1957. CCR followed with a cover of Screamin' Jay Hawkins's 1956 hit "I Put a Spell on You." The third was "Proud Mary," an original written by Fogerty that climbed to No. 2 on *Billboard*'s pop chart. Eager to put another song on the charts that would strategically ascend while "Proud Mary" was in descent, Fogerty wrote "Bad Moon Rising."

After the single of "Bad Moon Rising" was released in April 1969, it, too, climbed to No. 2. With its astrological lunar reference and warnings of bad things to come, the song was thought to reflect both the cosmic ethos of the hippie movement and the foreboding late 1960s. In truth, the song poked fun at astrology and had little to do with current events.

John Fogerty
(Creedence Clearwater Revival lead vocalist, lead guitarist, and songwriter)

In 1967, I bought a little notebook to jot down song title ideas. I was living in the San Francisco Bay Area, and the band had just changed its name from the Golliwogs to Creedence Clearwater Revival. During the Summer of Love in '67, the hippie movement was becoming quite a thing. Astrology was the rage, especially phrases like "Capricorn rising" and "the moon is in the seventh house." I poked fun at that stuff, like we do with UFOs. When asked about my sign, I told people I was a double asparagus with a broccoli rising.

But after hearing all those astrological phrases along with lunar names like harvest moon, hunter's moon, and wolf moon, the idea of a "bad moon" popped into my head. I wrote it down in my new notebook. But when I looked at the phrase, it felt flat and incomplete. What's a bad moon? So I added the word "rising," to give it action and define its intentions. Next, I had to figure out how to turn it into a song.

Our first album under our new name came out in May '68. My cover of "Suzie Q" was our first hit, but it was a novelty song. Unless we had a solid follow-up, I worried we'd be a one-hit wonder. When the band recorded *Bayou Country*, our second album, in October '68, I knew our big single had to top our last one. "Proud Mary" was the first single released. As it shot up the charts, I felt we needed another single fast, even before recording our third album. "Proud Mary" would eventually slide, and I didn't want too much time to elapse between hits.

My intention was for us to get on the radio and never get off, like one long possession of the football. I started flipping through my notebook and landed on the phrase "bad moon rising." As a child, I loved the 1941 movie *The Devil and Daniel Webster*. In a nutshell, it's about a New Hampshire farmer who makes a pact with the Devil to enrich himself in exchange for his soul.

But when it was time for the Devil to collect, the farmer enlists the help of attorney Daniel Webster to get him out of the jam. What I remembered most is this furious storm the town endures. All of my lyrics for the song were inspired by that scene: "Don't go around tonight/Well it's bound to take your life/There's a bad moon on the rise."

The next verses were about the storm: "I hear hurricanes a-blowing/I know the end is coming soon/I fear rivers overflowing/I hear the voice of rage and ruin/Hope you got your things together/Hope you are quite prepared to die/Looks like we're in for nasty weather/One eye is taken for an eye."

I wrote the song's words and music in a small house that my then wife and I were renting in El Cerrito, California. There was a pocket room between the living room and kitchen that was about twelve feet square. It was my tiny songwriting sanctuary, more of a mental space than a true office or den. In that room, I figured out the chords to "Bad Moon Rising" on my Gibson ES-175, a jazz and country guitar.

One day in January '69, after I began showing the rest of the band what I had come up with for "Bad Moon Rising," I drove to Oakland to visit Fantasy Records to see how our albums and singles were selling. I parked my Peugeot in front of the building. When I came out about an hour later, someone had thrown a brick through the rear-door window. My Gibson and the little Fender Tremolux amp and speaker that I'd bought in tenth grade were gone.

I was heartbroken. I drove straight to a music store in nearby Albany. I'd heard that Jeff Beck, Jimmy Page, and Eric Clapton all played Les Paul guitars through a Marshall amp. In the store, I took down a Les Paul Custom and tuned all the strings down a whole note and strummed a great big D chord. It sounded great. I bought the Les Paul. It made "Bad Moon Rising" sound big and ominous.

In early February '69, the band flew down to RCA Studios in Los Angeles. I had written "Lodi" at the same time, so we'd have a song for the B-side of the new single. We went to RCA because that's where we had recorded our album, *Bayou Country*. That day, we just recorded the music. I purposefully didn't record my lead vocal or background vocals. The reason for this was my love as a kid for '50s singer-guitarist Gene Vincent. He used to do this to get great instrumentals. I wanted that same feel on "Bad Moon Rising."

As a result, the guys in the band didn't hear my vocal or even the song's melody until the record came out. We just focused on the music. On the session, I played my tuned-down Les Paul. Tom, my older brother, played his 1967 Rickenbacker 360 guitar. Stu Cook played a 1967 Fender Precision bass, and Doug Clifford played his Camco drums.

The instrumental arrangement I wrote was influenced by Elvis Presley's "I'm Left, You're Right, She's Gone." Even as a kid, I thought the 1955 Sun record was peculiarly melancholy. I loved Scotty Moore's guitar lick on there. It came from that early period in Elvis's career where they were kind of playing country but inventing rock 'n' roll at the same time.

On "Bad Moon Rising," I played that rockabilly lick, channeling Scotty Moore as best as I could. A week or so later, I returned to the studio to add my lead vocal and overdub the lead guitar parts so they'd be doubled on the record. I sang my lead vocal with slap-back echo to give my voice a Sun sound. Elvis was on my mind while I sang.

But the echo obscured my last line of the chorus. Instead of hearing "There's a bad moon on the rise," some people heard "There's a bathroom on the right." Now, when I perform the song, I poke fun at it by singing the incorrect lyrics.

In 1986, I was at a music awards event when out of nowhere, someone wrapped his arms around me from behind. "Give me back all my licks," he said, laughing. It was Scotty Moore. He knew I was a huge fan from the way I played on "Bad Moon Rising." When I turned to talk to him, I was metaphorically down on my knees thanking him. That's when I realized that between Elvis and *The Devil and Daniel Webster*, there's quite a bit of my childhood in that song.

Tommy James and the Shondells, from left, Ronnie Rosman, Mike Vale, Tommy James, Peter Lucia and Eddie Gray in New Jersey in 1968.

10: Crystal Blue Persuasion
TOMMY JAMES AND THE SHONDELLS
Released: June 1969

LSD was legal in the United States until late 1966, when California and Nevada banned the psychedelic drug. The country's remaining forty-eight states soon followed. But these laws didn't stop rock and soul artists from creating music that emulated the vibrant experience of an acid trip. Nor did the laws halt concert promoters, record-company art directors, and advertisers from using psychedelic imagery to market what they were selling. Among the many albums with trippy covers were Donovan's *Sunshine Superman*, Cream's *Disraeli Gears*, the Zombies' *Odessey and Oracle*, the Lemon Pipers' *Green Tambourine*, and the Beatles' *Sgt. Pepper*, to name just a few.

But not all songs with a psychedelic feel were about LSD. One example is Tommy James and the Shondells' "Crystal Blue Persuasion." The song first appeared on the group's late 1968 *Crimson & Clover* album, which had a psychedelic cover. Long thought to be a metaphor for a hallucinogenic experience, the song, with its dreamy, sunny feel, was in fact inspired by the euphoria of the Bible's Book of Revelation and the Young Rascals' 1967 hit "Groovin'."

The song's single wasn't released until June 1969 as an afterthought following the success of two other hit songs from the album—"Do Something to Me" (No. 38) and "Crimson and Clover" (No. 1). "Crystal Blue Persuasion" reached No. 2 on the *Billboard* pop chart, helped by horns that Tommy James added to the single version for a soulful, AM radio punch.

Tommy James
(Shondells founder, lead singer, guitarist, and songwriter)

In early 1968, I was performing with the Shondells at a small college down South. By then, we had ten charted hits, including a No. 1 with "Hanky Panky" and two in the Top 5—"I Think We're Alone Now" and "Mony Mony." During a meet and greet backstage after the show, a student with thick-rimmed glasses wearing a short-sleeve shirt and tie came up to me. Nervous, he handed me a sheet of notebook paper. At the top was a title: "Crystal Persuasion." The rest was a religious poem he had written, inspired by the New Testament's Book of Revelation. He urged me to keep it. Then he took off.

I folded the paper and put it in my pocket. I, too, had been struck by the Book of Revelation. I was brought up in the Catholic Church in Michigan, but religion wasn't that meaningful to me when I was little. Then, in '67, I became a born-again evangelical Christian after watching Billy Graham preach on TV. Graham's simple, elegant message hit me between the eyes. I noticed the student had used chapter 22 of the New Testament for inspiration: "And he showed me a pure river of water of life, clear as crystal, proceeding out of the throne of God."

Back at our hotel that night, bassist Mike Vale and guitarist Eddie Gray and I sat with our guitars writing songs. As we talked, Eddie was fooling around with this two-chord riff. I liked it and told the guys about the student's ethereal poem. As Eddie kept the riff going, we came up with secular lyrics that were in sync with the late '60s and our sound. As we jammed on the riff, I came up with: "Look over yonder/What do you see?/The sun is a-rising/Most definitely/A new day is coming/People are changing/Ain't it beautiful?"

I liked "crystal persuasion" for the chorus line, but it needed an extra syllable so the phrase would sing well. I suggested "blue," a soft, easygoing word. The guys agreed and the line became "crystal blue persuasion." It was all very late '60s. Mike came up with a couple of lines, I added more and Eddie played Spanish flamenco guitar parts for flavor while I picked up the two chords he had been playing.

We finished in about a half hour. The song kind of fell out of our faces. It was about peace, good, and brotherhood. We all loved "Groovin'" by the Young Rascals when it came out in '67. Unconsciously, we may have felt that song as we created a Latin vibe for "Crystal Blue Persuasion." We knew we had something, so that summer we went to New York to record it for our next album. It wound up being the toughest song I ever produced.

At Allegro Sound Studios, I had us record the basic rhythm track like a rock song. We used a full set of drums, three different keyboards, and a bunch of guitars. But when we listened back to the track, it was a drag. I had overproduced it. There was too much going on, and it lost the groove we had come up with in the hotel. So I spent the next month in the studio unproducing it.

At the mixing console with engineer Bruce Staple, I started by pulling out the drums except for my bongo. Then I pulled out all the guitars except my tremolo on an acoustic and my two-chord rhythm riff that I played on a Fender Jazzmaster. I left in Eddie's flamenco runs on his Martin acoustic and Mike's bass. All the keyboards were removed except Ronnie Rosman's Hammond organ. That worked. With the basic rhythm track in place, it was time to overdub, strategically. I didn't want to wind up with clutter again.

From the start, I played the bongo at the beginning to count off the beat for the guys so they knew when to come in. We kept the bongo for the song's intro. It created suspense and foreshadowed the Latin groove. On my lead vocal, I added tape delay, which repeated what I sang a fraction of a second later. The result was depth and dimension. We had been using tape delay on our music for some time. It kicked our records up a notch and was part of our signature sound.

For the background vocals, drummer Eddie, Mike, and I added our voices as we went along, singing in falsetto. The tape delay pulsed and made the voices sound hypnotic. But I still felt this wasn't enough. Songwriter Doc Pomus once told me, "We're not writing songs, we're writing records." In the studio, you're not just creating music but magic moments listeners will remember. So just before the third verse, I had the music and vocals change keys by going up a half step, from A to B-flat.

You can hear the shift just before we sing, "Maybe tomorrow/When he looks down/On every green field/And every town." By moving up a half step, you feel a release and a sense of euphoria. I also wanted a different feel at the end. Originally, the song just faded out. But I felt something more had to happen. So toward the end, when we repeatedly sang "crystal blue persuasion," the instruments start playing in double time, like a racing pulse, to close out.

The next day, I took a tape of the finished song up to our label. Morris Levy, the head of Roulette Records and a gruff street guy, loved Latin jazz. He listened and flipped. He said, "I like that. Where'd ya come up with that one?" He played it for everyone he knew.

Ahead of the album's release in December 1968, we put out "Do Something to Me" in October and then "Crimson and Clover" in November. Then the label wanted to put out "Crystal Blue Persuasion" as a single in June '69. I went back into the studio to edit the four-minute album version to a slightly shorter single. I did several mixes before realizing the third verse needed a soulful punch for radio airplay.

I'd been fascinated by the horns on Hugh Masekela's No. 1 single of "Grazing in the Grass" that came out in May '68. So I added horn riffs as background in our third verse. They're only on the single. I also recorded another lead vocal track on top of my existing one to widen it. The song had to have a big, commercial sound to be an AM radio hit.

I never heard from the nervous student with the poem. That's how the good Lord works. Subtle things happen in life that don't seem important, but they turn out to be.

Diana Ross in Los Angeles in 1975.

11: Ain't No Mountain High Enough
DIANA ROSS
Released: July 1970

Written by Nickolas Ashford and Valerie Simpson in 1966 for Motown's Tamla Records, "Ain't No Mountain High Enough" was recorded first by Tammi Terrell and Marvin Gaye in 1967. It was the first in a series of duets by Terrell and Gaye, who were positioned on recordings and on TV as a romantic couple singing love songs to each other. As one sang, the other responded, and their duet format became highly successful even though, in the studio, Terrell typically recorded her parts first and Gaye's vocal was overdubbed later. Their single of "Ain't No Mountain High Enough" peaked at No. 19 on *Billboard*'s pop chart.

In 1969, as Diana Ross's popularity surged, she was considered by Motown to be more valuable as a solo artist than the Supremes' lead singer. Conflict within the group had already heated up as the trio's chart success declined in 1968 soon after their chief songwriters, Lamont Dozier and brothers Brian and Eddie Holland, left Motown. The time had come for Motown to position Ross as a superstar. She left the Supremes in early 1970.

For her first album—*Diana Ross*—the singer was urged to rerecord "Ain't No Mountain High Enough." There was some hesitation on her part, since the song had already been a hit and Ross wouldn't be singing to a male partner. As a result, the song needed a dramatic update. To give it a majestic feel, an arrangement was written that turned the song into a power ballad, with Ross's vocal starting off soft and building to a crescendo before sailing into a euphoric finale. The move to cover and rearrange the song turned out to be a smart one. The single hit No. 1 on the *Billboard* pop chart.

Valerie Simpson
(pianist, background singer, and cowriter)

I first met Nick Ashford in church in 1962. He had just graduated from high school in Michigan and came to New York to be a dancer. But his auditions didn't work out, and he wound up homeless. He was staying at a friend's apartment on Manhattan's Upper West Side. I was still a senior in high school then and sang in the choir at the White Rock Baptist Church in Harlem. I also sang in the Followers, a gospel vocal group. One day, I saw Nick standing in the back of our church as we sang. He was there looking for a hot meal.

By then, Nick was singing with a New York gospel group. After we were introduced by his friend, I talked him into joining the Followers. In early '63, the Followers performed at Sweet Chariot on West 46th Street. We had a nice run there until May, when the club was picketed by a Harlem church. The minister felt gospel had no place in a club. The experience informed Nick and me to stick together as songwriters. Nick was the perfect mouthpiece for my melodies, and my piano inspired his lyrics. It was an easy relationship.

Our first hit, "Let's Go Get Stoned," was written with Joshie Armstead for the Coasters in 1965. Ray Charles recorded the song a year later and had a No. 1 R&B hit. The song's success brought us to the attention of songwriter Eddie Holland at Motown. To do well there, Nick and I knew we needed a great song. Nick told me about lyrics he had recently written while walking down Central Park West. During his walk, he worried about whether he'd be able to remain in the city. That's when he noticed that the buildings along the park looked like mountains.

Words came to him: "Ain't no mountain high enough/Ain't no val-ley low enough/Ain't no river wide enough/To keep me from getting to you." The "you" here meant success. I loved the lines, and we used them to write a love song. When we were done, we recorded a demo with me on piano and Nick singing. Motown loved it and wanted the song for singer Tammi Terrell. She hadn't had a big hit yet.

Paul Riser
(arranger-conductor)

I first heard the demo in my Motown office in late '66. I liked it. The song had sensitivity and strength. The first thing I did was record the rhythm track with the Funk Brothers, the label's house band. That famous rattlesnake sound in the introduction—"tick-a-tick-a-tick"—was Uriel Jones hitting the metal rim of his snare drum with his sticks. I wanted those there to build suspense before Tammi's lead vocal came in.

After Tammi recorded her vocal, the producers decided the single would be stronger as a duet. Months earlier, Marvin had a hit with Kim Weston on "It Takes Two." So Marvin was added to Tammi's record to help its odds on the charts. Marvin was amazing. He overdubbed his vocal so it wrapped around hers, as if the two of them were in love, singing to each other in the studio.

Mary Wilson
(Supremes founding vocalist)

Tammi had a great record with "Ain't No Mountain High Enough." In October '67, she collapsed onstage while performing with Marvin. Doctors later diagnosed she had a brain tumor, which kept her from touring. The following spring, the Supremes—Diana Ross, me, and Cindy Birdsong, who had replaced Florence Ballard months earlier—recorded "Ain't No Moun-tain High Enough" for a duet album with the Temptations. On the song, Diana sang the vocal with Dennis Edwards, who had just joined the Temps.

I don't recall us performing the duet on the road. It was too intricate for the Supremes and Temps to sing together onstage. Besides, there wasn't much point rehearsing it. There were rumors that Diana was about to leave the Supremes to become a solo artist.

Simpson

When Diana was planning to leave the Supremes in the fall of '69, [Motown founder] Berry Gordy asked Nick and me to produce her first album. Nick and I wanted one of our songs to run longer than the usual three minutes. At the time, artists such as Isaac Hayes were doing this. We decided to try it with "Mountain." But we needed a different approach so it sounded new. Nick suggested we have Diana narrate an extended verse. He thought she had a great speaking voice, so he wrote new lyrics.

Once his monologue for Diana was completed, I worked on a new structure for the song. I created an introduction that began as an instrumental and led into a choir that set up Diana's spoken voice. We delayed the song's familiar chorus—"Ain't no mountain high enough/Ain't no valley low enough"—until about four minutes into the song and treated it as the climax. We held the chorus back because listeners already knew it and expected it would come eventually.

Riser

When Valerie and Nick gave me their new piano-vocal demo, it was precisely structured. Listening to Valerie's piano, I felt the song called for a majestic, symphonic approach. Since the chorus didn't come until late, I wanted the choir in the introduction to sing the chorus as "ahhhs." This worked like a Broadway musical overture, teasing what was coming later in the song.

Simpson

When we began to record, we did the rhythm track first at Motown. I played piano with the Funk Brothers studio musicians. That's me on the record throughout.

Eddie Willis
(Motown guitarist)

Valerie's piano was cold-blooded. Man, she could really play. She told each of us what to do, and we stayed close to what she wanted. Even though there were three of us on guitar, we never got in each other's way.

Riser

After the rhythm track was done, we flew to New York to record the strings and brass.

Simpson

After New York, we overdubbed the choir parts and background vocals at Motown. For the choir, Joshie Armstead sang the top notes, I sang in the middle, and Nick was on the bottom. On the record, you can hear Joshie singing like her life depended on it. Then I overdubbed the Andantes, Motown's studio vocal group, filling in around us.

When all the music and background vocals were on tape, we had Diana come in to record her vocal. I wanted everything done so she'd hear all of it in her headset. We really got the best out of her. Producing is about getting something special out of an artist. We stretched Diana. She could do it, and she didn't mind going for it.

But when we gave the song's final 6:18 mix to Berry, he felt it took too long to get to the chorus. Nick and I thought about it and listened to it several times. We agreed we didn't want to move things around. Nick said to Berry, "It's like an orgasm. You don't have it immediately. It builds."

That was fine for the album, but Berry insisted we at least cut it down for the single. Nick and I resisted at first, so Berry held off releasing it as the album's first single. Instead, he released Diana's "Reach Out and Touch (Somebody's Hand)." Eventually I edited the song down to 3:32 so we could get it out. But many radio DJs played the album version instead. Nick and I felt vindicated.

When I hear Diana's version today, I'm proud of how it came out. I'm also amused by how many people think the original and Diana's solo version are two completely different songs with the same title. Proof that Nick and I accomplished our goal—creating a new version for Diana's solo debut.

In the years that followed, something happened between Nick and myself. I'll just say that when you're writing love songs all day long with someone, you can wind up falling in love. We did, and Nick and I married in 1974.

Black Sabbath, from left, Bill Ward, Tony Iommi, Ozzy Osbourne and Geezer Butler, in 1970.

12: Paranoid
BLACK SABBATH
Released: August 1970

One of the earliest hard-rock bands to influence the emergence of heavy metal in the 1970s was Black Sabbath. Formed in Birmingham, England, in 1968, the band went through a series of name changes until August 1969, when they took the name Black Sabbath. The name's inspiration has several different backstories, but several band members have agreed that bassist Geezer Butler first came up with it after waking up from a nightmare. With the new name in place, the band's goal was to create music and imagery that would mimic horror movies and capitalize on the genre's popularity.

In early 1971, Black Sabbath released its second album, *Paranoid*, in the United States. The band became one of the first to pioneer what guitarist Tony Iommi called heavy rock. The subgenre is marked by a massive metallic sound driven by power-chord guitar riffs, wailing guitar solos, distortion, shrieking vocals, and dark, Gothic imagery.

Written by all four band members, the album's title song was released as a single in September 1970. While it only reached No. 61 on the *Billboard* pop chart, the song's FM popularity helped push the album to No. 12. The single and album versions were identical, both clocking in at 2:48.

Ozzy Osbourne
(Black Sabbath lead singer and cowriter)

Growing up in the Aston section of Birmingham, England, I had one pair of pants. Our house was tiny, and my mum and dad were factory workers with six kids. We had zero. At home, we'd put on family shows. My sisters sang, and we'd eventually get around to a singalong. But I didn't take singing seriously until I heard the Beatles.

You have to understand, the arrival of the Beatles was like going to bed one night when everything was gray and dismal and waking up to a world that was sunny and alive. The Beatles painted a bright future for kids. I imagined Paul McCartney marrying one of my sisters.

As soon as I was able, I worked. I had jobs in a slaughterhouse, in factories, and on building sites. But I couldn't seem to hold on to a single one. My first "musical" job was testing car horns. My mother used to work on the factory floor of a company that made car parts. I'd be there in a soundproof booth listening to different types of horns. It drove me nuts.

I wasn't cut out to work nine to five. I couldn't do it. My attention deficit problem made working a monotonous job impossible. When I was seventeen, my father went into debt to buy me a small sixty-watt Vox speaker system with a microphone. That got me gigs. No other area band then had a singer with his own PA system.

In 1967, I joined a band with local guys. We called ourselves Rare Breed. Then we were Earth. In '69, [bassist and lyricist] Geezer Butler came up with a new name, Black Sabbath, mentioning it first on a ferry returning home from gigs in Hamburg, Germany. He said Earth wasn't a powerful enough name. At Birmingham pubs, we played hard rock and tried to change the vibe. We never called our music heavy metal. I never got my head around that term. It's meaningless.

We just played rock in an uncommercial way. The only competition we had then was Deep Purple, Led Zeppelin, and maybe Leslie West's

Mountain. There was nobody else like us. We were punks before punks. Eventually, in 1969, we were signed to Vertigo Records. We recorded our first album, *Black Sabbath*, in no time in late '69. We could do it fast because we had broken in our songs at gigs on the road before we recorded.

Tony [Iommi] would come up with whacked-out riffs like no other guitarist. Whenever he came up with a riff for a song, I'd go, "You ain't gonna top that one. That's unbelievable." But he would, every time. Geezer was very clever with words. When we finished recording songs for our second album in London, Rodger Bain, our producer, said we needed one more, about three minutes long. He said, "Just jam something."

Tom Allom
(recording engineer)

It was evening when Rodger noticed we needed another song. Tony stayed behind at Regent Sound Studios on Tottenham Court Road to work on the riff. The rest of us went off to a pub on nearby University Street. Before long, Tony came by. He said he had come up with an idea. We had another round and went back to the studio.

Osbourne

Tony played us the riff, and I hummed to get the pattern of the song for the melody. I can't play a musical instrument, I don't read music, and I didn't write the lyrics on this song. But I have this natural sense of melody. Sometimes, if I couldn't hum a better melody than what Tony was playing, I'd just join him on his riff. That's what I did on "Paranoid" [Osbourne scats the melody].

Allom

We recorded the band's instrumental tracks for "Paranoid," and Ozzy's scatting, at Regent, where I worked as a staff engineer. We only had a twelve-input console and a small array of mikes. Bill Ward's drums were handled with four mikes. Tony's guitar in that tiny studio was phenomenally loud. We just stuck two mikes six inches from his two cabinets. Each held four, twelve-inch speakers.

Osbourne

Once I had the song's melody, Geezer wrote lyrics for it. He came up with the title—"Paranoid." I kind of knew what paranoid meant. It was a word being used a lot around then. People would say, "Oh, he's paranoid." But I wasn't really sure. I said to Geeze, "What does 'paranoid' mean?" He freaked out that I didn't know.

Allom

Ozzy's lead vocal on "Paranoid" was done about a week later at Island Studios on Basing Street in Notting Hill. Ozzy put on the headphones and recorded his vocal. He kind of followed Tony's guitar riff. The way Ozzy set the melody in sync with the guitar riff was brilliant.

Osbourne

I recorded the words Geeze wrote out. But at the time, I didn't know what they meant either. I just knew the song made me feel good. My vocal on "Paranoid" was pure emotion. It's the way I sing. The soul came from where I grew up, where life was poor and freaking painful.

Allom

Rodger had this way of producing Sabbath that was very simple and straightforward. It was pretty dry—not too much reverb. Just a little bit of a slap-back delay on Ozzy's voice to give it an Elvis Presley feel.

Osbourne

Originally, the title of our second album was going to be Walpurgis, which was the name of one of our songs. It was some kind of pagan thing. We figured we'd play off a black magic theme, a witches' night or something. At some point, Rodger said, "What does 'Walpurgis' mean? Why don't you call it 'War Pigs'?" I thought to myself, "What's a war pig?"

But rather than call the album "War Pigs," the record company changed it to "Paranoid." Once they heard the song, they realized it had potential as a single. But the artwork was already done, so they kept the war pigs on the cover. After the single came out in the U.K. in the fall of 1970, we sang "Paranoid" on Britain's *Top of the Pops* TV show. I have no idea if the audience got what we were doing. The song was so different from any of the other pop acts on the show.

"Paranoid" is a part of me now. I sing it at every gig. It's my encore and my anthem. It's ingrained into my soul. "Paranoid" is Ozzy, and Ozzy is "Paranoid."

The Grateful Dead, clockwise from top left, Bob Weir, Phil Lesh, Bill Kreutzmann, Ron "Pigpen" McKernan, Mickey Hart and Jerry Garcia in 1970.

13: Truckin'
GRATEFUL DEAD
Released: November 1970

Few rock bands toured as often or performed longer concerts than the Grateful Dead. Starting in 1967, you'd be hard-pressed to find a venue where they weren't on the poster or handbill. If a festival called to book them, the Dead would be there. The San Francisco band understood early the value of word of mouth and thrived on jamming for loyal audiences, which began following the group from concert to concert. These traveling audience members became known as Deadheads.

In 1969 and early '70, the Grateful Dead were on a particularly grueling national tour, in some cases playing multiple sets over multiple nights at the same venue. Their calendar was full. To save money, they stayed at budget hotels and motels. Their song "Truckin'" detailed the band's travels—and their troubles—during those months.

Recorded for the Dead's *American Beauty* album in September 1970, "Truckin'" was released two months later as an edited single and peaked at No. 64 on *Billboard*'s pop chart. When FM radio embraced the song's longer album version, the song became a counterculture anthem, helping *American Beauty* reach No. 30 on the album chart.

Bob Weir

(Grateful Dead lead singer, rhythm guitarist, and cowriter)

While we were on tour in early March 1970, Robert Hunter, a friend and superb lyricist who traveled with us on the road, pulled a lyric sheet out of his luggage and gave it to Jerry [Garcia]. Though Robert was a terrific guitarist, he didn't play with us. He'd come up with words for songs and we'd craft music and vocal harmonies for them. On this particular day, Hunter's title at the top said "Truckin'." Jerry liked what he read, and we planned to work on the music as soon as we had some downtime.

The word "truckin'" goes back to music of the 1930s. But Hunter probably grabbed the title from Mr. Natural, one of artist R. Crumb's underground comic characters. Mr. Natural had a bunch of sayings. One of them was "Keep on Truckin'," which was the spirit of our song—keep boogying on. At first, the meaning of Hunter's lyrics was a mystery to us. But the words became clear the more we read them. For example, Hunter included our New Orleans incident two months earlier in January.

After we'd played a gig at the Warehouse there, we returned to our hotel to find that the cops had searched our rooms and found our stash. A bunch of us were arrested, but a settlement was reached. Hunter's lyric was "Busted, down on Bourbon Street/Set up, like a bowlin' pin/ Knocked down, it gets to wearin' thin/They just won't let you be."

In the verse "Dallas, got a soft machine/Houston, too close to New Orleans/New York got the ways and means/But just won't let you be," Dallas's "soft machine" was the police there. Houston being "too close to New Orleans" was about avoiding another bust. The "doo-dah man" later in the song is from R. Crumb's comics, but it can be whoever you think it is. You're at liberty to make up your own doo-dah man there [laughs].

As for "What in the world ever became of Sweet Jane?/She lost her sparkle, you know she isn't the same," I don't know who "Sweet Jane" was. I have a feeling it wasn't Janis Joplin. It was just some sorority girl who found her way into a little dead-end alley in the hippie culture. Each of us had our own individual Sweet Jane and probably still do.

The "reds" in the line "Livin' on reds, vitamin C, and cocaine/All a friend can say is, 'Ain't it a shame?'" were red Seconal pills. The bikers were using them as a recreational drug. We took them to overcome insomnia. Given how much coffee we drank to be up for shows, a little Seconal at night was the only thing that knocked us out fast.

In late March 1970, we finally had time to work on the song's music. We were booked to play a theme park in Dania Beach, Florida, called Pirates World. At our motel, we had the afternoon off, so the band sat by the pool. I don't believe Hunter was there. There weren't any tourists at the motel so we had the pool to ourselves. Jerry, bassist Phil Lesh, and I sat on the diving board with our acoustic guitars and came up with a melody to go with Hunter's words.

As we worked, we came up with this bluesy shuffle. We moved back and forth from the diving board to a table to write things down. The melody had to work in my register, so we put it in the key of E. We outlined much of the song that afternoon. The melody came fairly quickly. Then we came up with choral parts for the melody, an approach we had picked up from the Swan Silvertones, a gospel group we loved and listened to.

The choruses were easy for me to sing the lead, but the verses were hell. Some of them were straight-up tongue twisters, like "Most of the cats that you meet on the streets speak of true love." Give it a try. You're not going to get through it. At first, I complained bitterly about how those dense verses were going to go. Jerry's response was, "Sing 'em like Chuck Berry in 'School Days.'" Jerry meant I should use Chuck's rapid-fire delivery and enunciation to fit a lot of words into each measure.

I can't say I gave it much thought, but I did give it a college try. I know I don't sound much like Chuck Berry on the recording [laughs]. We kept refining the music and tightening the choruses [sings]: "Truckin', up to Buffalo/Been thinkin', you got to mellow slow/Takes time, you pick a place to go/And just keep truckin' on."

The writing of the song took us only about two and a half hours, if that. The vocal harmony was a little trickier. I have to credit Phil for coming up with the harmony. Jon Hendricks, the jazz singer from the vocalese group Lambert, Hendricks & Ross, also played a role. Three years earlier, in 1967, when we called ourselves the Warlocks, we backed Jon on a single called "Fire in the City." Jon was producing it for a documentary.

Jon was cool. He got what he wanted out of us—vocal harmony—and we learned from him. He's a vocalese singer and composer and one of the best at coming up with lyrics for instrumental jazz solos. Jon's mind and mouth are so fast that he's able to get a lot of words into each measure with perfect enunciation. Just being in his presence made us think. "Truckin'" has that same vocalese and vocal harmony feel in places. I thought of Jon as we worked on the song.

We never divided up harmony parts to sing in specific ranges. Instead, each of us just looked for great-sounding notes. If you listen carefully, you'll hear that sometimes I'm on the high notes and sometimes the lowest ones. We rehearsed the harmony vocals, but the painstaking part was ensuring we could do it the same way each time. Once we were happy with what we had, we recorded a demo tape for reference.

We first performed "Truckin'" in August 1970 at the Fillmore West in San Francisco. We didn't have time to go into rehearsal space to work on things. We did that live, while touring. But the song was always a challenge for me. You had to hope you were having a good night to get the lyric out cleanly. If the band started too fast, I knew I was going to have a rough time of it.

We recorded "Truckin'" at Wally Heider Studios in San Francisco in September 1970 for our *American Beauty* album. We set up in a circle, but we had to get Phil's bass away from Billy Kreutzmann's drums. Phil liked to play loud in the studio, so we had to put him over in the corner. For "Truckin'," we had to baffle ourselves off a bit. We built a little fort of soundproofed partitions around Billy's drums to keep the rest of the band's instruments and vocals from bleeding into his microphones.

We were only minimally successful at that. This is one of the reasons why we famously didn't make good studio records. We played too goddamn loud in there. On "Truckin'," I played my Gibson ES-335. It was my basic guitar then. Not until recently have I changed guitars much between songs.

Today, when I sing "Truckin'," I go back to that time through my character's eyes. It's sort of a fantasy version of what my life was like then and what I was observing on the road. When I'm singing the song, I generally don't have any thoughts. I'm not even there. My character is. I take a break while my character tells his story.

In those rare moments when I do think about what I'm singing, I usually wish I had a few new verses. But I don't feel at liberty to write them myself. I'll have to give Hunter a buzz to see if he has anything for me. [Robert Hunter died in 2019, two years after this interview.]

Alice Cooper in London in 1971.

14: I'm Eighteen
ALICE COOPER
Released: November 1970

The Crazy World of Arthur Brown may have launched shock rock, but the band Alice Cooper took the form to Broadway levels. The elaborate theatrical skits played out onstage complete with props such as a guillotine and an electric chair gave audiences something to look at as well as listen to. But Alice Cooper's brand of horror had a dark, humorous edge and was more akin to *Tales from the Crypt* comics than revolting realism. The morbid jolt was just enough to rile up an audience, not make it sick.

Alice Cooper had a rocky start in 1969. Their first two albums were disasters in terms of sales, and as the date to record their third album approached, the effort clearly was do-or-die. If they hoped to record a fourth, Alice Cooper had to get it together and write and record at least one major hit. So they took their best shot. Their new label, Warner Bros., was so cautious, it released the single months before the album was even completed. The strategy was to see how the song did and then make a decision about the band's fate. If Alice Cooper's best effort died on the *Billboard* pop chart, Warner Bros. was certainly going to pull the plug on both a fourth album and the band.

When that single, "I'm Eighteen," was released in November 1970, it climbed to No. 21. Its respectable performance convinced Warner Bros. that Alice Cooper had legs and that the band had found a way to tap into the youth culture's appetite for rock theater. The band's third album, *Love It to Death*, was completed and came out in March 1971, rising to No. 35 on the *Billboard* album chart. Alice Cooper won a stay of execution.

Alice Cooper
(Alice Cooper lead singer and cowriter)

After our albums *Pretties for You* and *Easy Action* were released in 1969 and early '70, we became anxious. Our first barely charted at No. 193 and the second didn't chart at all. Shep Gordon, our manager, suggested we relocate from Los Angeles to the Midwest, where we had a following.

Michael Bruce
(Alice Cooper rhythm guitarist and cowriter)

Touring in the Midwest in early '70, we had stayed at motels. During our downtime, I came up with songs on my guitar. One of them was called "I Wish I Was 18 Again." I hadn't been home in a couple of years, and I missed Phoenix. I had the song's three-chord riff—E minor, C major, and D major—but my lyric was a little silly [he sings]: "Be my high school girl/Be the only one/I wish I was 18 again." I knew that wasn't going to last [laughs]. I used the song to warm up in dressing rooms before shows. Eventually the band began using my riff as an eight-minute soundcheck jam.

Dennis Dunaway
(Alice Cooper bassist and cowriter)

In the early spring of '70, we were in New York to shoot our performance scenes for the film *Diary of a Mad Housewife*. At the Gorham Hotel, I looked across West 55th Street at the City Center theater. All the posters outside were for the Joffrey Ballet's spring season. On the poster was a scary white-faced clown with thick makeup around his eyes and squiggly lines coming out like spokes. I told Alice he should do his eyes that way. At first, he wasn't into it, but he was open. We bought eyeliner at a nearby cosmetics store and applied it at the hotel. That was the start of Alice's spider eyes.

Bruce

Back in the Midwest, the band wanted to start performing our sound-check jam for audiences. But my original lyric was too cumbersome. Alice rewrote it.

Cooper

My lyrics were about coming of age, confusion, and frustration. It became an angst song, like the Who's "My Generation." In some ways it's bleak: "I got a baby's brain and an old man's heart/Took eighteen years to get this far." When I wrote the lyric, I was twenty-two, so I had to think back to what it was like to turn eighteen: "Don't always know what I'm talkin' about/Feels like I'm livin' in the middle of doubt." By then, we needed a place to live in the Midwest and to rehearse 24/7. Our road manager, Leo Fenn, found us a ranch near Pontiac, Michigan.

Bruce

The place had a four-bedroom farmhouse with a kitchen and an empty barn out back. Behind that was an indoor horse paddock, with a large, enclosed room that was perfect for rehearsing.

Shep Gordon
(manager)

The band just needed a smart record producer. The Guess Who was a Canadian hard-rock band with hits like "No Time" and "American Woman" on the pop charts. The guy who produced their records was Jack Richardson. I went up to Toronto to see him.

Bob Ezrin
(coproducer)

Jack didn't want to have anything to do with Alice Cooper. He didn't like their albums. To keep Shep happy, though, Jack told me to go to

New York to hear the band at Max's Kansas City and let them down easy. In early September of '70, I sat down at a table right in front of the stage at Max's Kansas City waiting for Alice to come on. Everyone in the place had spider eyes painted on like Alice.

At times, the band's music was powerful, what people called hard rock then. At other times it was whimsical and focused on theatrics. I loved it. After the set, I went upstairs and bounded into their dressing room. I said, "We're going to produce your next album." I also said their song "I'm Edgy" could be a hit. Drummer Neal Smith pointed out that Alice was actually singing "I'm Eighteen."

When I finally left at 3:00 a.m., I realized Jack was going to fire me for committing to produce a band he wanted me to blow off. In the morning, when I called him, Jack wasn't happy. But he said, "If you like the band that much, you produce them." Jack wanted me to start by recording just four songs. I went up to the band's Pontiac ranch to get the music in shape, what we call preproduction. The first song we tackled was "I'm Eighteen."

First, I had them play the original version the way they performed it onstage. There was a long introduction. I stopped them and said we had to get to the vocal much faster. I compressed the intro to just the three-chord riff. Then I had Glen Buxton play a lead guitar solo that flew into Alice's first verse: "Lines form on my face and hands/Lines form from the ups and downs." The biggest problem with the rest, though, was that everyone played all the time. The music had to be stripped down to just bass and drums with the vocal then built back up.

Cooper

Bob was brilliant. He kept telling us to dumb it down so we could shorten it. He wanted the listener to get it immediately.

Ezrin

At first there was pushback, but Alice was an advocate. He heard the results instantly. What I wanted from the band required a lot of practice. We routined it over and over until they got it right. Then we edited Alice's lyric to fit the tighter arrangement.

Cooper

We had been intent on being the Yardbirds and showing off our guitars. Bob said absolutely not. Glen Buxton's lead guitar needed to come at the right time and then drop out. The guitar couldn't interfere with the melody line or bass and drums. Bob stripped us down to what the Beatles had done. Bob was our George Martin.

Ezrin

After we had "I'm Eighteen" set, the band played it live at a Detroit gig. The audience went nuts.

Cooper

In the fall, we recorded "I'm Eighteen" and three other songs for our next album, *Love It to Death*, at RCA's Mid-American Recording Center in Chicago. Elvis had recorded there.

Bruce

We recorded in street clothes. Makeup was strictly a stage thing. I played my Gibson SG guitar. I have the hands of a boxer, so I don't have super-long fingers. That Gibson's frets were an easier target to hit playing rhythm.

Dunaway

I played a Gibson EB-0 bass. Coproducer Jack Richardson was there by then. At some point he turned over a metal ashtray in the booth and taped it to the console. Then he tapped the beat on the tray with a drumstick like a metronome so we'd hear it in our headphones. It kept us from speeding up.

Bruce

When Alice added his lead vocal to the instrumental track, Bob cleared the studio. He wanted an environment that would allow Alice to get into character emotionally while singing.

Ezrin

What most people don't know about the recording is that it's the product of multiple takes spliced together. Jack was an editing master and did the cuts.

Bruce

When the single came out in November 1970, Shep had everyone constantly call radio station CKLW in Windsor, Ontario, to request it. CKLW's signal reached south into the American Midwest and north, across the river, to Detroit.

Ezrin

The Midwest was highly receptive to "I'm Eighteen." Kids of assembly-line factory workers populated the region. By 1970, they began to see their dads with dead-end jobs and no prospects. This wasn't what they wanted to do. They wanted to matter.

Bruce

As the single gained traction, we recorded the rest of our third album, *Love It to Death*, which was a hit at No. 35 after it came out in March '71. Inside the album's gatefold, fish-eye photos of the band were placed in Alice's eyes. If you look closely, you'll see us in our Pontiac rehearsal space.

Cooper

Young rock artists were becoming a mirror of the chaos going on in American society. Our band was the frightening mirror, like the one that distorts at the fun house. But what we were doing had to have comedy. If you're singing about chaos and horror, you have to play it as tongue in cheek. Otherwise, the shock overshadows the music.

The last line of my lyric to "I'm Eighteen" was supposed to be "I'm eighteen and I hate it." But as I neared the end of my vocal in the studio, I decided to flip it to "I'm eighteen and I like it." I wanted to turn the teenage angst around. That was a surprise to everyone in the control booth. With my earlier lyric, the song was a good hard rocker. But by flipping the line, the song became a statement.

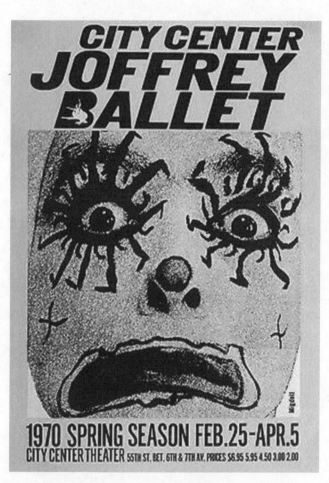

New York City Center poster from 1970 that inspired Alice Cooper's eye makeup.

Marc Bolan of T. Rex in 1972.

15: Bang a Gong (Get It On)
T. REX
Released: July 1971

Three years into a music career in London, guitarist Marc Bolan formed a two-man group in 1967 called Tyrannosaurus Rex. Enamored by the colorful psychedelic scene evolving in the city and taken with Donovan and Bob Dylan, the duo—Bolan and drummer Steve Peregrin Took—released three trippy acoustic folk-rock albums. Two reached the Top 15 in the U.K. The music was driven by Bolan's mystical and florid poetry. After replacing Took in late 1969 with drummer Mickey Finn, Bolan began exploring elemental rock and the electric guitar. They didn't have much choice. While Finn had the right rocker look, he couldn't duplicate Took's complex rhythm patterns.

By 1971, the duo expanded to four members and its name was shortened to T. Rex after producer Tony Visconti began using the abbreviation on his wall schedule. Deeply influenced by the trendy unisex clothing stores on King's Road and in Notting Hill, Bolan's fashion style became more flamboyant. As he wrote songs for the band's next album, *Electric Warrior,* one of them was "Bang a Gong (Get It On)," a cocky and camp rocker.

Most noteworthy was the band's appearance in 1971 on the BBC TV's weekly *Top of the Pops* music show. Bolan was dressed in a gray satin jacket and pink pants, sporting silver glitter teardrops under each eye. The performance would mark the start of glam rock—a form that mixed bubblegum-pop hooks, androgyny, and the faux sentimentalism of cabaret. "Get It On" became glam rock's first global hit, reaching No. 1 in the U.K. and No. 10 on *Billboard*'s pop chart in early 1972. Bolan would die in an auto accident in 1977.

Tony Visconti
(producer)

In 1967, I was offered a job that changed my life. Denny Cordell, a British record producer, asked me to join him in London as his recording assistant. I was twenty-three. I left New York for the U.K. in April '67. In London, I lived with Denny for a time. We produced British artists such as Manfred Mann, Georgie Fame, and Procol Harum. After a year, Denny gave me a nudge. To be successful, he said, I had to discover a group worth recording. By then, we were releasing records through Regal Zonophone.

On my first night of talent scouting in 1968, I went to London's UFO Club to see an acoustic psychedelic-folk duo—Marc Bolan and Steve Peregrin Took. They called themselves Tyrannosaurus Rex. After the set, I introduced myself to Marc and we had a lovely conversation. I gave him my card. The next morning, Marc and Steve came up to Denny's office. Marc sat on the floor and played the entire set from the night before.

After they left, Denny wasn't keen on them. I said I loved what I'd heard. Denny wanted to keep me happy, so he said, "They'll be our token underground group." For their first few albums, I just added overdubs and production touches. We released a handful of singles. Several landed on the British charts. Marc said he named the group Tyrannosaurus Rex so fans would remember them. Growing up, he loved Godzilla movies. In some ways, he saw himself as a tyrant lizard, as a nonhuman hero.

At some point in 1970, Marc noticed I had shortened the name to T. Rex on my calendar. He saw it as a betrayal. I told him it was a pain to write the full name all day long. So the duo became T. Rex. In the summer of 1970, a fashionable female friend of Marc's, Chelita Secunda, began taking him to London's King's Road to the boutique Granny Takes a Trip. He began dressing up for performances in women's shoes and mascara. He did this to stand out and connect with women in his audiences.

Over the summer of '70, T. Rex evolved. We released "Ride a White Swan" as a single, which went to No. 2 in the U.K. "Hot Love" hit No. 1 in early '71. By then, T. Rex had become an electric glam-rock band with Marc on lead vocal and guitars, Steve Currie on bass, Bill Legend on drums, and Mickey Finn on percussion.

Bill Legend
(T. Rex drummer)

When I joined T. Rex, Marc wanted to transition from the underground act he had as an acoustic duo to a four-piece rock 'n' roll band. Marc loved Elvis, Eddie Cochran, Chuck Berry, and other rockers from the '50s. So did I. Marc was an instigator and an innovator. He knew he attracted both sexes and played off of that, and his look was integral to the band. But behind the visuals, the music was pure rock.

Visconti

T. Rex's U.K. chart success led to a monthlong U.S. tour. In late March 1971, we flew to New York. There, Marc and I discussed the band's next album, *Electric Warrior*. Eager for product, T. Rex's new record label, Fly, wanted the band to record it while they were in the U.S. We booked time at New York's Media Sound and recorded "Jeepster" and a couple of other songs.

Legend

In New York, I bought a black Gretsch wooden snare drum for touring. It had a bigger, solid sound. At our hotel, Marc had me come to his room with the drum. He sat against the bed's headboard playing his guitar and singing "Get It On." I accompanied him, and we worked out a few drum ideas.

Visconti

In L.A., we stayed at Hyatt House on the Sunset Strip. Marc and I were in his room when he took out a notebook filled with lyrics. He pointed to a page and said he wanted to record a song he wrote called "Get It On." Marc played it for me several times on his acoustic guitar.

103

I sang background vocals and took detailed production notes. All of the song's chords were Chuck Berry's changes. It was all very rock 'n' roll. An hour later, when Marc and I finished, I knew we had a smash hit. Marc didn't explain his lyrics, but I knew they referenced three women he had been dating over the four years I'd known him:

"You're dirty and sweet, oh yeah/Well you're slim and you're weak" was likely about the woman Marc was dating when I met him. She never wore makeup and was incredibly sweet and very passive.

"Well, you're windy and wild/You've got the blues in your shoes and your stockings" was likely an American model who lived in London and was in *Hair*.

The verse that opens with "Well, you're built like a car/You've got a hub cap diamond star halo" was probably the woman who became his manager and driver.

Marc's phrase "bang a gong" may have been inspired by the gong that opened movies made by Rank Films in the U.K. Or it could have come from any number of those jungle movies he watched in the '50s, where someone bangs a gong to signal the start of a native ritual. I knew we had to get into an L.A. studio and record. We also needed background singers. Fortunately, we already knew Mark Volman and Howard Kaylan, cofounders of the Turtles.

We first met them in 1970 when they opened for Frank Zappa. Mark and Howard got us into Wally Heider Studios, where the band and I worked out an arrangement. First, I recorded a basic rhythm track with Bill's drums, Steve's bass, and Marc's rhythm guitar. This session included Marc's opening riff played on his white Stratocaster.

Legend

When we recorded, we set up facing each other. We wanted a live effect so we could feed off Marc's riff and each other.

Visconti

The T. Rex musicians were great together in the studio. They were so quick and precise. Steve had his bass part down by take number three, including his descending lick that Bowie wound up using on "Rebel Rebel" a few years later. As the band worked through "Get It On," they further modified it. I saw myself as the band's coach, the fifth member who was there at every step saying yes or no.

As soon as the basic rhythm track was done, Marc picked up his second guitar—a late-'60s Les Paul with an orange top. Marc played lead with it and used some cool guitar effects—a wah-wah pedal, a treble booster, and a Fuzz Face pedal for distortion. Marc sang a live take, but the band was so loud it couldn't be used. Once the backing track was good to go, Marc overdubbed a lead vocal. Marc liked slap-back echo, the kind you hear on early Elvis Presley records. So we added some echo to give his voice a little snap. The guitars also had slap-back echo.

At the fade, Marc sang Chuck Berry's line from "Little Queenie": "Well meanwhile, I'm still thinking …" That was impromptu, done during the session. The line surprised us, and everyone smiled. After I recorded Marc's and Howard's background falsetto vocals, we stopped and the band returned to London. The rest of "Get It On"—the piano, the saxes and strings overdubs, Mickey Finn's tambourine, and the mixing— were all done at London's Trident Studios in Soho.

I'm fairly certain Rick Wakeman played piano on the overdub. I had him play a glissando on the front end and in the middle. He's also playing some really cool rock 'n' roll eighth notes. Ian McDonald of King Crimson played all of the overdubbed saxes. He borrowed a baritone sax and we double-tracked it. On the second break before the concluding section of the song, he played an alto.

The single had to sound great on dull, lo-fi AM radio. So I mixed it bright and thumpy. I also tightened up the sound of Marc's guitars by compressing them on the mix. When the single hit No. 1 in the U.K. in '71, we knew it was bound for the U.S. But Chase, an American band, already had a record out called "Get It On." Our title was changed to "Bang a Gong (Get It On)."

When "Get It On" was released in '71 along with *Electric Warrior*, T. Rex became the biggest thing in the U.K. since the Beatles, and Marc epitomized glam.

Yes, clockwise from far left, Chris Squire, Rick Wakeman, Steve Howe, Alan White and Jon Anderson in 1972.

16. Roundabout
YES
Released: January 1972

Many formally trained musicians who came out of Britain's music and art schools in the late 1960s began to create a new form of rock that eschewed dance beats and pop hooks. Instead, they created a fusion of rock and classical that was geared to rococo performance. Inspired by the Beatles' and the Beach Boys' studio experiments on albums in 1966 and '67, as well as by Bob Dylan's observational poetry and Frank Zappa's spring-loaded abstraction, bands such as the Moody Blues, the Nice, and Procol Harum created a symphonic form that laid the groundwork for progressive rock. Bands that followed in the late 1960s, such as Jethro Tull, King Crimson, Gentle Giant, and Emerson, Lake & Palmer added Elizabethan and folk touches.

One of the most innovative and cutting-edge progressive rock bands in the early 1970s was Yes, thanks largely to *Fragile*, the group's fourth studio album, released in 1971. While the album placed the group's classical leanings front and center, the band had the good sense to energize the formality of the music by hiring Rick Wakeman. The keyboardist had intended to become a concert pianist but wound up mastering an early generation of synthesizers and electronic keyboards, making him very much in demand. Not only did his electric keyboards become dominant sounds on Yes albums, but they also became visual superstars in concert as Wakeman worked them with a spectacular, spiderlike attack.

"Roundabout" was *Fragile*'s sole released single and climbed to No. 13 on *Billboard*'s pop chart in early 1972, helping the album reach No. 4 for seven weeks. *Fragile* also was the band's first album to feature Wakeman's revolutionary style of keyboard playing.

Jon Anderson
(Yes lead singer and cowriter)

I began writing the lyrics to "Roundabout" while traveling with the band in a van through Scotland in late March 1971. Yes was on tour then, and we had just performed in Aviemore the night before. In the van, we were heading south to Glasgow, about a three-and-a-half-hour drive. There were mountains and lakes everywhere. I had smoked a joint, so everything was vivid and mystical. As we drove along, we encountered a fair number of "roundabouts," what you in the States call traffic circles. At one point, the road dropped into a deep valley and ran next to a large lake. Low clouds covered the mountain peaks. I took out my little notepad and started writing.

I wrote the lyrics in a free form and didn't edit the lines much. I just loved how words sounded when I put them together: "I'll be the roundabout/The words will make you out 'n' out" expressed how I felt as the song's words came to me fast, the way cars navigate roundabouts. I expected to be in the van for several hours, so I was spending "the day your way, call it morning driving through the sound of in 'n' out the valley."

"In and around the lake" was the road winding through the region. Down in the valley, the mountains seemed to "come out of the sky and stand there." I was married then, and I knew I'd see my wife in a day. "Twenty-four before my love you'll see/I'll be there with you."

Steve Howe
(Yes guitarist and cowriter)

In Glasgow, we checked in to our hotel, and Jon and I got together in my room with a cassette recorder. Eventually we had this minor-key feel for the verse that resolved in a major key for the chorus. But the song's biggest advance came that August in a London rehearsal studio, when keyboardist Rick Wakeman replaced Tony Kaye in the band. Rick was more interested in the technology direction we wanted to take.

Anderson

Rick revolutionized our sound. He added multiple keyboards, which gave us more textured possibilities. At the rehearsal studio, I sat on a chair in the middle of the band and listened to what they were developing. If what they were working on wasn't happening, I'd make suggestions. "Roundabout" wasn't difficult to sing. But as the band's vocalist, I needed to know where the song was going. They often looked to me to figure out what should come next so the vocal and instrumental worked together.

Howe

In September, when we went into Advision Studios in London to record "Roundabout," we used their sixteen-track tape machine, which let us layer the instruments. The song became pure magic.

Anderson

The rhythm track was recorded first, in segments. The band would rehearse one segment at a time and then record it. Then they'd move on to the next segment, always mindful of the song's progression and structure. Steve planned to open the song by playing something of a Scottish jig on his acoustic guitar. He had played it for me earlier at our hotel.

Howe

My opening acoustic guitar part was played on my 1953 Martin 00-18. But we felt the song needed something more dramatic to start. We found it with a backward piano note. When you strike a single piano note and hold it down, the sound starts loud and then fades away. We wanted that to happen in reverse. We recorded Rick holding down a piano note, and then we turned the tape reel over and started the song where the note was faintest. What you hear on the record is a note going from faint to loud, as if it's rushing toward you.

Rick Wakeman
(Yes keyboardist)

For the piano-note intro, I simultaneously played the lowest E on the studio's grand piano and the E an octave higher. The octave gave the note a fatter feel. Chris Squire wanted a funky sound on the bass, sort of a Sly and the Family Stone feel. I played organ arpeggios over the top with my right hand as my left hand mirrored Chris's bass notes to add weight.

Howe

When we finished the rhythm track, Chris overdubbed his bass track using my Gibson ES-150 electric guitar, which had a Charlie Christian pickup. It wasn't terribly loud, but it was effective, giving him an eight-string bass sound. On the organ, Rick was adventuresome, allowing the rest of us to see a wider sonic path and plenty of room for experimentation. Except for my acoustic Martin at the start and during the ballad passage in the middle and at the close, I used a 1961 blonde electric Gibson ES-5 Switchmaster throughout.

Wakeman

On most of "Roundabout," I played a Hammond C3 organ. Later, I overdubbed a Minimoog when the song slows to a ballad about five minutes in and Steve plays acoustic guitar. I also added a mellotron for flute sounds when Jon slowly sings "in and around the lake." The mellotron gave the passage a "Strawberry Fields" mood.

Anderson

Once the instrumental track was done, I went into the studio early one day with just the engineer and recorded my lead vocal while listening to the music through headphones. When the other guys came in, we recorded the harmonies. Finally, we reached a point where the song had to end. I thought, "Let's do something totally different and sing harmony, like the Byrds or the Beach Boys." I started singing, "Dah dah-dah-dah, dah, dah, dahhh." Then we all started singing that in harmony. We added it onto the end of the song. If you listen carefully, you can hear Rick singing three notes against the grain of what we were doing. They're the notes to "Three Blind Mice," and it sounded intriguing.

Howe

To close the song, I decided to mimic what I had done on my Martin guitar at the beginning. But I ended on an A-flat chord, which the ear doesn't really expect.

Anderson

A couple of days after we finished "Roundabout," the band went into the studio to listen to it on the big speakers. When the song finished, I thought, "Oh my gosh, it's so good." I looked around at everyone. It was an interesting feeling. My conscious self was glowing. I thought, "I can't believe this is happening in my life at this moment in time."

Jackson Browne in 1974.

17: Doctor My Eyes
JACKSON BROWNE
Released: March 1972

While progressive rock bands were making inroads in London and New York with electric keyboards and classical motifs, a new mellow movement was emerging on the West Coast that would turn Los Angeles into a rock album recording center. Singer-songwriters in L.A. enclaves such as Laurel Canyon and Echo Park were creating a new sound that merged country, folk, and rock with tight vocal harmonies. David Crosby, Stephen Stills, Graham Nash, Neil Young, and Joni Mitchell had already started the revolution in the late 1960s with manager David Geffen, who launched Asylum Records in 1971 to record the new sound.

One of the first artists to emerge in the second wave was singer-songwriter Jackson Browne. In the late 1960s, he wrote songs for others but, by 1971, at twenty-two, he decided to record his own songs. His first solo album, *Jackson Browne*, was recorded that summer and released in early 1972. His approach with country-influenced vocal harmonies and personal, introspective lyrics would catch the ear of the Eagles, a band that came to personify the sound of California rock in the 1970s.

The single "Doctor My Eyes" peaked at No. 8 on *Billboard*'s pop chart, and in 2019, Browne's eponymous first album was inducted into the Grammy Hall of Fame.

Jackson Browne
(guitarist, pianist, and songwriter)

In mid-1969, I was living in Los Angeles in a basement apartment in Echo Park. I had my grandfather's upright Fischer piano from the early 1900s. He was a printer and craftsman and had painted wildflowers on the front and the sides. One day, my good friends—songwriter Greg Copeland and his then wife, songwriter Pamela Polland—came by. She sat at my piano and played a song she had just written called "Mind Snap."

I kind of appropriated her piano riff for a song I was writing that became "Doctor My Eyes." I played the piano part with my thumbs an octave apart. No real piano player would do that, but I thought it was a cool way to suggest the rhythm I needed for the song. During the writing process, my eyes became infected and badly encrusted. I could barely see. I didn't know what was wrong with them.

I went to the doctor, and he gave me some medicine. It took a while for my eyes to return to normal. My eye trouble was the initial inspiration for the song's lyrics. But as I wrote them, the eye issue became a metaphor for lost innocence and for having seen too much: "Doctor, my eyes have seen the years/And the slow parade of fears without crying/ Now I want to understand."

I don't know what makes me write anything. Many of my songs are imagined. They come from somewhere. This song is not literally about going to the doctor to get my eyes fixed. It's a little more glib than that: "Doctor my eyes/Tell me what is wrong/Was I unwise to leave them open for so long?" The lyrics are sort of an understated remark about the loss of idealism. Back in '69, I don't think I ever played "Doctor My Eyes" for anybody. At the time, the clubs I played in never had a piano, and I just put the song aside.

I recorded my first album—*Jackson Browne*—for David Geffen's Asylum Records in the summer of '71 at Crystal Sound in L.A. Crystal was where James Taylor had recorded his third album, *Mud Slide Slim*, earlier that year. Along the way, I met James's recording engineer—Richard Orshoff. His engineering sounded great, and he was a warm and empathetic guy. I thought if James's producer, Peter Asher, liked working with Richard, he might be great for me.

From the start, I thought "Doctor My Eyes" was the album's one song that was short enough for a single. I also thought recording a single would be a perfunctory exercise and fun to try. David Crosby, a friend, agreed to sing background harmony on some of the album's songs. During the recording process, David Geffen played Graham Nash "Doctor My Eyes" and asked if he thought it could be a single. Graham said it might be if he added a high harmony vocal. That was the album's great break—having Crosby and Nash singing with me at a time when I was a totally unknown songwriter. It was quite a calling card at radio stations.

Before we started, I'd met drummer Russ Kunkel through a friend. Russ was a fantastic, innovative drummer who had recorded with James Taylor. He could arrange songs for acoustic musicians and make drums happen and sound completely natural. Russ said he liked my songs and urged me to call him when I went into the studio. That was an incredible windfall.

When we began recording the basic rhythm track for "Doctor My Eyes," I played piano, Leland Sklar was on bass, and Russ decided to play congas instead of drums. I had to change my piano part. Up until then, I played that dumb two-thumb part throughout the song. With these two amazing players, I had to find a piano part that would support what they were doing and the song. I decided to play straight fours—playing on every beat—like the Beatles did on a lot of their songs.

Once we had the basic rhythm track, I suggested Russ overdub a shuffle beat on the drums, to widen the sound of his congas. I also got guitarist Jesse Ed Davis to come in and overdub a solo. I was lucky to have him. He was part of a group of great session musicians from Tulsa, Oklahoma. I had met him through Pamela Polland, which is funny now that I think about it. Her riff was the song's foundation.

I originally called Jesse to play on my song "Nightingale." But when he listened to it, he asked if I had anything else. I played him "Doctor

My Eyes." He said, "Yeah, I can play on that." Once Jesse was in the studio, I played the tape of our basic rhythm track in his headphones. As he tuned up his guitar to the track, Richard was already recording him. Fortunately, Richard recorded everything Jesse played, including little tuning riffs we wound up using.

After Jesse overdubbed his solo in the middle of the song in one take, he began to pack up his guitar. I went into the studio and asked if he could add his guitar at the end, as the song was going out. Jesse plugged his guitar back in and added that part. As he packed up again, Richard went into the studio and asked if he could add some big whole notes under his solo and at the end for depth. Jesse happily did that, too. Then he was gone. We used every note he played.

After my album was finished, I went out on the road prior to its release in January '72. I didn't perform "Doctor My Eyes" in advance of the album or even after the single was a hit. It was just me and multi-instrumentalist David Lindley.

One day after the single reached the Top 10, I returned to L.A. from the road. The girl I was seeing picked me up at the airport. As we drove up La Brea Avenue, she said, "Watch this." She turned on the radio and "Doctor My Eyes" was playing. I have no idea how she did that, but we both cracked up.

It was so surreal to hear one of my songs that way. I had been focused on making an album. For years, I didn't think much of the song. It wasn't really representative of what I'd done. But then recently, I listened to a test pressing of the master for the album's reissue. When "Doctor My Eyes" came on, it knocked me out. I thought, "That's pretty good, that's not bad."

The Hollies, from left, Allan Clarke, Terry Sylvester, Bobby Elliott, Bernie Calvert and Tony Hicks in 1973.

18: Long Cool Woman In a Black Dress
THE HOLLIES
Released: April 1972

Disgruntled by the Hollies' unwillingness to record his songs, Graham Nash in 1968 quit the British pop group he had cofounded to form a singer-songwriter trio in Los Angeles with David Crosby and Stephen Stills. His departure for Crosby, Stills & Nash left a gaping hole in the Hollies' vocal harmonies. As Nash's success bloomed, the Hollies' other founder, Allan Clarke, was growing restless and also wanted to leave the group. But first, the band had an album to finish.

Distant Light was the band's eleventh album, but in the process of recording it in the spring and summer of 1971, they found themselves one song short of completion. Clarke suggested "Long Cool Woman in a Black Dress," a rockabilly noir he had cowritten weeks earlier with lyricist Roger Cook about a Prohibition-era FBI agent, a raid, and a woman who catches the protagonist's eye.

When the "Long Cool Woman" single was released in the United States in early 1972, it reached No. 2 on the *Billboard* pop chart—becoming the British band's highest-charting single in the United States since inception.

Roger Cook
(cowriter)

In June of 1971, Allan Clarke of the Hollies and I were at my office on Park Street in London. We frequently wrote songs together there. At around noon, we left to grab lunch at La Genova, near Marble Arch. After a bottle of wine and a brandy, Allan and I returned to my office to work on a song. At some point, we decided the song should be set in New York during Prohibition.

Both of us loved Hollywood films about speakeasy bad guys and cops smashing beer barrels and whiskey bottles in the streets. I was sitting at my upright piano and Allan was next to me on a chair with his guitar. After messing about on the keys for a bit, I started pounding out a melodramatic and slightly sinister blues riff with my right hand. It was in the key of C. As my pointer and middle finger played the C and E notes, my thumb moved from G to A to B-flat and back down to A. I can't lay claim to the chords. It's an old rock 'n' roll riff.

Allan Clarke
(Hollies lead singer, lead guitarist, and cowriter)

As Roger played his riff, I came up with a melody on my Fender Telecaster along with a simple chord sequence. We had brought that bottle of brandy back with us.

Cook

Bouncing ideas back and forth, Allan and I thought the song should be sung from the perspective of an FBI agent working undercover at a speakeasy. I wanted the lyric to have the tough-guy language you hear in gangster films. We came up with lines like "sitting in a nest of bad men" and "people who are doing wrong." We even avoided calling the place a speakeasy. We called it a "bootlegging boozer on the West Side." A "boozer" in London is slang for a pub that serves alcohol illegally after hours.

As the lyrics developed, the agent is about to call the district attorney to tip him off when he spots the speakeasy's female singer. The woman takes his breath away. "A pair of 45s made me open my eyes" has nothing to do with guns. It was tough-guy slang for the singer's bust. "Just a five-nine, beautiful, tall" describes her height and poise. Which is why the FBI agent is "a bad mess" after just one look. Remember, Allan and I were a little tipsy.

As soon as we came up with "She was a long cool woman in a black dress," Allan and I stopped and looked at each other. We had the song's title. The guy in the song named Charlie says, "I hope that you're able, boy." He's the agent's sidekick who saw him eye the woman. We chose the name Charlie because Allan and I were big fans of *On the Waterfront*. In the film, the Charlie character is Marlon Brando's brother and was played by Rod Steiger.

At this point in the lyric, something had to happen. So we came up with lines about police sirens wailing, everybody running, and a gun going off. As the cops sweep in to make their arrests, the FBI agent says, "The D.A. was pumpin' my left hand and she was holdin' my right." The agent had saved the long cool woman from arrest by saying she was his gal. Allan and I finished the song's lyric in less than two hours. I wrote it all out on three sheets of paper. In fact, I still have the sheets someplace, but I can't find them.

Shirley Burns and Carol Weston popped down a few times that afternoon. Shirley was George Martin's secretary and Carol was John Burgess's. George and John had cofounded AIR Studios two years earlier and had offices upstairs. Shirley and Carol liked the song but admitted they didn't understand a word of it.

Bobby Elliott
(Hollies drummer)

The Hollies were getting pressure from EMI in the U.K. and Epic in the States to deliver *Distant Light*, our next album. In the past, we had recorded at Abbey Road Studios, but Ron Richards, our producer, may have chosen AIR because he had helped George Martin and John Burgess start the company.

In July '71, all of the Hollies arrived at AIR Studios, but Ron called in sick. Allan said he had a song he wanted to play for us that might work. He sat on a stool and took out his Telecaster. As he played and sang the song, I joined in on drums and Bernie Calvert played his Fender bass. We decided to go ahead and produce it ourselves with the help of John Punter, our engineer.

Clarke

The guys liked the song, but we needed an intro. I came up with a guitar motif, but I wasn't influenced by Mason Williams's guitar on his 1968 hit "Classical Gas." I just pulled something out of the air and it sounded right. We recorded the song in the key of E. Originally, Tony Hicks was going to play lead guitar. But he thought that since it was my song, I should play lead.

So it was me, Bernie Calvert on bass, and Bobby Elliott on drums, with Tony overdubbing his rhythm guitar after. I used the same Telecaster with heavy strings that I had written the song on with Roger. Though the lyric's story was set in the 1920s, I wanted the song to sound like a '50s rocker, with that twang and urgency. By the mid-'60s, the Hollies didn't record much rock 'n' roll after the Beatles made it big. I missed the old sound.

On the vocal, my intention wasn't to sound like John Fogerty of Creedence Clearwater Revival. I was thinking of Elvis on his early songs, like "Mystery Train." I always liked recording with a bit of echo on my voice. It gave me a better feel of what I was singing. I wanted that same echo for "Long Cool Woman." Punter liked it so much that he added quite a bit more when we recorded to give me a big rockabilly sound.

Elliott

We were all Elvis fans so we were sold on that Sun Records sound. It was called slap-back echo. Punter created a slight delay using two tapes so that Allan's vocal slapped back in less than a second, producing a dry echo effect.

Clarke

While recording, I goofed on a line. I sang, "Well suddenly we heard the sirens/And everybody started to run/A-jumping out of doors and tables." It was supposed be "Jumping out of doors and windows," but "tables" sounded good so we left it in. My guitar on the record was double-tracked—meaning I recorded my guitar part and then over-dubbed the exact same notes on top, giving the Telecaster a chunky sound. After I sang the song's last line, "Cause that long cool woman had it all," I repeated "had it all" seven different times until the fade-out. I was channeling Elvis, shout-singing the phrase.

Elliott

When we finished, I overdubbed two hard drum shots—one in the middle of Allan's intro and again just before his guitar riff starts. I did this for dramatic effect by hitting the bass drum, the large tom-tom, and the snare drum all at once.

Clarke

When Ron returned to work, he listened to the tape and said, "You'll have to change the echo. I don't like it." I insisted it stay as is. We went back and forth, but eventually he gave in. None of us took the song seriously. We never envisioned it as a single. It was just a song to finish off the album.

Cook

Two last interesting twists. First, when Allan and I came up with the idea of a long cool woman, I had Billie Holiday in mind for the nightclub singer. I loved her voice. Second, in 2005, I was having lunch at the U.S. Capitol in Washington, D.C. I was there on behalf of the Nashville Songwriters Association International to urge Congress to improve the copyright laws for songwriters and artists. At some point, our hosts asked me to sing a couple of songs I cowrote. One was "Long Cool Woman."

When I finished, a guy came up and showed me his badge. He was an FBI agent watching over Congress. He said, "That's our song, man." He said that agents loved the first two lines: "Saturday night I was downtown/Working for the FBI." Apparently, when the single came out in 1972, they played it over the two-way radio for all the agents to hear.

Bernie Taupin and Elton John in New York in 1970.

19: Rocket Man
ELTON JOHN
Released: April 1972

At age fifteen, Elton John began playing piano at a local pub in Northwood Hills, England, and jamming in his newly formed Bluesology band. In the mid-1960s Bluesology backed touring R&B artists. Bernie Taupin, at the same age, left school with dreams of becoming a journalist. After leaving that job, he spent his teenage years drifting around Lincolnshire. In 1967, at age seventeen, he answered an ad placed by Liberty Records' London A&R executive Ray Williams seeking talent. John wound up answering the same ad later in the day. When John mentioned he composed music but couldn't write lyrics, he was handed an envelope of lyrics left behind by Taupin.

The pair began collaborating regularly in 1969, when John's first album, *Empty Sky*, was released. As songwriters, Taupin would provide John with lyrics, and John would create music for them on his piano. When John released his fifth studio album, *Honky Château*, in 1972, the album reached No. 1 on the *Billboard* chart in the United States and was the first of his six consecutive No. 1 albums in America with Taupin.

Included on the album was one of John and Taupin's most captivating power ballads—"Rocket Man." After the single was released in April 1972, it reached No. 6 on *Billboard*'s pop chart.

Bernie Taupin
(lyricist)

In mid-1971, I was in England driving north to visit my parents in Lincolnshire. I had moved to the States a year earlier and hadn't been home in a while. After exiting the M1 motorway, I had to take back roads to my parents' village. By then, the sun had set and it was pitch-black. I remember the stars were out.

I had recently reread Ray Bradbury's *The Illustrated Man*, his 1951 collection of science-fiction short stories. My favorite was "The Rocket Man." The story is about an astronaut who spends three months at a time in his rocket away from his wife and son. He's torn. He wants to be home with his family, but he also wants to be up among the stars. Eventually, his rocket falls into the sun.

During my drive, I thought about the Bradbury story. I also thought about the 1970 song "Rocket Man" that Tom Rapp had written and recorded with his band, Pearls Before Swine. It was a literal retelling of the Bradbury story. What appealed to me most about the Bradbury story wasn't the character's yearning or his tragic outcome but the drudgery of being an astronaut.

In '71, the future of space flight was exhilarating. America was putting astronauts on the moon. Yet twenty years earlier, Bradbury had envisioned future astronauts as little more than intergalactic truck drivers, burning themselves out alone, far from home.

Driving the back roads, I began writing a song in my head about the drudgery of being an astronaut. As I thought about how to start the song, the first verse came to me at once: "She packed my bags last night pre-flight/Zero hour 9 a.m./And I'm gonna be high as a kite by then." But I didn't have a pad or pen in the car. I also couldn't dictate the words or call someone to take them down. Cellphone technology didn't exist yet.

So I repeated the lyrics over and over. I was trying not to lose my train of thought as I raced to my parents' house. When I arrived, I rushed in without saying hello. I was hunting for a pen and paper. I had never written that way before. Usually I'd come up with a line and build from there. In this case, words to an entire verse fell out of my mind and onto the page. The words had such a rhythmic cadence.

Honestly, I wasn't sure if what I had written down was a verse or a chorus. But since I hadn't seen my parents in some time, I set the initial "Rocket Man" lyrics aside. I can't recall exactly where I wrote the remaining verses or the chorus: "And I think it's gonna be a long, long time/'Til touchdown brings me round again to find/I'm not the man they think I am at home/Oh no, no, no, I'm a rocket man." I do know I finished the lyrics before I presented them to Elton in late '71. That's how we worked. My lyrics always came before Elton's music.

When I first came down to London in 1967 to look for work as a lyricist, at seventeen, I wasn't proficient on anything. I still can't play piano. And I'm not a very good guitar player. I met Elton through an ad in the *New Musical Express* newspaper. In the early days, before he recorded his first album in 1969, we lived at his mother's flat in the Northwood Hills section of London.

There was an upright piano in the living room. I'd sit on my bed in the back bedroom and write lyrics. Once I had something, I'd walk down the hallway to the living room and say to Elton, "Here, try this one." Then I'd go back to my room to write the next song as he wrote the music to the one I had given him. It was like an assembly line, like factory work [Taupin laughs].

Elton had recorded his first four studio albums at Dick James and Trident Studios in London. We couldn't afford to write together there because of the expense of studio time so we worked at our London flat. For *Honky Château*, his fifth studio album, in '72, we lived and wrote at the Château d'Hérouville outside Paris, where the album was recorded. As always, Elton and I worked there in separate spaces, with the words coming first.

127

I probably completed the lyrics to "Rocket Man" at the Château in late 1971, just before Elton began recording the album in January '72. He never questioned the meaning of any of my lyrics. He might say, "I don't understand this, and I don't know if I can work with it." But he never challenged my interpretation or the art of what I do.

In some respects, "Rocket Man" is a song of fragments. It's a short song with four short verses and lots of air to give it an ambient feel of space. But it's not poetry. I'd rather not be regarded as a poet. Unfortunately, I've borne that cross for years. Leonard Cohen is probably the only lyricist who can be called a poet. Some say Bob Dylan, but I think the songs Dylan has written that are regarded as poetry are more avant-garde, possibly in the Allen Ginsberg realm.

I'm a lyricist, and there's a big difference. My words are meant to be set to music. After I capture what's on my mind, I don't go back and overthink what I've written. Everything I write is pretty immediate. If any of the words or lines on "Rocket Man" were moved around, I'm sure I did that before I gave Elton the lyric sheet.

During the recording of "Rocket Man," I sat in the control booth and just observed. I felt very inadequate in the studio. I was a little intimidated by producer Gus Dudgeon. He was so technically advanced. I was afraid if I said something I would be laughed at. When I heard Elton's recording of "Rocket Man" played back for the first time on the monitor speakers, I was thrilled.

It was an amazing feeling to hear my lyrics turned into something special. The music gave my words a living, beating heart. You never get that feeling solely from the words. That feeling comes from the magic of music and melody—and arrangements and great musicians.

When "Rocket Man" came out in April '72, most people weren't aware of Pearls Before Swine's song. So critics pointed to David Bowie's "Space Oddity" as an obvious influence. But Bowie's 1969 song had no relevance to me whatsoever. I wasn't listening to pop music on the radio then. I was listening to Chicago blues, hard-core country, and mostly American-made music.

Looking back, the only line on "Rocket Man" that still bothers me a little is "Mars ain't the kind of place to raise your kids/In fact it's cold as hell." Mars's temperature is about as far from hell as you can get.

There's also a good chance that Elton stretched out my opening chorus line. I believe I wrote: "And I think it's gonna be a long time." Elton made it a "long, long time" so it would sing better. It's the same on "Bennie and the Jets." I didn't write "Buh-buh-buh Bennie." Those are Elton's tweaks that make our songs hits.

The Spinners, from left, Philippe Wynne, Bobbie Smith (front), Pervis Jackson, Billy Henderson and Henry Fambrough in 1974.

20: I'll Be Around
THE SPINNERS
Released: July 1972

In 1969, Philadelphia began to emerge as the center of a new form of soul that paired vocal harmony groups with lush, romantic orchestral arrangements. At the heart of this sound was Thom Bell, a classically trained musician and a songwriter and arranger. He produced artists such as the Delfonics in the late 1960s and the Stylistics in the early 1970s. In 1972, he took on the Spinners, who had left Motown for Atlantic Records.

One of the first songs Bell produced for the group was "I'll Be Around," which not only would set the tone for Philadelphia International Records in 1972 but also was among the first hits to feature a sophisticated dance beat that was copied and embellished in the music industry, giving rise to disco in 1973 and '74.

When the Spinners' "I'll Be Around" was released as a single in August 1972, it appeared on the B-side of the group's first Atlantic single. After radio DJs discovered the song and began playing it, the single climbed to No. 3 on the *Billboard* pop chart and to No. 1 on the R&B chart.

Thom Bell
(composer and producer)

One Friday afternoon in early '72, I was at Philadelphia's Sigma Sound Studios producing a Stylistics record. When we finished, Vince Montana, a superb percussionist and a friend, started teasing me. "Man, Thommy, I bet you can't write a simple song with three chords, like the old doo-wop stuff." I laughed and said, "Doo-wop was nice, Vince, but we've evolved." He said, "Yeah, but I still bet you can't do it. You need three legs to dance to some of this stuff."

Back at my office that evening, I couldn't shake Vince's challenge. I turned to my piano and played a series of three-chord combinations. Eventually I landed on E major 7, G-sharp minor, and F-sharp major 6 [Bell illustrates on the piano]. I realized I had the start of a song for Bobby Smith, the Spinners' lead singer. The Spinners had just signed with Atlantic, and I was producing two songs for them—"How Could I Let You Get Away" and "Just You and Me Baby." I wanted a third, for insurance.

What I loved about Bobby's voice is that he had an unusual vibrato and rarely sang on the beat. The melody and rhythm that I came up with was perfect for his voice. When I was done, I needed a lyric. But there was a problem. My writing partner, lyricist Linda Creed, was leaving on her honeymoon and I couldn't wait until she returned. The Spinners were coming into the studio that Tuesday to try out all three songs.

So the next morning, on Saturday, I went into my office and found lyricist Phil Hurtt, Bunny Sigler's writing partner, in another office. I played Phil the song on the piano. Then I gave him a cassette tape of me playing piano and humming the melody. I told Phil the title I had in mind—"I'll Be Around"—which was based on my melody. I didn't tell him what kind of story line I wanted. I left that to him.

Phil Hurtt
(lyricist)

That evening, I was watching the 76ers basketball game with the sound down and listening to Thommy's tape. I started writing the lyric based on his title. As soon as I came up with the first line, "This is our fork in the road," the rest came fast. [Hurtt sings a verse]: "You made your choice, now it's up to me/To bow out gracefully/Though you hold the key, but baby/Whenever you call me, I'll be there."

My lyric was about a guy who loves his girl, but he understands that she's confused and wants to date someone else. Instead of getting angry, he lets her go. He's hurt, but he's betting she'll come back. He's giving her space and offers a safety net. He knows there isn't much he can do if she wants to leave. His play is to be there if things don't work out for her. It was an unusual theme then from a guy's perspective.

Bell

As soon as I heard Phil's opening lines—"This is our fork in the road/Love's last episode/There's nowhere to go, oh no"—I loved it. The romantic story line was perfect for the Spinners. Now that I had the song's words, I wanted to be sure the song worked for the guys. The Spinners had a distinct, vulnerable sound. When Bobby and the Spinners came in that Tuesday, I played piano and sang Phil's words. Then Bobby and I went over the lead vocal part.

Once he was set, I worked with the rest of the Spinners. I sang each of the background notes I wanted them to sing, and they tried them out. Before they left, I recorded each Spinner singing his part and gave them each a tape. They had just come off the road and were heading home to Detroit for two weeks to rest. By practicing their parts at home, we'd save time and money when they came back to record.

When the Spinners left, I began writing and arranging the basic rhythm-track arrangement. After I finished, I brought the musicians in to record. On the intro, I had session guitarist Norman Harris open with three notes using octaves resolving in an E major 7 chord. Then I answered his line with three chords on the Clavinet, which sounds like an electrified harpsichord.

I wanted the Spinners to record more up-tempo dance stuff, so I had the drummer, Earl Young, emphasize the second and fourth beats. The flavor he came up with was fantastic. It became the start of the Philly dance beat that was adapted for many disco hits that came later.

Earl Young
(drummer)

As a session drummer, I had to have a thousand different beats in my head. I didn't do solos or stick-spinning stuff. I played grooves. My job was to come up with a beat that made the lead vocalist want to sing, so you could hear that energy and excitement in his voice. On "I'll Be Around," I created a medium-tempo dance beat. I hit the snare and floor tom-tom at the same time on the second and fourth beats to give them a fatter sound. Meanwhile, I played what I call my Native-American beat on the bass drum—two hits on the first beat and a one hit on the second, repeating the pattern on the third and fourth beats. This gave the song its groove.

Bell

When the Spinners came in to record, they put on headphones and added their vocals to the rhythm track. Once the vocal track was combined with the rhythm track, it was time to overdub the horns. After I recorded their parts, Don Renaldo and his strings overdubbed my "sweetening" arrangement. Then I overdubbed myself playing tambourine on the second and fourth beats to add a little shimmer.

I also added female background vocals. The Spinners were great, but they had low voices. The song needed a greater vocal range. I auditioned about twenty singers and hired Barbara Ingram, Evette Benton, and Carla Benson. They were students at Glassboro State College in New Jersey. I found them through my first wife, who was best friends with Barbara's older sister.

This was the first time I used female background singers with the Spinners. After "I'll Be Around," I used them on everything I produced. They became known as the Sweethearts of Sigma. By the end of the year, with "I'll Be Around" a hit, Atlantic had me produce the rest of the tracks for *Spinners*, the group's first album for the label, released in April 1973.

Hurtt

The first time I heard "I'll Be Around" on the radio, I loved it. The only change I noticed in my lyric was the addition of the word "once": "And love can burn once again, but I know you know." I didn't write that word in my original lyric. Bobby Smith must have added it so the line would be easier to sing at that tempo. Hey, it worked. My kids called the song "tuition." In the 1980s, they were in college, and whenever they heard it, they'd call and say, "Hey, Dad, cha-ching!"

Bell

In November '72, I saw Vince Montana at one of my recording sessions. I said, "Hey, remember that three-chord song you said I couldn't write? 'I'll Be Around' is No. 1 on the R&B chart and No. 3 on the pop side." Vince looked down, shook his head, and just laughed. Hey, if Vince hadn't challenged me that day, I probably never would have written that song.

The Temptations, from left, Otis Williams, Dennis Edwards, Melvin Franklin, Damon Harris and Richard Street in 1973.

21: Papa Was a Rollin' Stone

THE TEMPTATIONS
Released: September 1972

For years, Motown avoided recording socially conscious soul. The label's music from the start was about love, fitting in, and upward mobility. But as the 1960s grew more divisive over civil rights and the Vietnam War, a growing number of soul artists recorded songs for their labels about the struggle for equality and the plight of the inner city. Motown's fear was that politically charged music would turn off its mainstream market and could put the company's brand at risk. Finally in 1968, the label relented, and Diana Ross & the Supremes recorded "Love Child," which reached No. 1 on the *Billboard* pop chart.

By 1971, the label had released a good number of songs with socially conscious themes. Among them was "Papa Was a Rollin' Stone," about a father who abandoned his family from the perspective of a child. Originally recorded by the Undisputed Truth, their version only reached No. 63 on *Billboard*'s pop chart and No. 24 on the R&B chart after being released in early 1972.

Rerecorded by the Temptations in mid-1972 with a new arrangement, the psychedelic-soul ballad with a heavy bass line became a No. 1 *Billboard* pop hit. The song won two Grammys and was inducted into the Grammy Hall of Fame in 1999.

Barrett Strong
(lyricist)

In mid-1971, Norman Whitfield called me at home. We were a Motown songwriting team and lived just three or four blocks from each other in Detroit. He had a groove he wanted me to hear that needed lyrics. When Norman came over, he played me a tape he had recorded with the Funk Brothers, Motown's studio musicians. The music was for a song he was working on for the Undisputed Truth, a Motown group.

Norman said he wanted lyrics that were fun, not serious, so listeners would have a good time with it. But as I listened over and over after Norman left, I didn't hear the music the way he did. There was something about the bass line that spoke to me. It was the sound of someone confused about something and was trying to make sense of it.

The more I listened, the more situations I encountered as a child came back to me. I recalled kids whose fathers had abandoned their mothers coming to me for advice. They didn't understand why it happened or how to deal with it. Even though I was little, I was wise, like an old man. My father was a minister. He'd talk to me about life situations like that all the time. His stories stayed with me.

One day, a friend from across the street was at my back door crying. He wanted to know why his father wasn't around. I knew the reason but had to say something to calm him down. I told him, "Your papa's just a rolling stone." "Rolling stone" was a phrase used all the time in my neighborhood going back to the '50s. It meant a guy who couldn't settle down, even if he had a wife and kids. It was from the old proverb "A rolling stone gathers no moss."

Working at my piano, I came up with a story about children whose father had died and are asking about the neighborhood gossip: "Hey, Mama, is it true what they say/That Papa never worked a day in his life?/And Mama, there's some bad talk goin' around town/Sayin' that Papa had three outside children and another wife/And that ain't right."

My chorus was the mother's response: "Papa was a rollin' stone/Wherever he laid his hat was his home/And when he died/All he left us was alone."

138

That's the way it generally happens. A child asks his mother why his father is like that. Then the child has to live with what he's told. In the song, the mother rationalizes the father's behavior and blames it on his nature, even though they're left with nothing. It's about hopelessness and hope.

When I finished the lyrics, Norman liked the narrative, even though it was serious, not fun. After the Undisputed Truth recorded "Papa" and it was released in May '72, the record didn't do well on the charts. Norman convinced Berry Gordy [Motown's founder] to let him rework the music for the Temptations. Norman went back into the studio in the spring of 1972 with the Funk Brothers to start from scratch.

Paul Riser

(arranger)

I didn't arrange the Undisputed Truth's version of "Papa." That was David Van De Pitte. After Norman had the Funk Brothers come up with a new basic rhythm track for the Temptations, he asked me to arrange their version. He gave me a raw, unmastered tape of what they had come up with. When I first listened to the tape, I didn't think much of the new version. The bass intro lasted just over four minutes. I remember thinking, "When is this thing going to end?" I thought the song was over when the bass stopped. [Note: Of the three bassists listed on the album—Bob Babbitt, James Jamerson, and Leroy Taylor—the one who played on the song remains unknown.]

Strong

Norman wanted that extended bass line because nobody else had done anything like it at the time. The line originally lasted ten minutes but he edited it down to four. It was too good to stop.

Riser

The more I listened to the tape, the more intrigued I became. To me, the bass conveyed mystery and suspense. So I arranged the song like a movie score. The soundtrack to *Shaft* was a big influence. I had seen the film a year earlier when it came out and loved what my friend, arranger Johnny Allen, did with the orchestration. The bass on "Papa" had a similar feel.

I wanted to use strings throughout the song to build suspense. I wrote a string arrangement that wrapped around the bass to enhance the line. I brought in musicians from the Detroit Symphony, with Gordon Staples as concertmaster. I used nine violins, four violas, three cellos, and a harp.

I introduced the strings early in the song—in the fifth measure—to set the tone. Throughout the song, I had the strings play tremolos to hover above the music and add tension. That approach worked perfectly, especially when combined with the harp and Earl Van Dyke's Fender Rhodes electric piano. "Wah Wah" Watson's guitar and Maurice Davis's trumpet were overdubbed later.

Otis Williams
(Temptations founding member and baritone singer)

One evening in early 1972, the Temptations—Dennis Edwards, Melvin Franklin, Richard Street, Damon Harris, and me—were in Motown's recording studio. Norman played us the new rhythm track for "Papa Was a Rollin' Stone." To be truthful, we almost didn't record the song. The guys had enough of Norman and Barrett's psychedelic soul. "Papa" came after a long string of similar songs for us—including "Cloud Nine," "I Can't Get Next to You," "Ball of Confusion," and "Psychedelic Shack."

When we toured, fans constantly asked us when we were going back to ballads like "My Girl" and "I Wish It Would Rain." All of us wanted to return to more romantic songs. In the studio that evening, we listened to Norman's tape. At the end, I said, "Come on, Norman. We're tired of that stuff." Norman said, "No, no, it's gonna be a hit." For about twenty minutes, there was a back-and-forth.

Norman said, "Please fellas, come on, come on." I knew Norman best and could see he wasn't gonna let up. I said, "Come on y'all. Let's give it a try." As a vocal group, we grabbed the background quick. But the main lead part by Dennis Edwards needed a different tone. The song called for him to sing the lyrics with a bad attitude, which wasn't his thing.

Dennis hadn't heard the Undisputed Truth's single and didn't like "Papa's" opening line. His father had died the previous September 3, and he thought Norman and Barrett were poking at him: "It was the third of September/That day I'll always remember, yes I will/'Cause that was the day that my daddy died/I never got a chance to see him."

Norman insisted the line was completely coincidental. He also had the ingenious idea to have Richard, Melvin, and Damon sing lead lines so it sounded like a bunch of children were asking their mama about their father. Norman typically kept lead singers in the studio until "no o'clock" [Williams laughs]. You'd walk out whenever Norman felt he had what he needed. Norman asked Dennis for quite a few takes.

I was there when Maurice Davis recorded his trumpet part. Just as he was getting ready to leave the studio after he recorded, Norman had an idea. "Before you go, try this," he said. Some new gadget had just come out that had an echo on it. After Maurice hooked it up to his trumpet, he rerecorded his solos.

Riser

The gadget made Maurice's trumpet sound like kids crying or a police siren—a shrill flavor from the streets. It was another voice in the song and another part of the dialogue between the instruments.

Strong

The song works because the lyrics reflect reality. People have conversations like that every day. That's why it rings true. On the music side, Norman knew the song needed a big statement, so he had that long bass solo. Norman also knew all along we needed the Temptations on that song. The guy was a magician.

Roberta Flack in 1973.

22: Killing Me Softly With His Song

ROBERTA FLACK

Released: January 1973

Roberta Flack didn't set out to become a performer. Though she had played organ and piano in church growing up in North Carolina, she attended Howard University intending to become a music teacher. Soon after Flack became a grad student in music, her father suddenly died and she took a job teaching music and English. While teaching in Washington, D.C., Flack began to sing and accompany herself on piano at local clubs. She was discovered by soul-jazz pianist Les McCann, who arranged for her to audition at Atlantic.

From 1969 to 1971, Flack recorded a series of songs that either didn't chart or didn't chart spectacularly well. Then in 1972, she recorded a Scottish folk song called "The First Time Ever I Saw Your Face," which went to No. 1 on the *Billboard* pop chart. Her next single was "Where Is the Love," recorded as a duet with Donny Hathaway. It reached No. 5.

In 1973, while on a flight, she heard a folk song through her headset connected to the airplane's audio system. On a napkin, she re-ordered the lyrics and sketched an arrangement to "Killing Me Softly with His Song." Her version went to No. 1 for five weeks on the *Billboard* pop chart. Flack won two Grammys, and the song won Song of the Year and was inducted into the Grammy Hall of Fame in 1999. The song's lyricist, Norman Gimbel, died just prior to these interviews.

Charles Fox
(composer)

When I was eighteen in the late 1950s, I spent two years in Paris studying composition with Nadia Boulanger. By the early 1960s, I was a New York pianist with a background in classical, jazz, and Latin music. Then in 1967, I composed and scored the music for my first movie, *The Incident*, a film noir. *Barbarella* followed and, in 1969, producer Stanley Jaffe asked me to come out to Hollywood to score the Paramount film *Goodbye, Columbus*. That's when I saw my life coming together as a composer.

In '69, I was asked to score and write songs for the movie *Pufnstuf*, based on the children's TV series. But I needed a lyricist. BMI executive Ron Anton suggested Norman Gimbel. Norman had written English lyrics for bossa nova hits, such as "The Girl from Ipanema" and Michel Legrand's "Watch What Happens" and "I Will Wait for You." Norman and I hit it off.

By 1971, we wanted to develop songs for a female singer and get the songs recorded, the way Burt Bacharach and Hal David did with Dionne Warwick. We went to clubs and auditioned quite a few. Then someone recommended Lori Lieberman. We heard her and loved her sound. She had a beautiful alto voice. Norman and I started writing for her. Lori recorded song demos, and we made a deal with Capitol to produce four albums. We soon had nine songs in the can for the first one. Capitol was enthusiastic but wanted a tenth song.

Norman came over to my house in Encino. As I sat at my grand piano, Norman stood in the piano's curve facing me. He skimmed through his notebook of ideas. At some point, he looked up and said, "What about this—'Kill us softly with some blues?'" Norman said the line came from an Argentine novel called *Hopscotch*, by Julio Cortázar, published in English in 1966. Pianist and composer-arranger Lalo Schifrin had given him the book.

I liked the "kill us softly" part, but "with some blues" sounded dated. By '71, pop music had entered the folk-rock era of singer-songwriters like James Taylor, Carly Simon, and Joni Mitchell. Norman thought for a second and agreed. "What about 'Killing me softly with his song'?" I liked it. Norman went home to Beverly Hills. A few hours later, he called with the song's words. I wrote them all down. His lyrics opened with a verse: "I heard he sang a good song, I heard he had a style/And so I came to see him, to listen for a while/And there he was, this young boy, a stranger to my eyes."

The verse was followed by the chorus: "Strumming my pain with his fingers/Singing my life with his words/Killing me softly with his song/Telling my whole life with his words/Killing me softly with his song."

When I set to work on the music, I repeated the lyric "killing me softly with his song" because I needed an extra musical phrase to complete the melody I wrote. I also added pauses in two lines: "Telling my whole life [pause] with his words/killing me softly [pause] with his song." The pauses provide the lyric with a moment of reflection. That's part of the storytelling process from the composer's viewpoint.

As I wrote, Norman's lyrics guided my melody and harmony. But I was also writing for Lori. I could hear her singing the song in my ear. So I wrote the music as an introspective ballad. About a half hour later, I was done. The next morning, we asked Lori to come over. I played the piano and sang the song for her. She said the song reminded her of hearing Don McLean perform and being moved by his songs. She had seen him recently at an L.A. club. Then I played the song as Lori sang from a lyric sheet Norman had handed her.

Lori Lieberman
(folk singer)

Hearing Don McLean perform his song "Empty Chairs" affected me deeply. I wrote a poem about how I felt right then and there. Later that night, I called Norman and read him my poem. He thought it would match one of the titles he had written in his notebook of ideas. Over the course of the next two days, Norman asked me many questions about my experience. I answered them to help get the lyric just right. I've always been proud to be instrumental in the creation of "Killing Me Softly." I want nothing other than to be acknowledged for my part in the inception of this beautiful song.

Fox

We recorded the song in 1972 at Western Recorders in Hollywood. Lori played guitar in concert but not on the song's recording or the album. For that, I contracted studio guitarists. I arranged "Killing Me Softly," and Norman and I coproduced. I played a piano introduction, two guitars joined, and then Lori started singing the first verse. When we turned in the album, Capitol thought "Killing Me Softly" should be the single. To promote the album, Capitol programmed the song on American Airlines. Back then, airlines had different music channels—rock, classical, pop. Their playlists were on loops. Passengers couldn't skip songs or go back. You had to listen all the way through before the playlist repeated.

Roberta Flack
(singer, pianist, and arranger)

In 1972, I was on a flight from New York to Los Angeles and was listening to the plane's music channels. That's where I first heard Lori Lieberman's version of "Killing Me Softly." I probably heard it four times on the flight. The lyrics were haunting and the chord changes were lush. I could feel the song and knew I could tell the song's story my way.

Parts of the song reminded me of my life, of the pain that comes with loving someone deeply, of feeling moved by music, which is the universal language. More than anything, music makes us feel. As I listened, I jotted down the lyrics on a napkin. I also wrote down music lines and made notes on how I was going to arrange the song.

Fox

Back then, I was working on several Paramount projects at once. I had an office on the studio lot and spent a lot of time in their music library. One day, as I walked through the library, someone said I had a phone call. When I picked up the receiver, Roberta Flack was on the other end. Roberta said, "We haven't met but I'm going to sing your song." I was floored. Her cover of "The First Time Ever I Saw Your Face" had just won two Grammys.

Months later, I read a review that said Roberta performed "Killing Me Softly" during a concert run at L.A.'s Dorothy Chandler Pavilion the night before. I said to Norman, "Let's go down and see her." We went, and I could hear that she was developing her own way with the song. She sounded beautiful, but it wasn't yet the record that became a big hit.

Flack

In the studio, I gave my arrangement a 2/4 feel and took it a little faster than the original. I wanted a groove that deepened the song's meaning. The groove is the heartbeat of a song. Grady Tate played drums and Ralph MacDonald was on percussion. I also decided to open the song with the chorus rather than the first verse. "Strumming my pain with his fingers" was such a strong line. The rest of the chorus was powerful and set the song's tone.

I arranged my background singers like a choir. I grew up in the church. The harmonies never left me. They deeply influence all of my music. I also decided to play the electric piano rather than an acoustic piano. It has a more soothing sound at times. I felt it expressed what I felt in a way that the acoustic piano could not. If you listen carefully, you realize that the song is based on circles. It never ends. I chose to end the song on a major sixth chord instead of a seventh. To the ear, the sixth ends the cycle and the song.

Fox

Roberta's record became my first big hit. Since then, there have been hundreds of versions, including one by the Fugees in 1996. But Roberta's remains the one that's continually played around the world. There obviously was magic in her voice and in her arrangement decisions. As soon as the song opens and you hear her voice, you have to listen to it. Many years later, in 2004, when I was being inducted into the Songwriters Hall of Fame, Roberta agreed to present me with my award. Earlier in the day, after the rehearsal, she and I were alone in the hotel ballroom.

I said to her, "Roberta, how lucky for me that you found the song." Roberta, who's a very beautiful, spiritual person, said, "No, Charles, the song found me."

Deep Purple, clockwise from top left, Ian Paice, Ritchie Blackmore, Roger Glover, Jon Lord and Ian Gillan in the early 1970s.

23: Smoke on the Water

DEEP PURPLE

Released: May 1973

Loud, aggressive, and powered by the electric guitar, hard rock had a slow birth. Early bands that laid the groundwork in the 1960s included the Kinks, the Who, the Yardbirds, the Rolling Stones, Cream, Blue Cheer, and the Jimi Hendrix Experience. By the early 1970s, with the advent of album-oriented FM radio and concerts held in arenas, British bands such as Led Zeppelin, Black Sabbath, and Deep Purple took rock to the next level, with an emphasis on wailing vocals and commanding guitar riffs and solos.

Formed in London in 1968, Deep Purple started as a psychedelic rock band and then became a progressive rock ensemble before switching to hard rock in 1970 with their *Deep Purple in Rock* album. Their first major hit in the U.S. was "Smoke on the Water." The song's guitar chords that dominate the introduction remain one of hard rock's most iconic and enduring opening riffs.

When "Smoke on the Water" was released as a single in May 1973, it climbed to No. 4 on *Billboard*'s pop chart and helped lift *Machine Head*, the album on which it appeared, to No. 7. The single, written by all five band members, was inducted into the Grammy Hall of Fame in 2017.

Ian Paice

(Deep Purple drummer and cowriter)

In late November 1971, Deep Purple flew to Geneva, Switzerland, and drove to Montreux. Our friend and Swiss concert promoter Claude Nobs had invited us to record our sixth studio album at the Montreux Casino, on Lake Geneva. We were fed up with traditional recording studios. Most of them were outdated for our needs. The control rooms were cutting-edge, but the recording spaces were too small to capture our big stage sound accurately.

We had played the Casino earlier that year, and the space was ideal. But we needed a solid control booth for our recording engineer. So for December, we rented the Rolling Stones Mobile Studio—a control booth built into a large truck. It rolled into Montreux the night of December 3.

The next afternoon, we went to the Casino to hear Frank Zappa and the Mothers of Invention perform. We had never seen them live, and we wanted to hear how the music sounded in the hall. The Casino was a wood building with tropical island decor and around two thousand seats. Toward the end of the concert, someone behind us shot off a flare that soared into the rafters. The heat from the phosphorous light ignited a fire.

Frank Zappa, God bless him, went to the microphone and announced, "Fire! If you'd kindly move calmly toward the exit, ladies and gentlemen. Calmly." Then he smashed some of the ballroom windows with his Gibson guitar so people could escape faster. There was a gentle panic, but everyone got out.

Ian Gillan

(Deep Purple lead singer and cowriter)

Once outside, we walked to the Hôtel Eden Palace Au Lac a short distance away. In the bar-restaurant, we ordered drinks and watched the Casino burn. At some point, Roger Glover, our bassist, said, "Look at the smoke on the water." There was a downdraft from the mountains that shoveled the thick smoke from the fire across the lake. It looked like a film set, with the flames shooting upward.

Paice

Sitting there in the restaurant, two things went through my mind: I was happy we got out safely, and I began to realize that the place where we were supposed to record no longer existed. The next morning, Claude found us space at Le Pavillon, a grand theater near the Casino that was closed for the winter. The Stones' mobile unit parked outside, our gear was set up inside, and we started jamming late that afternoon for a sound check.

Roger Glover
(Deep Purple bassist and cowriter)

Once our sound was together, Martin Birch, our engineer in the mobile unit, began recording the jam.

Ritchie Blackmore
(Deep Purple guitarist and cowriter)

Ian Paice and I had started the jam by trying out things. At one point, he played this driving rhythm on the drums. I responded with the riff that wound up opening the record. Then Ian and I jammed on it before everyone else joined in. For the riff, I played two notes at the same time, starting with the G on top and D below. I played that with my thumb and first finger, not with a pick. The riff then moved along using the same spread between the two notes.

I used a black Stratocaster with a maple neck. The guitar was plugged in to a Hornby-Skewes Treble Booster that ran into a Marshall amp and speaker. The Hornby gave the guitar a vibrating, throaty sound coming through the speaker. Then I added chords to the riff for the rest of the song. My Strat was strung with bendable Clifford Essex guitar strings that Eric Clapton had recommended.

Paice

On the intro, as Ritchie played his riff, I played sixteenth notes on the hi-hat. For the body of the song, I played little twelve-note skips on the hi-hat to give the basic beat a roll, like a wave. Without the mild swing, the beat would have lost its rhythmic interest.

Glover

With that riff set, we built out the instrumental arrangement. We left room for verses, a chorus, and a guitar solo. I used a black-and-white Rickenbacker 4001 electric bass that I had bought earlier that year during our American tour. When I played it through my Marshall amp and speakers, it turned out to be raspier on the high notes and too distorted for my liking. But I had no choice. I only had the one bass with me and that Marshall stack.

There was no overdubbing on top of the bass. When the bass makes its entry, I'm playing E, F, F-sharp, and G. It couldn't be a simpler bass line. By midnight, the band had the riff and basic rhythm track down and started going for an actual take. But we had a problem. Our high volume had awakened the town and someone called the police.

Paice

After we finished recording a complete take of the instrumental, we learned that the roadies had been struggling to hold the doors shut with the police pushing on the other side. When the police finally came in, they told us to close down and leave. We labeled the reel we had just recorded "Title #1." It would become the instrumental backing track for "Smoke on the Water."

Glover

Clearly, recording at Le Pavillon was out. Claude found us sizable space at the Grand Hôtel de Territet a few kilometers out of town. It was closed for the season. The front doors opened into a large foyer, which led to a long corridor with high ceilings. It was ideal, but we needed to isolate and insulate the space.

Paice

To contain the sound, a carpenter put up a wooden wall to seal off the corridor where we planned to record. Then the roadies dragged mattresses from the rooms and put them up against the corridor windows. We also screwed in red lights to create a concert atmosphere. After we finished recording six songs for the album, we still needed one more. We pulled out "Title #1," which just needed a lyric and guitar solo.

Glover

Ian Gillan and I wrote the words while sitting on a bench in the corridor. I borrowed Ritchie's Stratocaster to pick out the tune as Martin, our engineer, played the "Title #1" tape through Ian's and my headphones. We called the song "Smoke on the Water" and had the lyric simply tell the story of what we had witnessed at the Casino—that we had gone to see the Mothers and the place burned down. We wrote the words in about twenty minutes.

Gillan

"Funky Claude" was Claude Nobs. "Swiss time was running out" was about finishing before we had to give up the "Rolling truck Stones thing." "With a few red lights/A few old beds/We made a place to sweat" refers to the red bulbs, the mattresses against the windows, and the space where we recorded the album. Then I overdubbed my vocal while listening to the "Title #1" track through my headphones. Ritchie had played the chorus in a minor key but I decided to sing it major, for the contrast.

Paice

The whoosh you hear on my drums at the end was done by hand in the booth. It's called flanging. We had two copies of the drum track playing back in sync with each other. When you applied gentle hand pressure to one of the tape reels, you momentarily slowed it down, increasing the degree of separation between them and producing that sound.

Glover

When we finished "Smoke on the Water," we didn't think it was that special. It was good enough for the album, but we had put most of our efforts into "Never Before," which was going to be our first single. That delayed our efforts for "Smoke on the Water" until a year after the album came out. I guess we just figured the song was an afterthought and that our fans would think of it the same way. Boy, were we wrong.

Todd Rundgren performing on TV's *Midnight Special* in 1973.

24: Hello It's Me
TODD RUNDGREN
Released: September 1973

Todd Rundgren doesn't fit into any single category of rock or pop. He's an amalgamation of them all. He began by cofounding the psychedelic rock band Nazz in 1967, left two years later to start a solo career, slipped comfortably into glam in the early 1970s and then progressive rock with Utopia before pioneering other forms as a producer of albums and songs by other groups. Later, he would become an early adopter of technology with music videos and computer software.

One of his first original songs was "Hello It's Me," written in 1967 about a painful high school breakup. He initially recorded the song in 1968 as a slow ballad with Nazz, though he wasn't the lead singer. In late 1971, while recording the solo album *Something/Anything?* he updated his song with a bouncier pop arrangement.

"Hello It's Me" peaked at No. 5 on *Billboard*'s pop chart after its release in 1973 and became Rundgren's biggest-selling solo hit, remaining on the chart for twenty weeks.

Todd Rundgren
(lead singer, pianist, and songwriter)

In the summer of 1967, I was sitting in a wheelchair. Nothing was wrong. I had cofounded Nazz months earlier and was living in our manager's townhouse in downtown Philadelphia. All of us in the band lived there. I found the wheelchair in a corner. I liked to roll around in it and balance myself on two wheels. Motion focused my energy. Up until then, Nazz had been playing cover songs. But we realized that if we wanted to attract a record deal and become successful, we needed original material.

One day, while sitting in the wheelchair, I was listening to jazz organist Jimmy Smith's recording of "When Johnny Comes Marching Home." The organ intro was intriguing. I picked up my electric guitar, a Gibson SG, and began trying to figure out Smith's descending chords. After I came up with an interpretation of the chords, I realized they could be the basis of an original song. Over the coming days, I developed a melody. Burt Bacharach was a big influence, especially his music for Dionne Warwick. The song "Walk On By" still knocks me out.

Once the music for my song was set, I turned to writing the lyrics. I thought back to early 1966, when I was still in high school. Senior year had been an emotional time. I had a crush on a girl named Linda, and we started seeing each other. She probably liked me because I was the only guy in school with long hair. We became close and hugged and kissed a lot at parties. One day in May '66, a friend dropped us off at Linda's house and I walked her to the front door. Her father, who was outside, hated me on sight. He turned the garden hose on me. Long hair on a guy was a political statement back then and a red flag for parents.

A day or two later, Linda told me she was forbidden to see me anymore. Just like that, she stopped talking to me and wouldn't take my calls. I adored her and was heartbroken, almost suicidal. That Christmas, I wanted to make a final gesture to win her back. I saved up and bought her a pantsuit. When I went to her house, the only person there was her sister, who invited me in. When I left, I realized I had to stop this. Writing my song in '67, I decided to make the lyrics about our breakup.

But instead of being the victim, I turned the song's story around so I was breaking up with her. This gave me a little power and allowed me to imagine how I might have done things differently over the phone.

I opened with "Hello, it's me/I've thought about us for a long, long time/Maybe I think too much but something's wrong/There's something here, doesn't last too long/Maybe I shouldn't think of you as mine." To ease the blow, I wrote a bridge about why the breakup was good for her: "It's important to me/That you know you are free/'Cause I never want to make you change for me." I guess in some ways it's how I would have wanted to be let down. As I continued to work on the song, I channeled other influences, including the Beatles and Beach Boys and their stacks of vocal harmonies.

Admittedly, to write a song like this, you had to be especially insecure. I didn't have a girlfriend all the way up through high school. Linda had been my first real relationship. Nazz recorded "Hello It's Me" on our first album in April 1968. Robert "Stewkey" Antoni, our keyboard player, sang the lead vocal. I envisioned the song as a ballad, but it became a dirge. I played the vibes on the recording, not the guitar. A guitar felt inappropriate, and I wasn't a ballad player. My guitar heroes were Eric Clapton and Pete Townshend. Vibes also gave the song a cooler, more atmospheric feel. The vocal harmony derived from major and minor seventh chords I learned fooling around on the piano in the high school auditorium after school. I didn't read music and still can't.

In 1969, I left Nazz to go out on my own as a producer and solo artist. By 1971, I lived in New York and had recorded enough material for three LP sides. I didn't intend *Something/Anything?* to be a double album. But I found a songwriting formula and got into a jag. I needed songs for the fourth side, so I decided to update "Hello It's Me." One Sunday morning, I called organist Mark "Moogy" Klingman and asked him to put together a recording session at New York's Record Plant that afternoon. By then, I envisioned the song faster and more sophisticated than the Nazz original. Carole King's *Tapestry* had just come out and its bouncy, melancholy sound was an influence.

At the Record Plant's top-floor studio, everything came together. Moogy brought in horns for the session—saxophonist Michael Brecker,

161

trumpeter Randy Brecker, and trombonist Barry Rogers. He also brought in five background singers. I established the feel for the song and taught everyone the chords before we recorded. On the 4:42 album version, you hear studio chatter and then a couple of false starts. I wanted to include sounds from the studio to give the song a live atmosphere.

I played eighth notes throughout on the piano, and Moogy played organ chords on top of those notes. My eighth notes provided urgency, a racing pulse under the whole thing rather than the original's sleepy conga. I wanted to put some life into the new version. Moogy's organ gave the song a breezy feel and filled out the spaces. The backup singers' parts weren't overly complicated until the very end, when I had them sing "think of me" a cappella several times.

Funny thing is the instruments that got the shortest shrift were the guitars. We used Rick Derringer and Robbie Kogel. I wanted them to sound as if the guitars had been an afterthought. "Hello It's Me" was done in a single take. I'm not sure if it was the first take, but there was no overdubbing or splicing. Everyone was in the studio at the same time. It happened just as you hear it.

Thirty years later, I was in Oklahoma to perform. On the afternoon before the concert, the phone in my hotel room rang. When I answered it, a woman's voice on the other end said, "Hi Todd? It's Linda. Do you remember me from high school?" There was a long pause on my end. When we finally began to talk, she told me she lived in the area, that she was married and had kids. My voice didn't warm up, and I avoided talking about the old days. I was pretty businesslike.

I told Linda I'd put her on the guest list for seats. She thanked me and we said goodbye. I added her name but I didn't include a pass for backstage access. Our lives had gone in two different directions and we really had nothing to say to each other. I think I also wanted to hold on to the image I had of her in high school. I never told her she was the inspiration for the song.

Daryl Hall, left, and John Oates of Hall & Oates in 1975.

25: She's Gone
HALL & OATES
Released: November 1973
Reissued: July 1976

Daryl Hall and John Oates met at Temple University in Philadelphia in the late 1960s. As musicians, they both had a keen awareness of the city's many vocal-harmony and romantic-soul groups. When Hall and Oates teamed up in 1967, they began as a soul cover band. In 1972, they signed with Atlantic Records just as the label was becoming a force in the emergence of Philadelphia soul. Hall & Oates's second album for the label, *Abandoned Luncheonette*, was released in 1973 and included their soulful ballad "She's Gone." But the song's single only managed to reach No. 60 on the *Billboard* pop chart.

After Hall & Oates released their hitless third album, *War Babies*, they were dropped by Atlantic. Then RCA signed the duo. Following the release in 1975 of *Daryl Hall & John Oates*—also known as the silver album—and the success of "Sara Smile," which had climbed to No. 4, Atlantic decided to reissue its single of "She's Gone."

By 1975, Philadelphia soul had already begun to dominate the charts thanks in part to hits produced by Philadelphia International Records. With the momentum of "Sara Smile," the reissue of "She's Gone" climbed to No. 7.

John Oates

(guitarist, singer, and cowriter)

I wasn't in love with our Manhattan neighborhood when Daryl and I moved up from Philadelphia in 1972 to gig and record for Atlantic. We lived uptown, in a second-floor apartment on 82nd Street and York Avenue. I wished we lived in Greenwich Village instead. A lot more was going on downtown, and I was often there at clubs.

One night in Greenwich Village, I ended up at the Pink Teacup on Bleecker Street at 2:00 a.m. On the weekends, the restaurant was open all night. After I was seated, in came this gal in a pink tutu with cowboy boots but no coat. Hardly anyone was there, so we started talking. She said her name was Freddy Littlebird. Hey, it was the early '70s.

At some point, I asked her if she wanted to get together that Sunday night on New Year's Eve. She said yes, so I gave her my address on the Upper East Side. Daryl was going to be away that weekend. But on Sunday, Freddy never showed. Bummed, I sat on our sofa strumming my acoustic guitar. Maybe she forgot or lost the address. Or she found something better to do. Or maybe, like me, she didn't care for the Upper East Side.

Either way, Freddy wasn't coming. She was gone. So I started singing a folky refrain about being stood up that sounded like a good chorus for a song:

"She's gone/I better learn how to face it/She's gone/I'd pay the devil to replace her/She's gone/What went wrong?"

A day or two later, Daryl returned. We sat around playing things and jamming. I told him the story about Freddy. He laughed. I said, "Check this out" and played him the "She's Gone" chorus.

Daryl Hall

(singer, keyboardist, and cowriter)

In 1972, my first wife, Bryna, and I separated. We had married in 1969 but the relationship wasn't working. It was a romantic shock period for me. When I returned to New York a few days after New Year's Eve, John played me the chorus of a song he was working on. As he strummed and sang "she's gone," the song was folky with the feel of Cat Stevens's "Wild World."

I liked it, but I'm much more R&B. I said, "Let's try it in another groove." I sat down at my Wurlitzer electric piano and played the keyboard lick you hear on the record's intro. John and I pooled our romantic sorrows, and I began coming up with lyrics for the verses. My marriage was dissolving, and everyone I knew was telling me not to worry, that I was going to be all right. None of that was helping: "Everybody's high on consolation/Everybody's trying to tell me what is right for me."

My family was religious, and we had attended a progressive Methodist church when I was little. That's where I sang growing up and learned about showbiz: "My daddy tried to bore me with a sermon/ But it's plain to see that they can't comfort me."

Oates

My chorus was about a girl who had come and gone. Daryl's verses were about lost love. We always took a universal subject and personalized it so someone listening could absorb it.

Hall

It's hard to describe songwriting's creative flashes. I tend to take little things from life when I write. After my marriage fell apart, I felt awful and it showed: "Get up in the morning, look in the mirror/I'm worn as a toothbrush hangin' in the stand/My face ain't lookin' any younger/Now I can see love's taken her toll on me."

The rest of the song's lyrics came together quickly. We immediately wanted to use it on our second Atlantic album.

When we went into Atlantic Studios in mid-'73 to record *Abandoned Luncheonette*, I played two measures of the "She's Gone" intro on the Wurlitzer for producer Arif Mardin. "That's wonderful," he said. We went forward and recorded it. For the session, Arif pulled together great studio musicians—bassist Steve Gelfand, drummer Bernard Purdie, percussionist Ralph MacDonald, and saxophonist Joe Farrell. Guitarist and keyboardist Chris Bond came with us, and Arif wrote the string and horn arrangements.

Oates

Purdie set the pace when he counted off the tempo for "She's Gone." He's so good that whatever he played that day was going to be perfect. We settled into his groove. It was like riding a wave.

Hall

The intro instrumental opened with me playing two bass notes with my left hand on my Wurlitzer followed by chords with my right. Steve on bass mirrored my left hand and made the line sound like a heartbeat.

Oates

Chris played the moaning guitar solo on the intro. I had a wah-wah pedal so I used it while playing my '58 Fender Stratocaster in reaction to what Daryl was doing on the keyboard. We were early synthesizer experimenters. On the intro, Chris added what sounds like electronic drops landing in water on an ARP 2600. It's a monophonic synthesizer, meaning you could only play one note at a time on the keyboard. You'd hit a note and use a dial or bar to create an audio effect. At the end of the intro, Chris added a high-pitched sound on the Arp that trails off.

Hall

John and I always overdubbed our own background vocals. Here, we arranged them so they'd sound like a gospel choir.

Oates

Our vocal harmony is all about texture. What makes our voices unique are the contrasts. Daryl's voice cuts. I'm softer and there's a thickness to it. The result combines thickness and edge.

Hall

I extended the intro for twenty measures. I wanted to create a mood and really set it in there. Then Arif overdubbed his string section arrangement. Strings in the verses intensified the mood's emotional confusion and suspense. By contrast, they play more of a sweetening role on the chorus. Halfway into the song, Arif overdubbed a terrific saxophone solo by Joe Farrell, who was playing with a lot of jazz fusion bands then.

After the solo, Arif suggested the music build to a climax. He had our instrumental modulate in half steps from the key of E to F, F-sharp, and then to G, with John's guitar wailing at the top. When Arif told me what he wanted to do, I thought, "What a crazy idea." But it was unbelievable. I was so taken with the crescendo that instead of hitting a B with my voice, I leapt to a D-flat when singing "She's gone, oh-whoa-oh I, I better learn how to pray."

How we ended the song wasn't planned. John and I just started exchanging "She's gones," like a call-and-response. We didn't rehearse that. It just felt right when we started doing it. John and I and Arif wanted the song's romantic sentiment to evolve. Early in the song, the vocal sounds despondent and directionless. But by the end, with the orchestral build and burst, the mood was more of a shrug and the feeling of moving on.

After *Abandoned Luncheonette* and the "She's Gone" 45 were released in late 1973, the single only charted at No. 60. We were disappointed. FM radio had gotten behind the album and it was big in college dorms. But the whole idea of white guys singing R&B wasn't appealing yet on a mass scale. You have to remember how unique we were at the time.

The following year, the vocal group Tavares recorded our song. Their version went to No. 1 on the R&B chart. I was pissed off that someone else had aced our song. "There it goes," I thought. In 1975, John and I moved to RCA. But our first album for the label with the silver cover confused people. We appeared to have makeup on our cheeks and around our eyes, so people didn't know what we were—glam, disco, rock, R&B, straight, gay. Now I look back and I'm proud we were shattering people's perceptions.

When the single of "Sara Smile" became huge, Atlantic re-released "She's Gone." This time it went to No. 7. We had just entered our I-told-you-so period. As for Bryna, I'm guessing she knew "She's Gone" was about us. But I wouldn't know. When we separated, we didn't keep in contact.

Oates

After Freddy stood me up, I saw her here and there in the Village in the months ahead. I never asked her why she didn't show New Year's Eve. By then, Daryl and I were touring. Talk about she's gone—I was gone. The past didn't matter much to me anymore.

Redbone, from left, Lolly Vegas, Pat Vegas, Pete DePoe and Tony Bellamy in 1971.

26: Come and Get Your Love

REDBONE

Released: January 1974

Native Americans' vast contribution to the development of R&B and rock is woefully underappreciated. The list of rock artists with Native American heritage is long and includes Howlin' Wolf, Link Wray, Robbie Robertson of the Band, Buffy Sainte-Marie, Rita Coolidge, Jimi Hendrix, Jesse Ed Davis, Jamie Luis Gomez of the Black Eyed Peas, Jimmy Carl Black of Frank Zappa's Mothers of Invention, Willy DeVille, Gary Duncan of Quicksilver Messenger Service, Anthrax's Joey Belladonna, and the Ventures' Nokie Edwards.

Formed in 1969 by brothers Pat and Lolly Vegas, Redbone was one of the first Native American rock bands in the post-Beatles era. The Vegas brothers had started as a cover band act in Sunset Strip clubs in West Hollywood in the early 1960s. When Redbone was formed, the band consisted of Pat Vegas on bass, Lolly Vegas on lead guitar, Peter DePoe on drums, and rhythm guitarist Robert Anthony Avila, whose stage name was Tony Bellamy. All were Native American.

"Come and Get Your Love" was credited to Lolly Vegas and released as a single from the band's fifth album, *Wovoka*. While *Wovoka* only reached No. 66 on the *Billboard* album chart, "Come and Get Your Love," with its ancestral dance beat, peaked at No. 5 on *Billboard's* pop chart in 1974.

Pat Vegas
(Redbone bassist, arranger, coproducer)

My father and mother met during the Depression in Texas and moved onto an Indian reservation in Arizona. When I was a year old in 1942, we moved with my older brother, Lolly, to Fresno, California, where my father found a job working in the Coalinga Oil Field. Our family name was Vasquez. We were descendants of Native American tribes of the Southwest and proud of our heritage. My mother's father, Antonio Beltrán, was a musician. So was everyone in his family. His sister was Lola Beltrán, Mexico's most famous ranchera singer and a favorite of Linda Ronstadt.

My grandfather had a guitar he played all the time at family gatherings. He kept it on top of his armoire. He said, "When you can reach that guitar, it's yours." A few days later, when I was five, I stood on a chair, took down the guitar, and started practicing. My brother already was playing guitar. He played it like a piano, picking at the strings with all four fingers at once. We formed our first local band when I was fourteen, playing Top 40 hits. Soon I had to switch to bass. We couldn't find a bass player who could keep up with our unusual rhythms.

By then, my parents had divorced. When my mom remarried, we added my stepfather's last name to ours—Vasquez-Vega. In the early 1960s, Lolly and I formed the Avantis, a surf-rock band, and looked for work at clubs on the Sunset Strip in Los Angeles. But many club owners told us they didn't hire Chicanos, Indians, or Blacks for their house bands. At Gazzarri's, the owner, Bill Gazzarri, liked us. He added an *s* to our last name, and we performed there as Pat & Lolly Vegas.

As our reputations grew, we worked as songwriters, arrangers, and studio musicians in Hollywood and Las Vegas. We played on records by

Sonny & Cher, James Brown, Tina Turner, and others. We also released singles and an album for Mercury in '66—*Pat & Lolly Vegas: At the Haunted House*. The Haunted House was an L.A. discotheque. In 1969, Lolly and I decided to form a rock band that embraced our Native American heritage. We needed a name.

My grandfather was from Texarkana, Texas, and had played guitar in a five-piece Cajun band on the weekends right over the Louisiana border. When I was little, he told me about the tribes uniting to fight and defeat General Custer at the Battle of the Little Bighorn in 1876. Afterward, he said, our people were on the run and went first to Canada and intermingled with the Acadians. Then they relocated to southwestern Louisiana, where many Cajuns lived. Lolly and I chose Redbone to pay tribute to our people for their courage and bravery.

One night, in 1973, Lolly called me at around 3:00 a.m. He asked me to come over. He had an idea for a song and wanted help. I grabbed my bass and tape recorder and went over to his house in Hollywood. Lolly played me what he had—a few plain chords, from C to D to B to E to A. It was a little singsong-y and needed an arrangement. We also had to change some of the lyrics. They needed to be smarter.

I told him to leave me alone in the room with it. The first thing I did was come up with the bass line. It immediately turned the song around. Then I altered the chord voicings and gave them a rhythmic feel. As I worked on the song and the arrangement, I thought about how Native Americans were always depicted in Westerns as bad guys being chased by the cavalry. I wanted the song to change that image.

My brother had called the song "I Want to Give You My Love." I changed it to "Come and Get Your Love." We wanted to show that our people were about love, not about massacring. By then, I had been in the room for hours putting the song together, getting the right rhythm and taping the music on my recorder. When the demo was perfect, I played Lolly the tape. He loved it. We also worked on the words. We opened the first verse with the word "hail," like glory to the world: "Hail/What's the matter with your hair, yeah-yeah/Hail/What's the matter with your mind/And your sign and-ah oh-oh-ohhh."

The song's verses refer to the excuses people back then came up with to explain why they were feeling out of sorts. Worrying about your state of mind, your astrological sign, your hair—they all got in the way of natural, honest feelings: "Hail/Nothin' the matter with your head/ Baby, find it, come on and find it/Hail, with-it baby, 'cause you're fine/ And you're mine, and you look so divine." The chorus—"Come and get your love"—is about pure love, without all the overthinking and trendy phrases.

The following day, Lolly and I went into Devonshire Sound Studios in L.A. with Tony Bellamy, our guitarist, and Pete DePoe on drums. Butch Rillera, who would become our next drummer, overdubbed background vocals. The beat was a joint effort, with Pete laying it down while we fine-tuned it. What we came up with was a Native American dance beat. When you dance to the Indian tom-tom, it's a straight beat with an emphasis on the upbeat—"don don-don, don don-don." Not "don-don don-don," like in the movies.

On the recording, after the opening drumbeat, my Fender Precision bass line mirrored Pete's tom-tom dance beat. If you listen carefully, the bass line drives the song. Lolly played an electrified sitar that Bob Bogle and Don Wilson of the Ventures had given me at a party as a gift. They were good friends. At the end of the chorus—"Come and get your love"—Lolly switched to his Fender Telecaster and played a wailing bluesy line.

We also wanted strings for drama. So Lolly and I got together with arranger Gene Page and told him where the strings should and shouldn't play. We used four strings and doubled them—meaning they recorded their part twice for a fuller sound. The song was on our fifth album, *Wovoka*. When the album came out in late '73, I brought it over to my mom's house in Salinas. As soon as "Come and Get Your Love" came on, she got up and started doing a tribal dance. She heard the beat and was so proud.

When the song reached No. 5 in April '74, I was thrilled. People were finally getting to know what we could do. We had proved that a Native American band could sing about love and have a pop hit on its own terms. We toured that year and played the song on TV's *Midnight Special* and *In Concert*. Tony dressed in a traditional Native American costume, with a bustle of eagle feathers on his back. He opened the song with a tribal dance.

On the road, when we'd first come out onstage in traditional Native American outfits, people in the front rows freaked and backed up about four feet. It was funny. They'd seen too many Westerns.

Gordon Lightfoot in Toronto in 1977.

27: Sundown
GORDON LIGHTFOOT
Released: March 1974

Three years older than Bob Dylan, Gordon Lightfoot has long been Canada's most revered folk singer-songwriter. Dylan has recorded Lightfoot's songs, as have many artists who treasure Lightfoot's craft of writing poetic lyrics and setting them to impossibly beautiful music. When Dylan was asked in a 2009 interview by MTV producer Bill Flanagan which Gordon Lightfoot songs he liked, Dylan said, "'Shadows,' 'Sundown,' 'If You Could Read My Mind'—I can't think of any I don't like."

A prolific Canadian recording artist since 1962, Lightfoot became a country-folk sensation when "If You Could Read My Mind" crossed over to the U.S. charts in 1970 and reached No. 5 on the *Billboard* pop chart. In all, he has had fourteen charted hits, including "The Wreck of the Edmund Fitzgerald."

His biggest hit was "Sundown," released in 1974. The song about jealousy and a failing relationship reached No. 1 on the *Billboard* pop and easy listening charts. Twelve years later, Cathy Smith, the song's unnamed subject, pleaded no contest to injecting comedian John Belushi with a fatal dose of heroin and cocaine in Hollywood in 1982 and served fifteen months in prison. She died in August 2020.

Gordon Lightfoot
(guitarist, arranger, singer, and songwriter)

Jealousy isn't healthy for a relationship, but it tends to work out pretty well when writing a song. At least it did for me. In June 1973, I was living in Aurora, Ontario, about forty minutes north of Toronto. I wanted to see how I'd do writing in the country, on the quiet side of things. I was due to record my next album that fall and needed another bunch of songs.

In Aurora, I rented part of a small two-story house on land that no longer was being farmed. The space had a sizable music room where I could write and keep my instruments and records. At the time, I was living with a woman named Cathy. We first met in 1971 at a country-and-western lounge in Toronto's Edison Hotel. I had gone there to hear an artist backing singer George Jones.

At some point, I looked across the bar and saw her. Cathy was beautiful. When she passed me, I said hello. On her way back, she stopped to talk. We made a date to go out and, before long, we moved in together. Two years later, up at the Aurora farmhouse, our relationship was fading. My first wife and I were separated and soon to be divorced. I didn't want to jump back into marriage. Cathy was resentful or bored. Either way, we weren't getting along.

Late one afternoon in July, Cathy said she was going into Aurora for a night with her Toronto girlfriends. I wasn't happy about that. Neither of us had been prudent about some of the things we had done in the relationship. After she left, I watched the sun set slowly out back. I felt tremendous jealousy. Once the ball of orange disappeared behind the hills, I grabbed my Gibson B-45 twelve-string guitar and began writing a song. I came up with an E chord to use as a drone behind a melody. You can hear the drone chord throughout the song. That chord was my dread about what Cathy was up to at the local bars.

By then, I was sitting at my desk with the guitar in my lap and a pad and pen, looking out at my front yard toward the road. I wrote "Sundown" using just three chords. Once I had the melody, the lyrics came pretty quickly. Songs for me have a way of pulling themselves forward. Given the jealousy and emotional trauma I felt, I knew my relationship with Cathy was in trouble. As I wrote, I couldn't help imagining that Cathy was chatting up guys. That image turned up in the opening verse: "I can see her lying back in her satin dress/In a room where you do what you don't confess."

The same goes for "She's been lookin' like a queen in a sailor's dream/And she don't always say what she really means."

"A queen in a sailor's dream"—I was happy with that line. It's one of my favorites in the song.

The chorus—"Sundown, you better take care/If I find you been creepin' 'round my back stairs"—was aimed at the imaginary guy she met. If you're gonna pick up my girl, don't show up at my house, please.

"Sometimes I think it's a shame/When I get feelin' better when I'm feelin' no pain." That's about drinking to numb the emotional pain.

"I can picture every move that a man could make/Getting lost in her lovin' is your first mistake." In those lines, I'm imagining guys checking her out.

The sunset was so beautiful that evening it made me mellow and aware of what I was feeling and how saving the relationship was pretty much impossible. But I was happy the relationship was winding down. You can hear my two different emotions in the song—a sense of blues and relief. Once I got going on a song, I usually didn't stop until it was done.

Cathy returned alone by 2:00 a.m. All of that stuff I had cooked up in my head—it was imaginary. When she came in, I had finished "Sundown" and was already on to another song. In the weeks that followed, I finished writing the album's remaining songs. Then I wrote arrangements for them. I'd studied arranging at Westlake College of Music in Los Angeles right out of high school.

I knew from the start I wanted a big bass part for my bass player, John Stockfish. He was a great player. The same was true for guitarist Red Shea. We had worked as a trio for years. In November '73, we recorded at Eastern Sound Studio in Toronto. At the first session, we rehearsed the song. That's when John came up with that superlative bass line that drives the song. It sounds big because he was a big player.

I played rhythm guitar on the opening and throughout the song on my Gibson twelve-string. Red played lead on his Martin D-18 acoustic. His electric guitar solo in the middle and at the end was done on a Fender. I overdubbed all the background vocals on the chorus myself. I added two voices to my lead vocal—a high part and a middle one. Then I doubled them to widen the sound.

We recorded all of it without a click track keeping the beat. That's a natural feel on there, and it only took us two or three takes.

Lenny Waronker
(producer)

In Toronto, drummer Jimmy Gordon played the first take with an emphasis on the second and fourth beats. But something didn't sit right. Fortunately, the engineer I was working with—Lee Herschberg—was pretty damn smart. When Lee and I talked in the control booth between takes, he suggested we ease up on the backbeat.

So in the verses, I had Jimmy hit just the fourth beat. That opened up space so you could better hear Gordon's vocal and guitar part. Jimmy resumed hitting the second and fourth beats on the chorus. The first time Red Shea took his electric guitar solo in the middle of the song, it didn't sound cool enough. The lyrics had a lot of drama, so the solo needed a toughness or a vibe. Otherwise, it was going to turn out square.

I walked into the studio, and Red and I talked about it for a while. Then I had a suggestion: "What about Pops Staples? Let's go that route." Pops was the father of the Staple Singers and the group's guitarist. He liked playing with a lot of tremolo. So Red adjusted his settings, and the tremolo added a lot of character to his solo. It was an easy fix, and it worked.

At some point, Gordon wanted to overdub a tambourine accenting Jimmy's beat. I pushed back. I was worried the song would turn out too pop. But he overruled me. In L.A., I was at Amigo Studios mixing the song and album when producer Ted Templeman, one of my closest friends, stopped by. I played him the tambourine overdub on "Sundown." He said, "Are you kidding? Keep it. It's just right."

Gordon knew what he wanted and could hear everything in his head. "Sundown" had a vibe, it had a sound. The moment he overdubbed his background voices in the chorus, it was over. I knew then that the song was undeniable.

Lightfoot

After the summer in Aurora, Cathy and I moved back to Toronto. We were together for another year and split in mid-'74, after "Sundown" came out. She heard the song, but I never told her it was about her. In fact, it wasn't about her. It was about me. I was singing about the emotional stress I was going through leading up to our split. It was a tough breakup. Cathy had gotten to know my kids from my previous marriage. We had a good thing, but the relationship didn't have fidelity across the board.

Cathy Smith
(the song's inspiration)

Gordon was a wonderful writer, a great tunesmith, and a talented singer. I was lonely up there while he worked. I liked going out with my friends back then, so they came up from Toronto. Those were crazy times.

Lightfoot

After Cathy and I parted, I saw her from time to time in Toronto. But I didn't feel bad. It had to be done. I don't know if she figured out the song. She probably did. I never got into it with her. The Aurora farmhouse is gone now. It was torn down soon after to make room for Highway 404. But the sun still sets beautifully up there, especially in the summer.

10cc, from left, Eric Stewart, Lol Creme, Kevin Godley and Graham Gouldman in 1975.

28: I'm Not in Love
10cc
Released: May 1975

In 1975, romantic soul was giving way to disco in the United States, rock had embraced a new androgyny, and punk was churning away as a working-class backlash against glossy arena rock. In the U.K., pop was becoming more sophisticated, mixing flamboyant glitter rock with American soul. It was a period in the U.K. when imaginative pop bands took risks and sifted varying styles to create a sound that would stand out and win over the U.S. market.

One such band was 10cc. Formed in Manchester, England, in 1972, the art-rock quartet was comprised of four multi-instrumentalists who also happened to be two pairs of songwriters: Eric Stewart and Graham Gouldman, and Kevin Godley and Lol Creme. All four had been in a long series of British bands with different names since 1964. Once they changed their band's name to 10cc, they went on a tear, releasing twelve songs that appeared on the *Billboard* pop chart between 1973 and 1979.

In 1975, 10cc released "I'm Not in Love," its breakthrough hit. With a tape-loop vocal choir, a female voice whispering, "Be quiet, big boys don't cry," and a Moog-generated beat, the ethereal ballad about resisting romantic commitment reached No. 2 on *Billboard*'s pop chart. The hit also helped set the stage for the British synth-pop movement of the early '80s.

Eric Stewart
(10cc lead vocalist, keyboardist, and cowriter)

One morning in the fall of 1974, my wife, Gloria, and I were having breakfast at home in England. At some point, she said, "Why don't you say you love me so much anymore?" We had been married nine years by then. I said, "Look, if I say that every day, the words will lose their meaning, won't they?" She said, "No, they won't." We left it at that.

After breakfast, I went off to the living room, where I had a grand piano and my acoustic guitar. I began writing a song about saying "I love you" without actually saying it. As I worked on the lyrics, I tried to balance what Gloria wanted me to say and how saying it would trivialize how much I loved her. At first, I tried a contrast. I sang, "I'm not in love" followed by things like "It's because I adore you." But on paper, it seemed clichéd and trite.

Instead, I wrote about the conflict between feeling a certain way and avoiding expressing it. I created the melody by strumming chord arpeggios on my guitar. For the first eight-bar bridge, I wrote a contrasting line: "Don't feel let down, don't get hung up, we do what we can, do what we must." But it sounded a little lame. When I arrived at Strawberry Studios in Stockport, about twenty minutes from my home, Lol Creme and Kevin Godley were busy on another song. So Graham Gouldman and I worked on "I'm Not in Love." He came up with masterful chords.

Graham Gouldman
(10cc bassist and cowriter)

For an intro, I played an A-major 6 with a B on the bottom on my guitar, shifting to a B-major chord with the B still in the bass. To set up the first verse, I went to a G-sharp 7 with a G on the bottom, and then a C-sharp minor with an A in the bass. When Eric started to sing, I used an E-major chord with a G-sharp in the bass followed by a G-sharp 7, C-sharp minor, and C-sharp minor 7. We also needed a second eight-bar bridge. All at once, Eric and I came up with "Oooh, you'll wait a long time for me" along with the music and chords.

Stewart

When Graham and I finished, Kevin and Lol joined us, and we recorded our first run-through using a light bossa nova beat. But during the playback, Kevin wasn't happy with the bossa or my "Don't feel let down" lyrics for the first bridge. Lol agreed and suggested we drop them entirely and he'd simply play the bridge's melody on the piano.

Gouldman

One of the best things about 10cc was that no matter who wrote a song, the others had the right to make it better. That gave all of us creative freedom.

Kevin Godley
(10cc drummer)

For me, the bossa thing wasn't daring. We needed something bigger and more atmospheric and evocative. What I heard in my head was a wash of voices, a choir that would hover above the music, like the one I had heard in the movie *2001: A Space Odyssey*.

Lol Creme
(10cc keyboardist)

Kevin's choir idea was great but it would be costly. Instead, I suggested we record the voice parts ourselves. I said we could do it by singing thirteen notes in a chromatic scale and recording them onto thirteen different tape loops. Then we'd record the loops individually onto our sixteen-track tape machine.

Stewart

It was ingenious. But first we had to record the song's basic rhythm track and my lead vocal as a guide. We knew our choir notes would take up thirteen of the sixteen tracks on our recorder. This meant we had only three left for the rhythm track. On one track, I played the electric piano and sang the lead vocal. Graham played rhythm guitar on the second track. On the third, Kevin used a Minimoog set to sound like a bass drum. He tapped out a ballad groove on the Moog's keyboard that sounded like a heartbeat.

Once we recorded the rhythm track, we spent weeks recording our voices and transferring them onto our recorder. Then the four of us worked the mixing console's twenty-four volume faders with two hands to create a choir behind the rhythm track and my lead vocal. We loved the background voices so much we left all the faders up a little throughout the song to provide a white-noise atmosphere. To be sure our vocals were always there as background, I put a long strip of gaffer tape below all the faders to prevent them being brought down accidentally to zero.

Gouldman

We were taking a big chance on the choir concept. It had never been done this way before. But when we finished, the result was exciting. Our voices sounded like they were from another planet.

Creme

Even with the choir, the song needed texture. I suggested Graham overdub an eight-bar bass solo on the first bridge. Someone said, "A bass solo in a love song, in a ballad?" We decided it was worth a try. I also suggested we have a female voice whisper, "Get it together."

Stewart

At that very moment in our conversation, Cathy Redfern, the studio's receptionist, stuck her head in. She whispered, "Eric, there's someone on the phone for you" and left. Lol said, "That's it! Let's get Cathy to speak the words."

Creme

I went down the hall after Cathy. When I told her what we wanted, she protested a bit, saying she had never recorded anything before.

Cathy Redfern
  (studio receptionist)

I was twenty-one then. I adored the boys, and they treated me like their sister. When Lol told me their idea, I thought it might be a prank. They were always kidding around. But Lol picked me up and threw me over his shoulder. In the control room, the guys were serious. They told me it was a love song and that my line should sound like I was trying to convince my boyfriend to think clearly.

Creme

But the more I thought about that line, the more "Get it together" sounded harsh. So I changed it to "Be quiet, big boys don't cry," which felt softer and more comforting.

Redfern

I went into the studio with Kevin, who was there to steady me and give me a cue. We both put on headphones so we could hear the song. Kevin touched my arm when it was time to say the words.

Stewart

At first, Cathy's delivery wasn't musical enough. We said, "Go softer, go softer, Cathy. Whisper. Get closer to the mike." Then she got it. We were using a Neumann U67 mike and had put a foam "pop shield" over it to prevent the mike from picking up any pops when Cathy got close and said the words "big boys."

Redfern

Hearing my voice after was surreal. I couldn't believe it was me. I was thrilled.

Stewart

After Cathy's voice recording, we overdubbed Graham's bass guitar solo leading into Cathy's words and his playing underneath her lines. It was another beautiful atmospheric touch. Lol's piano melody that opens the bridge was the next overdub. The slap-back stereo echo that I added to the piano notes gave them a haunting sound. Still, Lol thought we needed one more twist.

Creme

I went out and bought a child's plastic toy music box. When you pulled the box's string, it played the English nursery rhyme "Boys and Girls Come Out to Play." We set up two mikes in the studio about twelve feet apart, for a stereo effect. Then I swung the little box over my head between the two mikes as it played the tune. We wound up with an eerie sound, shifting from one speaker to the other. After Eric added stereo echo, the effect at the song's fade-out was like someone whistling in a tunnel.

Stewart

Finally, I mixed everything we had recorded. The electronic-sounding "ah-ahhhs" throughout are single notes I used from the tape loops for a punctuation effect. When we finished the album, I drove Gloria to the studio. The wives of the other guys joined us. We turned out the lights and listened to the whole thing, playing it over and over for what seemed like hours. Everybody loved it.

On the drive home, Gloria asked what "I'm Not in Love" was about. I told her, "It's my answer to your question about why I didn't say 'I love you' more often." Gloria said the song was so beautiful and unforgettable. Then she said, "I'd still love if you'd say 'I love you' more often." From then on, I've said "I love you" to Gloria every night.

Bryan Ferry of Roxy Music in London in 1975.

29: Love Is the Drug
ROXY MUSIC
Released: October 1975

Among the most fascinating and influential pop-rock movements of the 1970s was new wave. This outgrowth of punk first emerged in the mid-1970s as a way for more dimensional artists with punk sensibilities to break free of punk's monochromatic look and minimalist sound by incorporating fashion imagery, art sensibilities, and pop influences. New-wave artists in the United States and the U.K. not only were attuned to the so-called underground music scene but also to the downtown art and fashion worlds, which began to develop at about the same time.

In the U.K., Roxy Music was one of the earliest bands to combine aspects of glam rock, the rawness of punk, and the moody seduction of English fashion pop. Formed by Bryan Ferry in 1970, Roxy Music began recording in 1972. The band of highly skilled musicians recorded and performed music that was both edgy and posh and, at times, tongue in cheek. Models were used on many of their album covers in an effort by the band to embrace fashion and glamour and catch the eye of record buyers.

In 1975, several years before the new-wave movement took hold, Roxy Music released "Love Is the Drug." The minor-key single from the band's prescient *Siren* album reached No. 30 on *Billboard*'s pop chart and was the band's highest-ranging U.S. single. It also influenced the music of Nile Rodgers, Kraftwerk, Talking Heads, Elvis Costello, U2, and the Smiths, among others.

Andy Mackay
(Roxy Music saxophonist and cowriter)

I first met Bryan Ferry in London in 1971. Mutual friends who had attended art school at the University of Reading introduced us. I had studied the oboe and alto saxophone there. In college, I hung out with the art crowd and formed a performance-art group in 1967. We staged happenings and performed avant-garde contemporary music along the lines of John Cage, La Monte Young, and Morton Feldman.

Bryan and I quickly discovered that we both were working part-time as schoolteachers. We had an immediate rapport, and soon we began playing together with bassist Graham Simpson in what would become Roxy Music. A short time after the band formed, I brought Brian Eno into the mix. I had met Brian years earlier through my performance-art group. Just before I met Bryan, I bought a VCS 3, a portable analog synthesizer. I continued to play oboe and sax in Roxy, but I found it difficult to play and operate the VCS at the same time. So I played and Brian Eno twiddled the knobs. We also were using the VCS in Roxy to treat and distort the vocals and oboe.

Bryan Ferry
(Roxy Music lead singer, keyboardist, and cowriter)

When we formed Roxy, we just wanted to make interesting music that expressed who we were and what we were. I wanted Roxy to reflect my various interests and musical styles and forms, especially art music by John Cage and others like him. So it was great when I met Andy and, subsequently, Brian Eno and the others. We all had similar interests. There was a combination of elements that we put together that sounded different from what everyone else was doing.

Mackay

At home in London in early '75, I came up with chords for an unusual song on my Wurlitzer electric piano. My chords had a distinctly English-y sound inspired by twentieth-century classical composers like Ralph Vaughan Williams. They had a folk-harmony feel influenced by early church music. The song I composed didn't have words or a title. When I played it for the band at the studio, my tempo was slow, with a majestic, sweeping feel, moving in a dreamy and ambient direction. Bryan [Ferry] and drummer Paul Thompson wanted to push it along, to make it more dance-y.

Ferry

In June 1975, we began recording *Siren*, our fifth Roxy Music album, at George Martin's AIR Studios on London's Oxford Street. Chris Thomas was producing. I was writing the words and music for many of the album's songs on my own. But at some point, Andy played me an interesting chord sequence that sounded very promising. It was different from the other songs I had in mind for the album. At first, Andy's song was very slow moving—a bit like a requiem. I remember thinking it might sound better if we sped it up a bit.

Mackay

As soon as the tempo picked up, bassist John Gustafson jumped in with an awesome bass line. Interactions followed between the bass and drums that produced a Latin feel along with Jamaican ska, which was big in London then. I added my alto sax briefly in the early part of the song and then played a riff during the chorus. I was influenced by R&B sax players like King Curtis and wanted a nonjazzy riff.

Chris, our producer, suggested I double-track my riff on the chorus, to give it dimension. He insisted I double-track precisely. Chris was the guy who pushed you to work hard. He also stopped me from playing any additional sax lines. Had he not been there, I probably would have wanted to play the sax all the way through the song. Playing it at the start and on the chorus was just enough.

Ferry

I played the Farfisa organ, and Andy and Eddie Jobson added the other keyboards. Andy's sax fanfare on the intro was striking, and Phil added some great chiming guitars on the chorus. Paul Thompson played a strong and simple drum part, and Chris added a shimmering Leslie effect on the snare. The bass part John carved out was very unusual—angular and abrasive. I loved what he did the moment I heard him play it. John was special. He had played in the Big Three, one of the Liverpool bands of the early 1960s. He was a very rock 'n' roll sort of guy. Years later, producer and Chic cofounder Nile Rodgers said that John's bass line was a big influence on his group's "Good Times" in 1979.

Mackay

When we finished recording the music, Bryan took a tape home to work on the lyrics. When they were done, he brought them into the studio, complete. He liked to hone his product and get it down to what he felt it should sound like.

Ferry

Back then, I lived on Ladbroke Road in Holland Park, West London. I tended to work through the night on lyrics, which I would write on notepads. Then I'd piece them together on my old beat-up typewriter. My lyrics for the song's opening were inspired by the Caribbean patois of our Trinidadian friend, Christian. He worked for Roxy doing wardrobe. Christian was a very amusing, laid-back guy. If there was ever a problem, Christian would say, "T'ain't no big t'ing."

I liked the phrase, so my opening lyrics to the song were: "T'ain't no big thing/To wait for the bell to ring/T'ain't no big thing/The toll of the bell."

The image I had in mind for the song was a young guy getting into his car and zooming off into town, looking for action at a club: "Late that night I parked my car/Staked my place in the singles bar/Face to face, toe to toe/Heart to heart as we hit the floor."

I don't know how I came up with the rest of the song's lyrics. As a songwriter, you kind of discover what a song is, or it imposes itself on you. It's always quite complicated. I just thought of them. The words weren't based on something I had read or heard.

"Love Is the Drug" turned out to be a fun, upbeat song with a jaunty feel—quite unusual for me, as a lot of my songs had a melancholy flavor. At some point, I thought the song needed a dramatic opening. Outside my house, I had a gravel drive, and the crunching sound of the gravel under my shoes was an inspiration.

I decided it might be a good idea to add some sound effects to the song's intro. This would help create a picture of someone jumping into his car, revving up, and heading off into town. We found the different sounds for the opening on various sound-effects recordings—a car door slamming shut, the engine starting, and so on. Then we overdubbed them.

Mackay

When Bryan brought his lyrics into the studio, he double-tracked his vocal in stark harmonies to give it a full feel. With "Love Is the Drug," we needed a song that would take us a little bit mainstream without compromising our artistic approach. We wanted to consolidate ourselves on *Siren* and have the result sound more like a rock album. We didn't want it to sound too strange. We needed to make some money and tour. North America had been hard for us. We were seen there as an art-rock band.

Ferry

There is a kind of mysterious and slightly subdued quality about the song. We also used an interesting sixth on the song's final chord. I always quite liked that. We didn't shoot a video for "Love Is the Drug." MTV was still six years away. But there is a television appearance of us performing the song up on YouTube. I wore a black eye patch in the video, but it wasn't a piratical fashion statement, as many people thought.

The day before our taping, I was sent to the hospital to have my eye looked at. I had walked into a door or something. I remember thinking, "Oh, God, we've got to do a television show tomorrow." Which we did despite my eye. In the video, if you look carefully, you can actually see a bandage with a dressing underneath. But the black patch did look good.

Phil Lynott of Thin Lizzy in Philadelphia in 1978.

30: The Boys Are Back in Town
THIN LIZZY
Released: April 1976

Up until 1976, Van Morrison's "Domino" had been the highest-charting *Billboard* hit by an Irish rocker, peaking at No. 9 in 1970. In Ireland, rock flourished in the 1960s with hits by Them, Taste, and Eire Apparent. The first two bands launched the careers of Van Morrison and Rory Gallagher, respectively. The last included Henry McCullough and Ernie Graham. Many Irish rock musicians in the 1960s started out playing in Irish show bands, which were cover bands made up of six or seven musicians. The music covered might be rock 'n' roll, country, Western swing, or even Dixieland jazz and would typically take place in ballrooms and dance halls. But by 1969, hard rock was emerging.

Thin Lizzy was an early Irish hard-rock band formed in February 1970. The band was named for Tin Lizzie, a robot featured in *The Dandy*, a popular British children's comic. The band altered the spelling to Thin Lizzy, adding the *h* as a nod to Dublin, where "thin" would be pronounced "t'in." After the band recorded its first album in London in January 1971, they moved there from Ireland for greater visibility and work opportunities. The three-man group was led by bassist Phil

Lynott. His mother, Philomena Lynott, would become a Manchester hotelier. His father was Cecil Parris, from British Guiana.

Thin Lizzy opened for more successful bands on tours but struggled to gain exposure outside of Ireland with their own singles and albums. Then in 1976, on the verge of collapse, the band released the single "The Boys Are Back in Town" from their sixth studio album, *Jailbreak*. The song, written by Lynott, reached No. 12 on the *Billboard* pop chart and today remains a popular sports-arena anthem in the United States and abroad.

Scott Gorham
(Thin Lizzy guitarist)

I grew up in Glendale, California. In 1971, my brother-in-law, drummer Bob Siebenberg, suggested I move to London on a work visa. He had just joined Supertramp. In London, I played in a few groups and then started Fast Buck, a pub band, in 1974. On Wednesday nights, I invited out-of-work musicians to play with us so I could meet more musicians. Ruan O'Lochlainn was one of those musicians.

At some point, Ruan mentioned that an Irish band in London was looking for a guitarist. Fast Buck wasn't going to last, so I called Chris O'Donnell, the Irish band's manager. Chris said the band was Thin Lizzy and that their guitarist had quit. He told me to go to Iroko, an African supper club in London's Haverstock Hill, where the band would audition me.

The club was staffed by African guys wearing flowery shirts and white trousers. I knew nothing about Thin Lizzy and had no idea what they looked like. Soon, a tall black guy came over to shake my hand and asked if I was Scott. At first, I thought he worked there. But it was Phil Lynott, Thin Lizzy's leader and bassist.

I auditioned, and Phil hired me, even though he had just hired guitarist Brian Robertson. It turned out Phil wanted two guitarists, in case one of us quit suddenly. Months after I joined, we recorded the band's fourth album, *Nightlife*. That was followed by *Fighting* in 1975. The albums didn't do particularly well. Our next album was do-or-die. We headed off to Farmyard Studios in Little Chalfont, about an hour northwest of London. We needed to work without distraction.

During our stay there, Phil asked what I thought of a chord progression he played on his bass. I told him it seemed a little simple. He worked on it, and soon he had a melody and lyrics. He called the song "G.I. Joe is Back." It was a weird anti-war song. The Vietnam War was over and American troops had been returning home. The song's melody and chords were good, but the lyrics needed work.

Chris O'Donnell
(Thin Lizzy band manager)

Around this time, I had been with the band at a gig in Manchester, England, when I noticed that most of the 900 people in the audience were young guys. I told Phil that these boys probably just got off work, they've had a couple of pints, and they wanted to be taken someplace with the music. Phil liked this idea—that the boys were together.

John Alcock
(producer)

Phil had a shoulder bag he carried around with a notebook that held his song ideas. At Farmyard Studios, when Phil wasn't playing, he worked on lyrics. At some point, Phil said he had changed the song to "The Boys Are Back in Town." It sounded less clumsy than "G.I. Joe Is Back," so it wasn't a controversial decision. With the new lyrics, drummer Brian Downey needed a new rhythm. I suggested a shuffle. Brian was very good at them. His shuffle helped Phil and Scott fall into a groove.

Gorham

"The boys are back in town" was almost like a soccer chant you'd hear on Saturday night. Mates getting together to take on the town. When Phil finished the lyrics, we tried the song. We took it faster than "G.I. Joe." The first verse's line, "They were askin' if you were around," is about a character named Johnny, who Phil used often in songs. The guy had been away and now he was back in town and ready to tear it up with the old gang.

The lines in the second verse—"And that time over at Johnny's place/Well, this chick got up and she slapped Johnny's face"—was an extension of the Johnny character. It was actually about a real guy who used to come to our gigs. He was a member of the Quality Street Gang, a group of rough guys in Manchester who ran clubs, bars, and car lots.

The reference to "Dino's Bar 'n' Grill" in the third verse had to do with Los Angeles. As a kid, Phil loved 77 *Sunset Strip*, the early '60s American TV detective series that aired in reruns on Irish television. For Phil, that show was the epitome of Hollywood. When we were in L.A. on our first American tour in 1975, Phil walked the Sunset Strip in West Hollywood looking for No. 77. That number didn't exist. When he asked a parking attendant, the guy pointed across the street at Dino's Lodge, which appeared on the show's opener. Phil added "bar 'n' grill" to Dino's because it sounded way better than "lodge" and more American.

O'Donnell

At the Farmyard, the band recorded demos of their new songs. Then we listened back. I stopped them on "The Boys Are Back." I thought it was a smash. The two guitars playing harmony in the middle and end didn't exist yet. But the song was everything I'd hoped for. I wanted John Alcock to produce because he was six foot four and had a commanding presence that the band would respect. He also helped design Ramport Studios, where he wanted to record.

Alcock

I loved Ramport. The space was owned by the Who and built in an old church hall with high ceilings and no carpeting. You'd get a lot of bounce in your sound there. I wanted to capture Thin Lizzy's live sound. They were always playing gigs and came across great onstage.

Will Reid Dick
(engineer)

John and I placed mikes about a foot away from Scott's and Brian's guitar speakers for that big live sensation. We also placed mikes at the other end of the room, to pick up the depth and dimension. John wanted a wall of guitars behind Phil's vocal. He had Scott and Brian overdub their guitar parts to thicken them up. I pushed the volume as much as possible.

Gorham

Phil said we needed a guitar harmony bit in the middle and at the end. I had Brian Downey's driving shuffle in my head so I added a rolling riff on there. Brian Robertson played harmony behind my melody, and he added a logical ending.

Alcock

After we had all the instrumental tracks, Phil came in and recorded his lead vocal. Then he recorded his "Boys are back in town" chant in the chorus. It sounds as if two guys in the band are singing the line followed by the other two echoing it. But it's really just Phil singing all the parts. At the end of the song, Phil decided to whisper, "The boys are back in town." This happens when the song is quiet, just before the guitars come back again and before the fade-out.

Gorham

I knew there was something special about Phil from the moment I shook his hand. Onstage, your eyes were glued to him. The guy had this magnetic quality. As Phil tried to emulate Jimi Hendrix, Jim Morrison, and his other heroes, he became increasingly dependent on alcohol. He turned to heroin by the early 1980s. By then, he'd often become sick and less dependable. Thin Lizzy broke up in '83.

In late 1985, I had done some recording and wanted a critique from Phil. One morning in early December I went over to his house. He answered the door in his bathrobe. He gave me a big hug. I played him my tape, and he took out his acoustic guitar and played along. Phil said we had to start writing songs again and that we should get the band back together. He was in terrible shape. I gave him a look like, "Hey, you're not ready." Phil saw that and said, "I'm gonna clean myself up now. It's gonna be great." I gave him a hug and left.

At the end of December, Phil's roadie, Big Charlie, called to tell me that Phil was in the hospital. On January 4, I was in the basement cleaning up when the phone rang. My wife picked up. I heard her gasp. When she got off, she told me it was Charlie. Phil had just died. I couldn't believe it and I sat down on the basement stairs. Then I cried my eyes out.

Steve Miller of the Steve Miller Band in 1972.

31 : Fly Like an Eagle
STEVE MILLER BAND
Released: August 1976

Steve Miller formed his Steve Miller Band in San Francisco in 1966. A year later, in June, the band appeared at the Monterey Pop Festival in Monterey, California, and they released their first album, *Children of the Future*, in 1968. A series of six albums followed, four of which charted decently on the *Billboard* 200. Then, in 1973, Miller released *The Joker*, an album that peaked at No. 2 while the title single was a No. 1 hit.

The follow-up album was *Fly Like an Eagle* in 1976. During the year, Miller had spent months experimenting on an early Roland synthesizer, which he used to give the album atmosphere and cohesion as a concept. The album produced three major hits, the title track, "Take the Money and Run," and "Rock'n Me."

After the single of "Fly Like an Eagle" was released in August 1976, it topped off at No. 2 on *Billboard*'s pop chart while the album of the same name reached No. 3.

Steve Miller
(Steve Miller Band guitarist, lead singer,
keyboardist, and songwriter)

By the end of 1973, I was pretty fried. We not only had toured about two hundred cities that year, we also recorded an album, *The Joker*. After its title single was released that fall, it went to No. 1, and the album reached No. 2. I needed some time to slow down, think, and write.

For much of '73, we had been booked into rock theaters and ballrooms that we called psychedelic dungeons. Audiences loved long-form rock, so performances became more like events than shows. Instead of short sets, we'd commonly play for three hours. That meant we needed songs that would let us stretch out and jam. "Fly Like an Eagle" was one of them.

I wrote the song at a string of Holiday Inns during the tour. Sitting on the bed in my room, I wrote the song in reaction to what I saw on the road. In '73, things hadn't gotten all juicy and '70s yet. American ground troops were returning home from Vietnam to a recession, and people were living on the streets. It was a bad time.

Originally, I wrote the lyrics as a political statement. The words were from the perspective of Native Americans and the despair they felt, especially after the Wounded Knee standoff with law enforcement earlier that year. It was a feeling and an idea, especially in the song's first chorus: "Time keeps on slipping, slippin' away/Time keeps on leaving me on this reservation."

The second chorus also touched on this: "I wanna fly like an eagle/ Let my spirit carry me/I wanna to fly like an eagle/From this reservation." Same with the verse: "What about the people livin' in the street/ What about the Indians on the reservation."

I didn't have other songs about social injustice in mind, like Marvin Gaye's "What's Going On" from '71. The energy from the group War probably had some influence, since I had played gigs with Eric Burdon and War. In '73, I had a different band than the one that would record "Fly Like an Eagle" in '75. That earlier band—we called it the Joker Band—had a gritty, funky feel.

So once I had the two choruses and a verse, I wanted to get a groove going. During a sound check, I got together with Gerald Johnson, our bassist, and John King, our drummer. Gerald was our groovemeister. When we had the right groove, Dickie Thompson layered in his organ. I also hooked up my guitar to an Echoplex so the notes would echo.

But "Fly Like an Eagle" was still in flux. As I sang the song on the road, I came up with new lyrics and kept the ones I liked best. At some point on tour, I broadened the lyrics' focus, replacing "reservation" with "revolution." I wanted to make the song's message more universal to reflect everyone who was suffering and wanted change.

I was always socially conscious. In the early 1960s, when I attended the University of Wisconsin at Madison, I joined the Student Nonviolent Coordinating Committee and traveled down South as a Freedom Rider. We'd ride public bus lines there to challenge racial segregation. I also demonstrated against the Vietnam War.

In early '74, when the tour was over and royalty checks started rolling in from "The Joker," I decided to take a year and a half off. I broke up the band and began woodshedding song ideas at my home studio in Novato, California. Writing and recording demos on my 3M eight-track tape recorder, I still felt the same way about the state of the world. I just didn't want to harp on it in my music. As I polished "Fly Like an Eagle," I realized I didn't want the song to sound bossy and preachy.

I wanted to put it on the good foot and make positive records. The word "revolution" was still in there as a lyric, but it was less pronounced. I also looked critically at the music. "Fly Like an Eagle" had been a great live jam on the road but the song wasn't cohesive or interesting enough yet to be a studio record. It needed more dimension and texture. Revising the song, I had a visual image of a mirror ball with light bouncing off of it. The song needed sparkle.

So I drove to my local music store in San Rafael and asked for the cheapest, dumbest synthesizer they had. Back then, players tweaked keyboards to get sophisticated horns and strings sounds. I wanted one with unhip presets like the sound of the wind, an oboe, and muted trumpet. I left with a Roland SH-2000.

At home, I hooked up the synthesizer to my Echoplex. I created effects on the keyboard that felt like an eagle taking off and flying. I'd long been fascinated by electronic music and using the studio as an instrument. When I was a kid, I listened to a lot of music by avant-garde composers like La Monte Young and Stockhausen. That's when I decided to add the Roland with spacey settings on all the songs for my next album. This included electronic segues between tunes so the music would be seamless.

By mid-1975, I had enough material and demos for an album. I put together a new band with Lonnie Turner on bass and Gary Mallaber on drums. We recorded the basic track for "Fly Like an Eagle" at CBS Studios in San Francisco, but the song didn't sound exciting enough and lacked a concert vibe. We rerecorded the song but still no luck.

The third time, we recorded the basic track at Pacific High Studios with Joachim Young on the Hammond B3 organ and nailed it. I recorded my Roland overdubs at CBS but decided to go up to Kaye-Smith Studios in Seattle to finalize the track. It was a modern studio with quad sound and the latest bells and whistles.

There, I hooked up the Echoplex to the Roland and added the spacey overdubs in the control room. The song finally sounded just right. For the album version, I created a "Space Intro" using the Roland's "wind" preset. I fed it through the Echoplex so the sound would build up on itself. After the wind, I played ascending glissandi on the Roland through the Echoplex, creating the feeling of elevation and flight.

My guitar riff that followed was similar to my riff on "My Dark Hour" in 1969. Nothing had happened with that song in terms of the charts, so the riff was fair game. I also wanted to add some spacey effects at the end. To do so, we needed to splice more tape onto the reel to extend it. But the studio was out of new tape. So Jim Gaines, who was doing the mastering, found a reel of used, two-inch tape that had been bulk erased. When you bulk erase, a machine spins the reel on top of a big magnet and wipes the tape clean.

But for some reason, the magnet didn't erase everything. Listening back to what I had overdubbed near the end—just after all that cosmic stuff but before the fade-out—we heard these beeps every few seconds.

They were like the beeps you hear when NASA controllers are talking to Apollo mission astronauts in space. The beeps were perfect. We kept them in. Also great was Joachim's organ, which warmed up the Roland's synthetic sound. The combination of the two different keyboards was really interesting.

I still have the Roland today. When we had toured in 1976 for *Fly Like an Eagle,* Byron Allred, our keyboard player, lugged around a 300-pound synthesizer that cost about $14,000. Along the way, it would slip out of tune each time we played an outdoor festival or stadium concert. The Roland always worked. I recently took the Roland out, put it on the counter in my studio, and hooked up the Echoplex. Then I switched it on, wondering how it would sound after all these years. I hit the tones I wanted. Like magic, out came exactly what's on the record.

Al Stewart in New York in 1981.

32: Year of the Cat
AL STEWART
Released: October 1976

Scottish singer-songwriter Al Stewart began his musical career in the British folk-revival movement of the 1960s. He first recorded in 1965 as a sideman on folk singer-songwriter Jackson C. Frank's first and only album. As a solo artist, Stewart's first four albums didn't attract much critical notice, though he began to develop a following in the U.K. His fifth album, *Past, Present and Future* (1975), was his first to be released in the United States, where it reached only No. 133 on the *Billboard* album chart. His next album, *Modern Times*, was the first in a string of releases to be produced by Alan Parsons. He then signed with RCA.

Al Stewart's *Year of the Cat* was his seventh studio album and was released in the United States in October 1976. The title track was catchy but the lyrics were enigmatic. They were inspired by a range of influences—including an English comedian who committed suicide, Bob Dylan's lyric writing, the movie *Casablanca*, a Vietnamese astrology book, and the novelist Somerset Maugham. To top it off, the song's lyrics detailed a mystical tryst in Morocco.

After the album was released, it climbed to No. 5 on the *Billboard* chart. The single peaked at No. 8 and its smooth sound and catchy melody helped make the song a mellow, yacht-rock classic.

Al Stewart
(multi-instrumentalist, lead singer, and songwriter)

In England in the 1960s, comedian Tony Hancock was a national TV sensation. He was self-critical and riddled with anxiety. Playing the underdog was part of his humor and charm. When I was twenty, in 1966, I went to see Hancock perform in Bournemouth. His monologue that evening was all about being a loser and why he may as well end it all right there onstage. The audience roared.

But I had this eerie feeling. What if he was serious? What if he truly was depressed and despondent? Two years later, while touring in Australia, Hancock committed suicide. His cry for help inspired me to write a song called "Foot of the Stage": "His tears fell down like rain/ At the foot of the stage." It had the same melody line that I used several years later for "Year of the Cat."

I worked in a strange way back then. I'd go into the studio and record all of the basic music for a song first. Then I'd write lyrics and add my vocal. My American record company, Janus, thought I was mad. I'd play them what I had on tape and they'd ask, "Where are the vocals?" I'd tell them I was working on them.

In 1974, when I played Janus executives "Foot of the Stage" with a reference vocal, they liked the music but pointed out that no one in the States knew who Tony Hancock was. So I kept the music but reworked the song as "Horse of the Year," about Princess Anne, Queen Elizabeth's daughter: "Princess Anne rode up on/The horse of the year." Again, the same melody.

Being a big fan of Bob Dylan, I knew he favored using lines like "paths of victory," "masters of war," "chimes of freedom," and so on. I liked "of" phrases because they made for imposing titles. "Horse of the Year" was an "of" song, but you really couldn't take it seriously. It was just fun. I needed a new idea.

In '75, I was dating a girl named Marion. One morning, in my London flat, Marion left a book of Vietnamese astrology open on the kitchen table. The chapter was entitled "Year of the Cat"—the Vietnamese zodiac name for 1975. I looked at my "Horse of the Year" title and the book's "Year of the Cat." The former sounded silly and the latter sounded really good. But I couldn't decide on the song's story line.

Later that morning, *Casablanca*, with Humphrey Bogart, came on the TV. I decided the song should be about something exotic that happened in the Year of the Cat: "On a morning from a Bogart movie/In a country where they turn back time/You go strolling through the crowd like Peter Lorre/Contemplating a crime."

I liked what I wrote, so I continued: "She comes out of the sun in a silk dress running/Like a watercolor in the rain/Don't bother asking for explanations/She'll just tell you that she came/In the year of the cat."

The woman in the song is nobody specific. She was just an abstract fantasy. And I'd never been to Morocco, where the action takes place. The song's story has a Somerset Maugham influence—the idea of going to exotic places, having interesting things happen to you, and going along with them. It's novelistic.

Dylan had this wonderful phrase: "I accept chaos. I'm not sure whether it accepts me." It's the idea that things come out of nowhere, change your life, and then go away again. The guy in the song tries to make sense of what's happening, but the woman doesn't give him time for questions as she locks her arm in his. She doesn't want to hear it. As Maria Schneider says in the film *Last Tango in Paris*, "It's better not knowing anything." That movie was in the ether for me then while I was writing the lyrics.

Even though the woman in the song has a feline quality when she suddenly appears, she's not a metaphor for the cat. The unfolding narrative just functions like an uninterrupted cinematic boom shot. Repeating "year of the cat" at end of each verse also was a Dylan thing. Many of his songs do this, like "Desolation Row," from 1965. He uses "desolation row" at the end of each long verse as a stylistic thing. I didn't think any more deeply about it. I just liked the way "year of the cat" sounded. It replaced "Horse of the Year" and "Foot of the Stage."

Songs have a funny way of becoming hits. I first met Alan Parsons in '74, around the time he was working with the glam band Cockney Rebel on the song "Make Me Smile," which went to No. 1 in the U.K. I was about to start to record my sixth album, *Modern Times*, the one before *Year of the Cat*. I didn't have a producer yet for it. I realized at that point that I'd made five albums that didn't sound particularly good. I asked Alan if he'd produce *Modern Times*. He agreed. If he hadn't also been there for *Year of the Cat*, the title song might have sounded very different.

The music evolved at the same time. My band then featured parts of two successful English groups. Keyboardist Peter Wood and guitarist Tim Renwick had been in the Sutherland Brothers. My rhythm section—George Ford on bass and Stuart Elliott on drums—came from Cockney Rebel. While we were on tour opening for Linda Ronstadt in '75, Peter would play this piano riff during our sound checks. I heard the riff at each of our concert stops. When I spoke with Peter about using the riff for a song, he wanted it to be strictly instrumental. I wanted to add lyrics to it. So I left Peter's piano riff intact for the intro to "Year of the Cat" and wrote lyrics for the rest. This way both of us as cowriters would be satisfied. The song's riff and chords came from Peter.

We recorded the song's basic tracks and overdubs at London's Abbey Road Studios in January '76. In the midsection, we added a series of solos. First came the strings arranged by Andrew Powell. These gave the song a cinematic quality. The acoustic guitar solo was by Tim, who created a folk feel. He then switched to electric guitar. He was followed by Phil Kenzie's alto saxophone solo.

I wasn't crazy about the commercial sound of the sax, but adding it to singer-songwriter records was hot then. In '75, Paul Simon had added a sax on "Still Crazy After All These Years" and so did Carole King on "Jazzman." Everyone else liked Phil's sax solo, so we left it. Then Peter added an electric keyboard solo. The vocal tracks were added in Los Angeles, at Davlen Sound Studios. Alan Parsons was working on another artist's album project there.

When Alan and I mixed the song for the album, I said, "Let me try something." I pushed up the volume fader with Ford's bass track so it was more pronounced. By adding more of Ford, you hear the power of the song.

I have no idea if Marion heard the song and connected it to her book of astrology. By the time the record came out, we'd broken up. She married a Frenchman and moved to Bordeaux. It seems she had the "Year of the Cat" experience. I wound up with a song.

Ann Wilson, left, and Nancy Wilson of Heart in Los Angeles in 1976.

33: Barracuda
HEART
Released: May 1977

The band Heart began as Army in Seattle in 1967. After a series of name changes over the years, the band landed on White Heart and then Heart in 1973. That year, Ann Wilson joined the band as lead vocalist. Her younger sister, guitarist Nancy Wilson, joined Heart a year later. A hard-rock band with two women out front, Heart also included two brothers—guitarist Roger Fisher and manager Mike Fisher. Heart's first million-selling album, *Dreamboat Annie*, was released in 1975 and produced three successful singles—"Magic Man," "Crazy on You," and the title track.

To promote the album, Mushroom Records placed an ad in trade and music magazines touting the success of the album and singles. The ad also hinted there was an intimate relationship between the band's sisters, Ann and Nancy Wilson. Outraged by record-industry sexism and sexual harassment in general, Ann wrote a poem expressing her humiliation and anger. The words were for a song she called "Barracuda."

Heart released "Barracuda" on their next album, *Little Queen*, in May 1977, for their new label, Portrait Records. The single, cowritten by four band members, reached No. 11 on *Billboard*'s pop chart and the album reached No. 9.

Michael Fisher
(Heart manager)

From Heart's start in 1972, I had a clear idea of how I thought the band should sound to be successful. My vision as creative director was to combine the female folk and R&B sophistication of Ann's lead vocal with the high-energy rock feel of my brother Roger's guitar and Steve Fossen's bass. In 1976, Heart was touring in support of its first studio album, *Dreamboat Annie*. On October 15, we were in East Lansing, Michigan, to open for Bob Seger & the Silver Bullet Band. Several hours before the concert, Heart was onstage rehearsing as we checked sound levels and lighting cues.

Roger Fisher
(Heart lead guitarist and cowriter)

At the sound check, Mike Derosier and I began jamming. We were just horsing around playing a galloping riff. I wasn't thinking of any outside influence. Eventually, I added chords.

Michael Derosier
(Heart drummer and cowriter)

Roger and I had a great beat and riff going. An inspiration for me was the feel that Nazareth had on their cover of Joni Mitchell's "This Flight Tonight."

Roger Fisher

As Mike Derosier and I developed the riff and beat, my brother, Mike, loved what we were doing and recorded it on a cassette tape.

Nancy Wilson
(Heart guitarist and cowriter)

With the success of "Magic Man" in the fall of '76, we began to have trouble with our Canadian label, Mushroom Records, which wound up folding in 1980. Ann and I had written "Magic Man," the band's first big hit. It reached No. 9 on *Billboard*'s pop chart. To promote the hit and the band, Mushroom designed a trade ad to look like the cover of a supermarket tabloid. The ad had a photo from our *Dreamboat Annie* cover shoot. Ann and I were cropped at our bare shoulders so it looked like we weren't wearing tops.

The ad's headline read: EXCLUSIVE, THE HEARTBREAKING STORY! REGIONAL HIT MUSHROOMS INTO MILLION SELLER. Then under the photo of Ann and me standing back-to-back, the headline read, "Heart's Wilson Sisters Confess: It Was Only Our First Time!" I freaked. Mushroom made it seem that my sister and I were incestuous lovers. I was furious.

Ann Wilson
(Heart lead vocalist and cowriter)

To Mushroom executives, it was a funny badass rock sales technique. For Nancy and me, who were raised by a feminist mother, we felt violated. Supermarket tabloids were toxic and never allowed in our home. We were really offended. So was the band.

Nancy Wilson

When we were kids, Ann and I moved around quite a bit. Our father, John, was a major in the Marine Corps and was stationed in Panama and Taiwan before we moved to Seattle, Washington, in the early '60s. Our mother, Lou, was tough, too. As a family, we were a fighting unit. From childhood, Ann and I felt powerful, capable, and good at our craft. We were outward bound and emboldened to prove ourselves. We had each other to lean on. It was insulting that men in the record industry thought our inclusion in the band was ornamental. Ann and I wrote many of the songs, and the industry treated us as second-class artists.

Ann Wilson

After our set in East Lansing and before Bob Seger went on, both bands were backstage milling around with record industry execs and hangers-on. Everyone was drinking and schmoozing. Suddenly, this guy who supplied local stores with records came up to me. He said, "Hey Ann, how's your lover?" I said, "Mike [Fisher] is great. He's right over there. Go say hi." He said, "No, no, your sister. You know." He was referring to the trade ad.

I saw red, but our mother raised us to be dignified with anger and not explode. I just shut down. I went to find Nancy. I felt humiliated. I told her what had happened. I've never been homophobic. I've always felt people can love whoever they want. But this was about being sleazy and insulting my family. It was maddening. The band was staying at the Hotel Pontchartrain in Detroit. After we drove back, I went up to my room and sat on the bed and began writing a poem about how I felt.

The poem took about an hour and would become the lyrics to the music that Roger and Mike Derosier had come up with at the sound check. The porpoise in the poem was Nancy: "Back over time, we were all trying for free/You met the porpoise and me . . . 'Sell me, sell you,' the porpoise said/Dive down deep now save my head."

Nancy and I were huge Beatles fans. When "I Am the Walrus" came out in 1967 on *Magical Mystery Tour*, Nancy and I called each other porpoise. Then we shortened it to "porp." We liked that porpoises were considered smarter than most ocean life. The "western pools" were our houses on the west coast of Oregon, where we could relax: "All that night and all the next/Swam without looking back/Made for the western pools, silly, silly fools!"

The word "barracuda" came last. I first tried tiger and snake, but they didn't have the same evil creepiness of a barracuda—a slimy fish with no morals lurking in the water waiting for its prey. When my poem was done and we were back home in Seattle in early December, Nancy and Roger came over to the house that Mike [Fisher] and I shared. Roger played the riff. I sang and fit my poem's words into what Roger played. As a lyricist, I was influenced by Bernie Taupin at the time.

Roger Fisher

To gracefully merge Ann's words with the music, the second measure of each verse was changed to a bar of five beats instead of four. It was keyboardist and guitarist Howard Leese's idea.

Michael Fisher

After the ad, the incident backstage, and Mushroom's lack of tour support and payment, we discovered that our producer, Mike Flicker, had left the label. When I found out, I knew Mushroom had breached our contract. We were free to leave and sign with Portrait, a CBS division.

"Barracuda" was recorded at Seattle's Kaye-Smith Studios. We recorded the song's basic rhythm track in one take with Roger, Nancy, Steve, Howard, and Mike Derosier in Studio A. Then, as Ann recorded her lead vocal in Studio A along with Nancy and Howard overdubbing background vocals, I worked with Roger on overdubbing his guitar solos and effects in Studio B.

Roger Fisher

I came up with these tremolo harmonics on my guitar—the ringing sound you hear each time my chugging riff stops. I also had a flanger that gave my Stratocaster a sweeping sound. At some point, I reached for something behind my amp. The close proximity of my guitar to the amp's tubes created a cool sweeping oscillation, like an alien attack. I used the sound toward the end of "Barracuda," where Howard and I answer each other's guitar chords.

Nancy Wilson

Song endings can be tough. Once you're on a galloping horse, it's hard to slow down. We tried a bunch of different things, but most felt corny or stupid. So we decided to snap it off abruptly. During the mix, each of us sat at the console and had our own fader. We slid them all up slowly as the end neared so the volume built. Then we just cut them off. It was like the slamming of a door. To this day, Roger's guitar on the recording is one of rock's most iconic sounds. I've tried to re-create it numerous times without much luck.

Ann Wilson

No matter where Heart toured in the '70s, we came across our share of sleazeballs. "Barracuda" is me coming unglued. I never cried over stuff like that. I just got deeply disturbed and angry and channeled it into my songwriting and vocals. When I recorded my lead vocal, I felt rage. You can hear it in my voice. In that photo of Nancy and me bare-shouldered, we were just showing that sisters could be friends. Instead, we became the objects of cheapness. We were made to feel worthless. Funny thing is, I wasn't really angry at that record guy while recording my vocal. I was more furious at the culture that gave him permission to say something like that to me.

Carly Simon and James Taylor in 1977.

34: Nobody Does It Better

CARLY SIMON
Released: July 1977

By 1974, four of the nine James Bond films produced had themes sung by women. Shirley Bassey sang two of them ("Goldfinger" and "Diamonds Are Forever"), Nancy Sinatra sang one ("You Only Live Twice"), and Lulu sang one ("The Man with the Golden Gun"). As for the composers of these nine Bond themes, all had been men. Linda McCartney wasn't originally credited as a cowriter with Paul McCartney on "Live and Let Die" until years later, and her specific role in the writing of the words or music is unclear.

In 1976, Carole Bayer Sager and Marvin Hamlisch wrote the theme for *The Spy Who Loved Me*, first in New York together and then Sager finished off the lyrics in Los Angeles. The song—"Nobody Does It Better"—marked the first time a woman was credited as the cowriter of a Bond theme. The song also became the first theme with lyrics positioned from a woman's perspective. Earlier themes sung by women were merely male-written narratives, while "Nobody Does It Better" was about one of 007's conquests rating his performance as a lover.

Sager and Hamlisch's first choice for the theme's vocalist was Carly Simon. In 1976, Simon was a high-profile feminist recording star with a string of hits who came across as both a strong and sensual public figure. At the time, she was married to James Taylor. When Simon's "Nobody Does It Better" was released as a single in July 1977, the sultry, powerful rendition climbed to No. 2 on *Billboard*'s pop chart. The soundtrack album was nominated for an Oscar.

Carole Bayer Sager
(lyricist)

In mid-1976, Marvin Hamlisch and I were at his New York apartment working on a song. It wasn't going too well. At the end of our writing session, Marvin said, "I'm going to London to work on the next James Bond film, *The Spy Who Loved Me*. When I get back, let's try again to write something." The Bond film title didn't sound great for a theme title. I said, "Oh wow, James Bond, yeah. If I was going to write a Bond theme, I think I'd call it 'Nobody Does It Better.'" The title had just popped into my head.

"I like that," Marvin said, turning back to the keyboard. Within ten minutes, he had a chorus melody written. I sat for another ten minutes and came up with the lyrics: "Nobody does it better/Makes me feel sad for the rest/Nobody does it half as good as you/Baby, you're the best."

Marvin also wrote the music for two verses, but there wasn't time to add lyrics. Marvin said he'd put the music on a cassette tape and leave it with me. "My biggest job will be to convince [Bond producer] Cubby Broccoli to take a chance on you," he said. I wasn't insulted. I knew they liked to stick with name brands. But I was hopeful. A few days later, Marvin called from London. I was given the go-ahead.

While Marvin was there scoring the film, I began working on lyrics for the verses and remaining choruses. Days later, I relocated to Los Angeles. By then, many of the people I wrote with had moved west. Also, my marriage to Andrew [Sager] wasn't working out. Space was a good thing.

I rented a house in West Hollywood. Over the next few weeks, I finished the lyrics and sent them to Marvin in London. I used the movie title just once—in the first verse—just to get it out of the way: "But like heaven above me/The spy who loved me/Is keepin' all my secrets safe tonight."

The song had a stronger feel coming from the female perspective. Instead of just being loved by a spy, she had an opinion about the quality of his performance and passion. I didn't set out to make a statement. It was just me, as a woman, thinking about Bond. He was such a cool, sexy hero. I also wanted his sensuality and the captivating power of his sexuality to be mystifying, leaving the woman baffled about how she wound up in love. I did this by having the singer pose two questions to Bond in the lyrics: "And nobody does it better/Though sometimes I wish someone could/Nobody does it quite the way you do/Why'd you have to be so good?

"The way that you hold me/Whenever you hold me/There's some kind of magic inside you/That keeps me from runnin'/But just keep it comin'/How'd you learn to do the things you do?"

Those questions reveal that she didn't want to fall for him but did. The questions also added female vulnerability and sensuality to the song, as if spoken in bed after.

Carly Simon was my first choice to sing the theme. Marvin agreed. Carly was sexy in her demeanor and bedroom voice. She promoted that image on the covers of her albums. Her voice had a lot of texture. It's smooth and strong and yet it has a great pop sensibility—not too serious and yet intensely sensitive and revealing. I told Marvin that if Carly came aboard, he should encourage her to ad-lib the line "James, you're the best." I wanted the duality of James Bond and James Taylor, her husband at the time. Marvin flew back to New York to play Carly our song.

Carly Simon
(singer)

In late 1976, my manager, Arlyne Rothberg, told me I was being considered for the next Bond theme. I was excited. Ever since *Goldfinger* in '64, I wanted to sing one. The theme always opened the film. I was pregnant with Ben at the time, and James Taylor and I were living on Central Park West. Arlyne told me who the songwriters were, but I didn't personally know Carole or Marvin then. She said Marvin wanted to stop up the next day to play it for me. I said, "Sure." But I goofed. I forgot that a new tax attorney was coming by with papers. I hadn't met him yet.

229

The next day, when the doorbell rang, it was the tax guy with heavy glasses in a black suit and tie. I went into the kitchen to make us tea. As the water boiled, I wondered why the tax guy was playing my piano. When I came out with the tea, the pianist turned out to be Marvin. I didn't realize he looked like an accountant. Marvin sang and played "Nobody Does It Better." Then I sang it back. I don't read music, but when I listen, the music sticks.

Before Marvin left, I told him how great the song was and that I'd love to record it. Then Ben was born in January, so I needed a little time before recording. In April '77, I had to be in L.A. While there, producer Richard Perry recorded my vocal for "Nobody Does It Better" with session musicians, including pianist Michael Omartian.

Michael Omartian
(studio pianist)

Marvin was in the studio, too, that day. He came up with the piano intro. I was on the Fender Rhodes electric piano. But Marvin's sense of time was off slightly. After many takes, Richard called Marvin into the control booth. He suggested Marvin let me take a shot at the piano. Marvin agreed. He wrote out the intro on a sheet of paper. Then I sat down at the piano and we nailed it in a take or two. Later, I overdubbed my Fender Rhodes part.

We also created a lengthy ending so the orchestrator would have plenty of room to arrange strings around Carly's vocal. During the recording of the outro, Carly ad-libbed and layered her vocal several times. "Bay-bee . . . you're . . . the best, sweet baby, dar-ling . . . you're . . . the best." That's where she worked in "James," though it's not clear whether it made the final edit.

Simon

As I recorded my vocal, I imagined how the movie would start. Bond films always had plenty of action before the theme song came on. I also felt Carole's female perspective in the lyrics. They fit me perfectly. Adding "James, you're the best" was the perfect homage.

230

Richard Hewson
   (arranger)

By 1977, I had already worked with producer Richard Perry on a number of albums by American artists. I also had orchestrated the Beatles' "The Long and Winding Road" and "I Me Mine." After I finished my arrangement, Marvin and I disagreed over the ending. I had added horns to the strings. It was a Bond theme and needed a brassy flourish. Marvin favored holding a single note until it faded. To his credit, Richard backed me up, and Marvin eventually agreed. I conducted the orchestra at Abbey Road Studios.

Simon

Marvin screened the film for us in New York on the evening of July 13—two weeks before the movie opened on July 27. Only a handful of us were there—Marvin and Carole, James and me, and our friends, drummer Russ Kunkel and his wife Leah—"Mama" Cass Elliot's sister—and their son, Nathaniel. The film began with Bond, played by Roger Moore, skiing down the Alps chased by bad guys with guns. To escape, Bond skied straight off a cliff. His Union Jack parachute opened and he descended. When the silhouette of a women's hands came up to cradle him, my theme began. I was breathless.

About five minutes after the end of my theme, the film and Marvin's score began to slow and then stopped completely. We were in the dark. A woman with a flashlight arrived and told us there had been a citywide blackout. She led us out. Since we were on the West Side, we all headed up to my apartment. We lit candles, and I opened the windows. Everyone stayed overnight. Marvin played the piano and we all sang. I kept getting ice from the deli downstairs. I sang "Nobody Does It Better" any number of ways. James sang, too. He loved the song.

It was wonderful and the only night like it in my life. There we were around the piano during the 1977 blackout. My blackout just happened to include James Taylor and James Bond.

Walter Becker and Donald Fagen of Steely Dan in 1977.

35: Peg
STEELY DAN
Released: November 1977

Formed in 1971, Steely Dan was the musical alter ego of keyboardist and lead vocalist Donald Fagen and guitarist, bassist, and background vocalist Walter Becker. The songwriting duo had attended Bard College together in the late 1960s and shared many intellectual passions, including science fiction, film noir and foreign movies, cheesy sleaze, Ray Charles, orchestral jazz, and an obsession with studio production and perfection. They both also trafficked in cynicism and irony. After being signed to ABC Records, the quintet Fagen and Becker assembled released *Can't Buy a Thrill* (1972), *Countdown to Ecstasy* (1973), and *Pretzel Logic* (1974). Then Fagen and Becker stopped touring and the original band dissolved. *Katy Lied* (1975) and *The Royal Scam* (1976) were recorded with studio musicians.

In 1977, Steely Dan released *Aja*, arguably Fagen and Becker's masterpiece. Nearly forty musicians appeared on the album and many more auditioned but didn't have the right feel or sound on solos and various corners of songs. Hit singles from the album included "Peg," "Deacon Blues," and "Josie." In 1978, *Aja* won a Grammy for Best Engineered Recording—Non-Classical, and it was inducted into the Grammy Hall of Fame in 2003.

"Peg" was the album's first single, peaking at No. 11 on *Billboard*'s pop chart. The song's funky blues and enigmatic lyrics epitomized the atmospheric jazz-rock sound pioneered by Fagen and Becker.

Donald Fagen
(Steely Dan keyboardist, lead vocalist, and cowriter)

Like most of the songs Walter [Becker] and I wrote for Steely Dan, "Peg" wasn't planned out. The music emerged from a blues riff I was working on and the lyrics were inspired by old movies Walter and I watched over the years. "Peg" began at home in Malibu in 1976. I was fooling around on my little upright piano, trying to figure out ways to arrange a blues song, like the ones I'd heard on Blue Note albums by jazz musicians such as Horace Silver with lots of fascinating chord changes.

Eventually, I came up with a riff that had a major-7 feel. Then Walter came over with his guitar. He suggested a chorus and a few other changes. Next, we turned to the lyrics. I had an *All About Eve* idea. Unlike in the movie, where Bette Davis has a young assistant, Eve, who manipulates her way to stardom, the main character in our song isn't a star but has starlet fever. On her way up, she ditched her boyfriend. All of the lyrics are from the perspective of the jilted boyfriend, who was still hanging around.

Imagine that "Peg" takes place at a seedy photo shoot in L.A. in the 1950s. The scene is seedy because show business is seedy. Even what most people think are the heights of show business still have the seediness of a vaudeville dressing room. The name we came up with for the starlet was Peg. There's no hidden meaning. We just wanted a dotted half note for that spot, and Peg was short enough to fit with the music. The song's lyrics open with the ex-boyfriend watching the starlet posing for pinup photos: "I've seen your picture/Your name in lights above it/ This is your big debut/It's like a dream come true/So won't you smile for the camera/I know they're gonna love it."

In the second verse, the ex is thinking back on their relationship. The ex kept one of her glossy photos in his drawer with a Dear John letter she sent him. But Walter and I didn't want to use "pinup." It didn't sing well. So we shortened it to "pin shot," a neologism that was even seedier than pinup: "I like your pin shot/I keep it with your letter/Done up in blueprint blue/It sure looks good on you/And when you smile for the camera/I know I'll love you better."

As for "blueprint blue," I took a mechanical engineering class in high school. I was terrible at it, but I loved the ammonia smell that came from the machine printing the blueprints. Walter and I threw the lines back and forth and laughed at the ones we came up with. We liked creating the sensation of a story through word fragments that weren't too literal. The chorus that followed was a kind of a karmic "you'll get yours" thing. Like, "What you've done to me will come back to you": "Peg, it will come back to you/Then, the shutter falls/You see it all in 3-D/It's your favorite foreign movie."

The chorus is about how the guy is imagining how things will turn out for the starlet down the road. The first line is a variation on "what goes up must come down." The second line is cinematic. The click of the camera's shutter changes the scene to some point in the future. Then the third and fourth lines imagine the starlet's washed-up scenarios— appearing in a cheesy 3-D film. Or she's in someone's favorite foreign movie, a big comedown from her aspirations.

And that was it. The song was compact and minimalist—two verses and a chorus that repeat. Then, Walter and I turned to the instrumentation and arrangement. In early '77, when we were ready to record *Aja*, we flew to New York to record "Peg" at A&R Studios. We wanted a local rhythm section with a sophisticated, aggressive New York feel. We used drummer Rick Marotta. We liked his sound on Aretha Franklin's 1974 album *Let Me in Your Life*. He was a very soulful player.

We already knew electric pianist Paul Griffin from New York. Keyboardist Don Grolnick and bassist Chuck Rainey had been on our previous album, *The Royal Scam*. The instrumental sound picture for "Peg" was light but mysterious. The intro needed a filmlike, caper quality—slightly whimsical but dark. For our intro, I had Paul play the Fender Rhodes electric piano and Don play the Clavinet in unison. We liked the odd sound of those two keyboards pressed together—the smoothness of one against the funkiness of the other.

Rick hit the bass drum only on the second beat, to build suspense. Steve Khan filled the spaces on the intro by playing open chords on his rhythm guitar. Then he played a riff in the verses. Chuck's bass was rock steady. He liked using his thumb on the E string and got some great popping effects. Listen to his bass on "Peg." It's full of life. When we finished recording the basic rhythm track, we returned to L.A. to overdub additional instruments for texture. Saxophonist Tom Scott told us he had this new electronic wind instrument called a Lyricon. It sort of sounded like an alto sax but warmer and not as shrill. We liked it.

Tom Scott
(saxophonist)

The Lyricon looked like a soprano sax and plugged into a small synthesizer console built into its case. I adjusted the console's bars and switches to give it a synth-generated sound of that era, adding my distinctive wind and breath nuances. At L.A.'s Village Recorders studio, Donald and Walter knew what they wanted and where in the song they wanted me to play. I played my lick after Donald sings, "I keep it with your letter" and resumed in the middle of the line "It sure looks good on you."

Fagen

Initially, the guitar solo that we wanted in the middle of the song was problematic. Walter took a shot, but he didn't like what he played. Then we went through about a half-dozen studio guitarists without any luck. The guitarists were all perfectly good improvisers, but we wanted a set piece. Someone suggested we try Jay Graydon.

Jay Graydon
(guitarist)

After I got the call, I brought my 1964 Gibson ES-335 and Fender Deluxe amp. My solo was recorded in three parts. I played what sounded like a steel guitar lick with pretty blues notes. Donald and Walter loved that. Whatever I played after that they didn't dig. So we kept the first part, and I took a chance and went up the neck, bent notes, and ran down with an arpeggio. They liked that, too, so we kept it. For the third section,

Donald asked me to play something fast. So I played a fast-ascending lick and then walked my way back down the neck. That was it.

Fagen

Because Jay's solo section contains an unprepared change in modes, it was almost a Stravinsky-like moment. You can hear Jay felt that solo emotionally. For background on the chorus, Walter and I had planned to handle the harmony instrumentally with four saxes. But background singer Michael McDonald was still working with us, so we decided instead to create the harmony by overdubbing four Michael McDonalds.

Michael McDonald
(background singer)

In the studio, Donald instructed me from the piano on the harmony notes he wanted me to sing behind his vocal. But instead of recording one note and then recording the next while listening to the first through headphones, I cheated. I said to Donald, "Give me the notes individually and let me record each one without hearing the others." This let me sing my background lyrics in pitch, without being thrown by the density. I kept the harmony lyrics simple: "Peg! Peg!/Then, shutter falls/All in 3-D/Foreign movie—Peg!"

Fagen

The notes I gave Michael were tightly spaced, producing a thick sound. Michael has this amazing tone. We liked how he echoed the lyric. After Walter became ill, just before he died in 2017, I did a U.K. summer tour without him. It was rough. I could feel his absence most strongly then. But over time, the present kind of absorbs the past. Walter and I were very proud of "Peg." Unlike some of our other stuff, we felt we'd achieved a special simplicity with the song. And it's easy on the ears. Walter liked that.

Ric Ocasek of the Cars in the early 1980s.

36: My Best Friend's Girl

THE CARS

Released: October 1978

Punk surged in popularity in the United States in 1976 and took on political overtones in the U.K. as the British economy faltered. The stripped-down form expressed rage and rebellion against institutions and mainstream rock. Punk made money for record companies, record chains, and downtown clubs in cities. But when live audiences started to dry up between 1976 and '77, record companies went looking for the next big thing. Seymour Stein, the chairman of Sire Records, felt that punk—with its look-alike spiked-hair acts, shredding guitars, and shrieking vocals—had overstayed its revolution. Replacing punk were a growing number of art-rock bands that retained aspects of punk but added pop and polish. Stein called the evolving movement "new wave," a term borrowed from the 1960s French film movement.

One of the earliest American bands to be recognized as new wave were the Cars. In late 1976, the band first emerged in Boston as Cap'n Swing. After being turned down by several record labels, leader Ric Ocasek retooled by bringing in new musicians and combining art-pop sophistication and a post-punk vocal delivery. The new band included

Ocasek (lead vocals and rhythm guitar), Elliot Easton (lead guitar), Greg Hawkes (keyboards), Benjamin Orr (bass), and David Robinson (drums). In 1976 and '77, the Cars toured in the Northeast and worked on original material. They soon came to attention of Maxanne Sartori, Boston's influential WBCN-FM disc jockey, who began playing tracks on the air from the band's demo tapes.

When the Cars' eponymous debut album was released in mid-1978, their second single, "My Best Friend's Girl," reached No. 35 on the *Billboard* pop chart, helping to send the album to No. 18.

Ric Ocasek
(Cars lead singer, rhythm guitarist, and songwriter)

In early 1972, I was living in an apartment above the garage of a house near Boston. The house was set back in the woods, and about twenty other people lived there. They shared common space and sometimes ate together. It was very Zen. The best thing about my apartment was private access to a basement under the garage. The basement's concrete walls were thick, and it was dry and quiet. I'd go down there with my acoustic guitar and cassette recorder, sit on the floor, and write songs.

Ben Orr soon joined me in Boston. We had been in a series of bands together in Ohio and Michigan in the '60s. Eventually we teamed with guitarist Elliot Easton and formed Cap'n Swing. In early 1976, WBCN-FM disc jockey Maxanne Sartori heard our Cap'n Swing demo at the station and began playing it on her radio show.

Maxanne Sartori
(Boston radio DJ)

I met Ric that spring at a concert he played on Boston's Newbury Street and we started hanging out. We tooled around in his VW Beetle and went to hear bands at Boston's Rathskeller. That fall, after Cap'n Swing played Max's Kansas City in New York, I suggested that Ric shift Ben Orr from singing lead vocal to playing bass and sharing lead vocals with Ric. I also suggested that Ric hire drummer David Robinson, who had more of a pop feel.

David Robinson

(Cars drummer)

In mid-'76, I was in DMZ, a Boston band, when Ric asked me to join a band he was restructuring. When I went over to Ric's basement to play with the band for the first time, everyone clicked. Shortly after I joined, Ric wanted to change the band's name. Cap'n Swing sounded like the name of a bar band. We came up with lists of names. On my list was the Cars. It was easy to remember and it wasn't pegged to a specific decade or sound. The name was meaningless and conjured up nothing, which was perfect. Ric liked the name. The Cars came at the beginning of the alphabet, which was great in record stores. It also was easy to spell and impossible to forget. Funny thing is I didn't even own a car at the time.

Ocasek

I loved Buddy Holly's songs. I first heard "That'll Be the Day" when I was thirteen, in 1957. Holly's guitar intro made me want to learn to play. I also loved Holly's voice. It was quirkier than everyone else's at the time and stood out. When I realized Holly wrote his own songs, I thought, "Yeah, that's what I want to do, write songs." Shortly after David joined us, I was down in my basement writing songs. One of them was "My Best Friend's Girl."

Nothing in that song happened to me personally. I just figured having a girlfriend stolen was probably something that happened to a lot of people. I wrote the words and music at the same time: "You're always dancing down the street/With your suede blue eyes/And every new boy that you meet/He doesn't know the real surprise."

The "suede blue eyes" line was a play on Carl Perkins's rockabilly song "Blue Suede Shoes." When I wrote, "You've got your nuclear boots/And your drip-dry glove," I envisioned the boots and gloves as a cool '50s fashion statement.

As for the last lines—"And when you bite your lip/It's some reaction to love"—they were an emotional gesture. I was reading a lot of poets then.

At some point, I realized my lyrics didn't include the words "my best friend's girl." So I pulled out the lyrics someone had typed up and added a chorus in the margin in pen: "She's my best friend's girl/She's my best friend's girl/But she used to be mine."

I liked the twist. Up until that point, you think the singer stole his best friend's girl based on how good he feels about her: "When she's dancing 'neath the starry sky/She'll make you flip." With the last line of the chorus, "But she used to be mine," you realize the guy didn't steal his best friend's girl. His friend stole her away from him.

Elliot Easton
(Cars lead guitarist)

After Ric wrote "My Best Friend's Girl" and some others, we got together in his basement with our instruments and amps. We sat in a semicircle and he played them for us. Then we rehearsed.

Ocasek

We played our first gig as the Cars in December 1976. Then in February '77, we recorded a demo of our new songs, including "My Best Friend's Girl," at Northern Studios in Maynard, Massachusetts. We made a copy of the demo and I gave the reel to Maxanne at WBCN. She played our demos of "Just What I Needed" and "My Best Friend's Girl" a lot on the air.

Sartori

The new band had a punchier, more cohesive sound. I began playing the demos of "Just What I Needed" and "My Best Friend's Girl" in March during my weekday slot, from 2:00 to 6:00 p.m. Calls poured in with positive comments. The Cars' sound was fresh. It wasn't punk, hard rock, or folk rock. I thought of it as "pure pop for now people," the title of a Nick Lowe album.

Ocasek

Like all FM DJs, Maxanne had to keep an official log of songs played on the air. Those logs made it into trade publications, where the source for our demo songs was listed as "tape." That caught the attention of record executives at several labels who approached us. We signed with Elektra. Every artist I loved was on Elektra—the Doors, the Stooges, the Incredible String Band, and so many others.

We toured for much of '77 to build an audience. Then Elektra paired us with British producer Roy Thomas Baker. He wanted to record our first album at George Martin's AIR Studios in London. We were thrilled. I had never been on a plane before. Everything about London was magical and cool. We recorded *The Cars* album in twelve days in February 1978.

Easton

George Martin came by the control booth periodically and stretched out on the sofa. One time during a playback, he said, "That's not too bad, actually." High praise coming from him.

Ocasek

In the studio, "My Best Friend's Girl" didn't need much. It was all there on the demo. But Roy made the song sound much bigger. It opens with me picking on notes in the middle position of my Fender Jazzmaster guitar. My guitar went through an Ampeg VT-22 amp, which let me turn up the middle part of my guitar. The Jazzmaster was perfect, with that thud-y sound.

The handclapping in the first verse was us clapping, not a synthesizer. Roy had brought in a forty-track recorder built by Stephens Electronics. Even though it broke down a lot, the two-inch tape machine let us use more mikes to make the album sound large. When we recorded vocal harmony on the line "Here she comes again," Roy had us record one set of vocals. He triplicated them so there were twenty-four voices. Then he used the Stephens machine to get them up to around seventy voices.

At one point, we said, "Roy, we can't do that," fearing the vocals would sound too synth-y. Roy said, "You'll get used to it." Roy placed mikes ten to fifteen feet away from us for a more dimensional sound. He knew how to do this from recording classical music.

Robinson

What made "My Best Friend's Girl" special was Elliot's guitar. It really elevated the joy level.

Easton

The inspiration for my rockabilly riff and solo was the guitar lick from the Beatles' "I Will." I mutated it a bit to counter Ric's strong eighth-note feel. While our song's melody chords are E, A, and B, I played E, C-sharp minor, F-sharp minor, and B, to offset them. I played my solo on a new Fender Telecaster I had brought to London along with my Martin D-35 acoustic and Gibson Les Paul Standard. The Fender was twangy to begin with, but we added a little slap-back echo so it sounded fatter and jumped.

Robinson

Roy loved loud drums. I had tuned them so they were boom-y and bass-y. I also had super-thin wood drum rims, which helped my tom-toms pop. I overdubbed timbales to add a Latin feel. They're the bright, metallic-sounding drums that appear just before we sing the chorus "She's my best friend's girl." After, Roy mixed the drums loud.

Ocasek

When we finished recording the song, it was a tick too slow. Roy wanted it a little faster. So he went back and sped up the tape, pushing the song up a key, from E to F. If my best friend had stolen my girl, I might have been hurt but I wouldn't have been out for revenge. It's not me. That's why the lyrics are observational and not bitter. Maybe it was all that peace and love at the communal house.

Ray Charles and Kenny Rogers in 1980.

37: The Gambler
KENNY ROGERS
Released: November 1978

In the 1970s, country music's popularity soared, turning hit-making artists into national sensations and TV variety-show hosts. Country artists had liberated themselves from Nashville's countrypolitan sound, tailoring the music to fit their personalities and experiences. Female singer-songwriters Dolly Parton, Loretta Lynn, and Tammy Wynette reshaped country music from the woman's perspective. Artists such as Merle Haggard, Willie Nelson, Waylon Jennings, and Kris Kristofferson launched the "outlaw" movement. But perhaps the decade's biggest and top-earning artist was Kenny Rogers, a vocalist whose 420-plus hits covered a wide variety of genres. His musical background shaped his eclecticism.

Rogers grew up poor in Texas. He played the upright and electric bass in a rock 'n' roll band before joining a jazz group backing singer Bobby Doyle. In 1966, he joined the large-ensemble folk group the New Christy Minstrels as a singer and bassist. A year later, Rogers and several band members left to form the psychedelic pop band the First Edition. By the early 1970s, the band known as Kenny Rogers and the First Edition had a country sound. After the band broke up in the mid-1970s, Rogers launched a solo career, recording successful duets. In 1978, he recorded

"The Gambler," a country-pop song written by Nashville composer Don Schlitz. The song became so identified with Rogers that the title became his nickname.

Released in November 1978, "The Gambler" became a No. 1 hit on *Billboard*'s country chart and reached No. 16 on the pop chart. Rogers and Schlitz both won Grammy Awards for the song.

Don Schlitz
(songwriter)

In 1973, after three freshman semesters at Duke University, I dropped out at age twenty and boarded a bus from Durham, North Carolina, to Nashville. I had just $89 in my pocket. I wanted to be a songwriter. To pay the bills, I took a job as a computer operator at Vanderbilt University. I worked the graveyard shift, from 11:00 p.m. to 7:00 a.m. My job was to call my boss if the giant computer went down, as it often did.

In the morning after work, I'd sometimes head off to the office of Bob McDill, one of the best songwriters in Nashville. He had agreed to see me regularly to hear my songs, critique them, and give me advice. It was my first real break. One day in August 1976, when I was twenty-three, I was at Bob's office and told him I was having trouble cranking out songs. Sitting behind his desk with his guitar, Bob showed me an open-D tuning on the guitar, so all six strings played a D-major chord.

By strumming three different chords using that tuning, Bob created a drone sound that was an ideal backdrop for writing songs. After I left Bob's office that morning, I walked a mile back to my studio apartment on Fairfax Avenue. Along the way, those three chords and that drone sound stuck in my head. I started writing the lyrics to a song.

The strumming sound in my head sounded like a train. So I wrote about a young guy on a train who meets an older gambler. I'd never been on a train before, but I was an avid reader and had a pretty good imagination. I wasn't really a poker player either, but I had played nickel-dime poker in high school and knew enough poker terms. By the time I arrived home, I had the song's story and most of the lyrics done in my head—all except for the last eight-line verse.

I titled the song "The Gambler." My tenth-grade English teacher had emphasized the importance of a title. The idea for the gambler may have been inspired by my father, who had died a couple of years earlier. My dad wasn't a gambler. He was a Durham, North Carolina, policeman and a great man. I wanted the song to feel like one of our talks, in which he stressed the importance of making good choices. Inside my apartment, I began to bang out the lyrics on my dad's L. C. Smith manual typewriter. For the song, I cast the gambler's advice in poker terms, but I didn't have a time period in mind. I typed out the chorus first: "You've got to know when to hold 'em/Know when to fold 'em/Know when to walk away/And know when to run/You never count your money/When you're sittin' at the table/There'll be time enough for countin'/When the dealin's done."

Then I wrote three verses—starting with the young man's narration about meeting the gambler: "On a warm summer's evenin'/On a train bound for nowhere/I met up with the gambler/We were both too tired to sleep."

The second verse is about the gambler noticing that the young man is struggling with a problem: "Son, I've made a life/Out of readin' people's faces/Knowin' what the cards were/By the way they held their eyes."

The third was about the gambler giving the young man some advice: "If you're gonna play the game, boy/You gotta learn to play it right."

I wrote the music at the same time I wrote the words. Days later, when I played "The Gambler" for songwriter Jim Rushing along with a bunch of my other incomplete songs, he said, "That's the one you ought to finish." It took six weeks to come up with the last eight-line verse: "And when he finished speakin'/He turned back toward the window/Crushed out his cigarette/Faded off to sleep/And somewhere in the darkness/The gambler, he broke even/But in his final words/I found an ace that I could keep."

When I was done, I played "The Gambler" for everyone who'd listen. I wanted to get a song published so badly. Jim introduced me to Paul Craft, who had a publishing company with Audie Ashworth, who produced J. J. Cale. Audie produced a demo of me playing and singing the song. Next, Audie and Paul published "The Gambler," and Paul and

Jim started performing it around town. But I still couldn't get the song recorded by a top artist. So Paul introduced me to Merlin Littlefield, who worked at ASCAP. Merlin sent my demo to producer Larry Butler, and Audie sent the demo to local radio stations.

Paul was close with singer Bobby Bare and told him about "The Gambler." After he played him my demo, Bobby recorded it. But the great Billy Sherrill, his producer, didn't think it was strong enough for a single. So it remained on Bobby's album that came out in April 1978.

Kenny Rogers
(singer)

I first heard "The Gambler" at a studio in Nashville in the spring of '78. My producer, Larry Butler, was looking for songs with hit potential for my next album. Larry played me Bobby Bare's version. As I recall, he also played me a demo that Johnny Cash made of the song. Larry was going to produce Johnny's recording a few weeks later. I liked the song, but after hearing Johnny's version, I realized I was in over my head. Johnny had a way with a song. A lot of people can tell the same story, but stylistically, each artist gives a song its own identity. I had to come at the song differently.

To me, the song's story sounded as if it took place on a train traveling through the Old West. I also liked the music's rollicking cadence. We decided to give it a try. As I looked down the lyric sheet and sang the song in my head, the first three verses seemed very long. So Larry and I moved up the chorus to create a break in the story. I left the arranging to Larry. He had the song open with an acoustic guitar solo. I liked that. He also modulated the key up a step at the start of the fourth verse, to shift gears and add a little drama.

[On June 16], the day I came in to Jack Clement Recording Studios to record my vocal, the music was already in place on the tape. I put on the headphones and sang to the instrumental track. We adjusted the music later as needed with overdubs.

Schlitz

I first heard Kenny's soulful version at Merlin's office just before it came out. Merlin had it on a tape. Kenny gave it life. It's his song now—and it's how I hear the song whenever I play it on my guitar. I gave my original lyric sheet to Jim Rushing, the songwriter who'd told me "The Gambler" was the one I should finish.

Rogers

As I recorded my vocal that day, Ray Charles came to mind. I had seen Ray in concert when I was a young boy in Houston. From then on, I knew exactly what I wanted to accomplish in life. Years later, I had an opportunity to collaborate and perform with Ray. That was a dream come true because it brought me full circle with my childhood aspiration. His concert had left a big impact on me. Ray was a mentor for many years, whether he knew it or not. Some of that came through on "The Gambler." While singing about the older gambler giving advice to the younger man on the train, I was thinking about Ray.

I'm still not sure why my version caught on as it did. I was a relatively new solo artist then, so I guess people were paying closer attention. Somewhere along the way, the song's title became my nickname. People still call me the Gambler. Funny thing is I'm not much of a poker player. Or a gambler.

Allee Willis with Maurice White of Earth, Wind & Fire in the early 1980s.

38: September
EARTH, WIND & FIRE
November 1978

Jazz-influenced funk-rock horn bands came into their own in the early 1970s. Inspired by Sly and the Family Stone and James Brown, horn bands included Kool & the Gang, the Crusaders, Chicago, Tower of Power, Blood Sweat & Tears, Chase, Parliament-Funkadelic, the Electric Flag, Ohio Players, Isis (an all-female horn band), War, Mandrill, and others. Perhaps the most successful of all was Earth, Wind & Fire.

Formed in 1970, the Los Angeles–based band released its self-titled first album in February 1971. That year, the band performed the soundtrack for Melvin Van Peebles' film *Sweet Sweetback's Baadasssss Song*. Four years later, Earth, Wind & Fire scored and recorded the soundtrack to a film entitled *That's the Way of the World*. Convinced the film would tank, the band and Columbia Records released the soundtrack album in March of that year—three months before the film's June premiere. The goal was to enter the marketplace and own the title before the movie's failure stigmatized it. As predicted, the movie bombed, but Earth, Wind & Fire's album shot to No. 1 on the *Billboard* pop and soul albums charts, launching the band's prolific career. To this day, most fans of the album aren't aware the music was for a movie.

At the peak of their popularity, in 1978, Earth, Wind & Fire needed a new, fresh single to include on its first album of greatest hits. "September" was written to help maximize the album's sales. Released as a single in November 1978, "September" reached No. 8 on *Billboard*'s pop chart and No. 1 on the R&B chart. *The Best of Earth, Wind & Fire, Vol. 1* peaked at No. 6.

Allee Willis
(lyricist)

I grew up in Detroit in the early 1960s. Every Saturday, my parents dropped me off at Motown's headquarters, a little house, to sit on the front lawn. You could hear the music leaking through the walls. Those are the only music lessons I ever took. To this day, I still don't know how to read, write, or play music. I just hear everything in my head, the way I did outside Motown.

In 1969, I moved to New York and interviewed at Columbia Records. I started as a secretary and soon was promoted to junior copywriter. One day, while listening to Gilbert O'Sullivan's "Alone Again (Naturally)" on the radio, I wrote my own lyrics to the song. Then I called a friend to come over to my place to play piano and turn my lyrics into a song. He brought over the sheet music to the Jackson 5's "Never Can Say Goodbye."

He flipped to the last page and played the chords from the end to the beginning, while I sang. That became my first song, "Ain't No Man Worth It." I wrote and sang two more songs by myself and took the three on a cassette tape to my boss in Columbia's advertising department. He loved them and took them to the head of Epic. I got signed to a record deal for the first ten songs I ever wrote. We started recording my album *Childstar* in 1972, and it was released in 1974.

During my tour to promote the album, I wasn't comfortable on stage. I decided the easiest thing to do was to be a songwriter and avoid the trauma of performing. Epic dropped me. In March 1976, I moved out to Los Angeles and took my songs to more than twenty music publishers to try and get a job as a songwriter. Finally, A&M's Almo/Irving Music gave me a deal. In my first eight weeks, eleven of my songs were recorded by other artists. But even though I had a great publishing deal, I was living on food stamps.

Then a friend introduced me to Verdine White, the bass player and a founding member of Earth, Wind & Fire. Verdine and I wrote two songs together for two different artists. Verdine kept saying, "I'm going to have my brother, Maurice, call you." I never thought that would happen because Earth, Wind & Fire was huge, and I was starving.

Verdine White
(Earth, Wind & Fire bassist and vocalist)

When Earth, Wind & Fire began working on our next album, *I Am*, in '78, Maurice needed someone to help him with song lyrics. I told him I had met a great lyricist.

Willis

One night my phone rang. Maurice was on the other end. He said, "Would you write the next Earth, Wind & Fire album with me?" I couldn't believe it. The next day I went to the space where Earth, Wind & Fire was rehearsing. Maurice came over and introduced himself. He handed me a sheet of notebook paper with a bunch of phrases he had written and the word "September" handwritten at the top. Earth, Wind & Fire guitarist Al McKay wrote the music. It was for their greatest hits record coming out before their next studio album *I Am*.

White

I had worked out the groove for the "September" bass line on my Fender Jazz Bass. The song wasn't called "September" yet, and the lyrics hadn't been written. It was just a groove that Al McKay had put together that felt really good.

Willis

"September" was the first song Maurice and I worked on at my office at Almo/Irving Music. I asked him about the significance of the twenty-first of September from his lyric sheet. He said, "I just like it." What bothered me most was his extensive use of "ba-dee-ya." It sounded like filler or a space-holder, like yadda-yadda. I said, "We're going to replace that with real words, right?" He said he liked them the way they sounded. I also felt the other phrases were a little singsong-y. While the words went with the happy feel of the music, they needed to be more intellectual.

For the first verse, Maurice had written down a bunch of disconnected lines: "Do you remember, the twenty-first night, September/ We were holding hands/Remember there was never a cloudy day/Our hearts were ringing with our souls in tune to singing."

I turned them into: "Do you remember, the twenty-first night of September?/Love was changing the minds of pretenders/While chasing the clouds away.

"Our hearts were ringing/In the key that our souls were singing/As we danced in the night, remember/How the stars stole the night away."

For the second verse, Maurice had written: "Remember there was never a cloudy day/I want to be with you/Shaping all of my time to be with you/Our life was a rhyme/Remember there's never a cloudy day."

I turned these phrases into: "My thoughts are with you/Holding hands with your heart, to see you/Only blue talk and love, remember/ How we knew love was here to stay.

"Now December/Found the love that we shared in September/Only blue talk and love, remember/The true love we share today."

What still bothered me was that "ba-dee-ya" appeared over twenty times in the song and kicked off each chorus. On the last night of recording, with "September" due at midnight, I went into the studio, dropped to my knees, and grabbed Maurice's thighs. I begged him to replace "ba-dee-ya" with real words. "Ba-dee-ya" remained.

But I learned the best lesson of my career that night. Never let the lyric get in the way of the groove. If the beat is there, the melody is there, and everything is working about the song, people listening will get what "ba-dee-ya" means. It's funny, most people still don't know the lyric being sung there. The biggest guesses have been "party on" and "all and all."

Maurice passed away in 2016. Two years later, I went to lunch in L.A. with his wife, Marilyn. Someone in the restaurant recognized me and came over and asked, "What's the significance of the twenty-first of September?" I told him what I had been saying for forty years: "There is no significance. That date just sang the best." Marilyn stopped me. She said, "Are you kidding? The twenty-first was the day that our son, Kahbran, was supposed to be born." Maurice never told me that. For decades, I had been disappointing people whose birthdays or weddings were on the twenty-first of September. Now they know.

Marilyn White
(wife of the late Maurice White, cowriter)

In the spring of 1978, after my doctor told me our child would likely be born on September twenty-first, I came home and told Maurice. He was so busy then. I had no idea if he'd remember. By July, I sensed we were having a boy. So we came up with a name—Kahbran—by adapting parts of the first and last name of Lebanese American writer-poet-artist Kahlil Gibran. But Kahbran was born early, on the first of August. While Maurice was working with Allee on the lyrics to "September" and recording the song, he never told me about his line "Do you remember, the twenty-first night of September?"

The first time I heard it was when he played me a tape of the finished song in our home studio, after Kahbran was born. My whole body smiled. It was like a secret message between us and our son. I said, "Oh my God, you remembered." "Yeah," Maurice said. "Yeah, I did."

Michael McDonald at home with his grandmother in 1979.

39: What a Fool Believes

THE DOOBIE BROTHERS

Released: January 1979

When the Doobie Brothers formed in San Jose, California, in 1970, they were a mainstream rock trio fronted by lead vocalist and guitarist Tom Johnston, drummer John Hartman, and bassist Greg Murphy. Initially called Pud, the band was stuck for a new name until a friend flippantly suggested the Doobie Brothers based on their fondness for pot—"doobie" being slang for a joint back then. Playing Northern California, the band developed a strong following. After their first album was released in 1971, the Doobie Brothers added members, including Jeff "Skunk" Baxter, who joined after his time with Steely Dan came to an end in 1974. The Doobie Brothers' hits between 1970 and 1975 included Johnston's "Listen to the Music" and "Long Train Runnin'" and Patrick Simmons's rootsy "Black Water."

By 1974, relentless touring and the pressures of writing and recording had taken a toll on Johnston's health. The following year, he had to leave the band while hospitalized for a bleeding ulcer. Baxter pulled in Steely Dan background vocalist Michael McDonald. The Doobie Brothers' next album in 1976 marked a major change in the band's sound. The R&B influence became more pronounced, especially with McDonald's vocal style and his songs such as "Takin' It to the Streets," and "It Keeps You Runnin,'" and a cover of Marvin Gaye's "Little Darling (I Need You)."

For the Doobie Brothers' eighth studio album, in 1978, a strong single was needed. McDonald set to work but the song didn't come easy. After writing one catchy verse, he was stuck. So he teamed up with Kenny Loggins and together they finished writing "What a Fool Believes." The single, released in January 1979 climbed to No. 1 on *Billboard*'s pop chart and became the band's biggest hit. The album, *Minute by Minute*, also went to No. 1. The song won three Grammys and the album won one.

Michael McDonald
(Doobie Brothers keyboardist, lead singer, and cowriter)

In early 1978, I was living in a house in the Studio City section of Los Angeles. I was singing lead and playing keyboards in the Doobie Brothers and doing a lot of songwriting on the grand piano in my living room. The riff for "What a Fool Believes" first fell into my hands while I was picking at a melody on the piano. Eventually I came up with the riff's rhythm and chords and had my opening verse.

Some of the verse's lyrics I wrote on an envelope while flying from New York to L.A.: "He came from somewhere back in her long ago/The sentimental fool don't see/Tryin' hard to recreate/What had yet to be created once in her life."

I also had a vague sense of the song's concept: A fool believes what he believes, and you can't change his mind. I used this idea as the basis for the song's story. It was about a couple who had broken up and after a period of absence reunited to talk.

At their sit-down, he's foolishly optimistic and believes they'll get back together. For her, it's just a cordial get-together to have a drink. In the song, I wanted to have the two of them express how they felt from their different perspectives. As for the feel, I thought it would be cool to write a song that was sharply rhythmic, like those '60s singles by the Four Seasons, the Four Tops, or Edwin Starr. But I couldn't seem to get beyond the one verse's riff, melody, and lyrics. So I set aside what I had.

By the spring of '78, the Doobie Brothers were preparing for our next album. I played a bunch of song fragments for our producer, Teddy Templeman. When I came to the riff and verse of "What a Fool Believes," he said, "What is that? You gotta finish it. That's a hit song." By then, I wasn't moved by it. I knew that being patient with a song idea is better than rushing it along. But we didn't have time to wait.

Tiran Porter, our bassist, mentioned he had run into singer-songwriter Kenny Loggins and said Kenny wanted to write with me. I was open. I didn't know Kenny, but I liked his music. I spoke to Kenny on the phone. He agreed to drive down the next day from his home in Encino. Before Kenny arrived, I was at the piano playing unfinished songs to see if they'd be good ones for us to work on. Just as I finished playing my verse to "What a Fool Believes," there was a knock at the door. I went to get Kenny, but before we said more than hello, he said, "What was that riff you just played?"

Kenny Loggins
(cowriter)

I parked on the street in front of Michael's house at around noon. As I removed my acoustic Taylor guitar from the car, I heard Michael's piano. His front door was open. Michael was playing and singing a verse. Before I knocked on his door, I had a melody and a lyric line for the bridge. When he stopped to get the door, my imagination kept going. Inside, I asked him to play the verse again. I said, "I think I know how the next part goes."

Michael sat at the piano and I sat in a chair next to him with my guitar. He replayed the verse. Then I sang and played him the bridge I had come up with outside: "She, had a place in his life/He never made her think twice." Then we went back and forth like a game of tennis to come up with the rest: "As he rises to her apology/Anybody else would surely know/He's watching her go."

As a collaborator, I had to figure out the kind of writer Michael was so I could adjust my approach. What stood out on the verse and bridge was his stride style on the keyboard. His left thumb moved around quite a bit and was always an octave or two below his right hand. Listening to him was like going to church.

I also noticed that on songs, Michael tended to shift from optimistic major chords to melancholy ones very quickly and beautifully. On the lyrics side, Michael never explained to me how he wanted the song's story to develop. He didn't even have a title. Instead, he was flexible.

McDonald

We weren't sure where the chorus should go or what it should say. That was the song's problem. Should the couple get back together or not? Kenny and I agreed that they shouldn't, that the story shouldn't resolve neatly. As we worked, I thought about Brenda Lee's "As Usual," a song about someone who can't seem to move on from a lost love. Kenny and I talked about how people in those situations tend to kid themselves. The fantasy of the relationship is often better than the reality.

We also realized the guy in the song we were working on should be the main character. Trying to get both characters to express different perspectives in the short time frame of a song was impractical. The woman was in the song's story, but she wouldn't participate. The guy was the one who was clueless and in turmoil.

Loggins

By 1:00 a.m., when we finished for the day, I had three or four cassettes filled with our approaches. We had finished everything except the chorus. We decided to pick it up the next day on the phone.

McDonald

The next day, I called Kenny. I was at the piano with my hands on the keyboard and the phone on my shoulder and under my chin. We agreed that sometimes you can't change what a fool believes. Sometimes you have to accept that this is who the person is. The chorus Kenny and I came up with reflected this: "But what a fool believes he sees/No wise man has the power to reason away/What seems to be/Is always better than nothing/And nothing at all keeps sending him . . ."

The woman in the song probably said things to him a million times hoping he'd understand how she felt, but it never registered. That's what the song is about, the human nature part, the simple act of listening to each other. That's when we titled the song "What a Fool Believes." Usually, it's best to have the title from the start, to give the song direction and purpose. In this case, it came at the end.

But when we recorded the song in August '78 at Amigo Studios at Warner Bros., we kept speeding up the tempo after the bridge. So Teddy, who had been a drummer in Harpers Bizarre in '66, sat at a second set of drums to lock us into the time. We also brought in plywood panels and put them on the floor under our feet. These allowed us to stomp four beats to the measure, to lock in a precise '60s, finger-snapping groove. You can't hear them on the recording because the sound was mixed out.

When we finished, Warner Bros. executives weren't crazy about the song or the album *Minute by Minute*. They didn't think it was cohesive and thought we were finished as a band. Teddy was the last man standing in our corner. He had picked "What a Fool Believes" as the album's first single. The rest of us had lost faith in it. Then all of a sudden, the album sold 100,000 copies and kept on going while "What a Fool Believes" became a huge hit. I was amazed. Everyone who thought they knew better was wrong, including me.

Loggins

In July '78, months before Michael and the Doobie Brothers released their recording of "What a Fool Believes," I released my version on *Nightwatch*, my second solo album. I was pretty happy with it. But in December, when I heard Michael's version on *Minute by Minute*, I thought it was amazing. Michael's feel, vocal harmonies, and stride keyboard made the song drop-dead perfect. I remember wishing I could have recorded mine again.

Elvis Costello in 1977.

40: Accidents Will Happen
ELVIS COSTELLO
Released: May 1979

As new wave flowered in the late 1970s, original songs by artists in the U.K. and the United States became more musically sophisticated and sardonic. Vocals by male new-wave performers often had a hiccup-y Buddy Holly feel, but the music and songs were ruthlessly nervous, like rockabilly with a chip on its shoulder. Songwriting also became more personal and cryptic. Instead of using universal themes, songs often focused on artists' pitfalls and flaws, archly cloaked in coded phrases and pop hooks that were far from formulaic.

One of the most prolific singer-songwriters of the new-wave era was Elvis Costello. Edgy and enigmatic, Costello had a clever complexity that was reminiscent of Tin Pan Alley greats from the 1930s and '40s who favored arch phrases and cosmopolitan wit. Costello's first album, *My Aim Is True*, was released in 1977 and did well in the U.K. but only reached No. 32 on the *Billboard* chart. His follow-up, *This Year's Model*, went to No. 4 in the U.K. but only climbed to No. 30 in the United States. Costello decided to open his third album, *Armed Forces*, with

"Accidents Will Happen," a song that glibly attempted to explain his early infidelities.

Recorded with his band the Attractions, the catchy song only reached No. 101 on the *Billboard* pop chart. But the album's popularity on FM radio helped thrust *Armed Forces* into the No. 10 slot on the *Billboard* chart for two weeks in March 1979, establishing Costello as a formidable songwriting force.

Elvis Costello
(guitarist, singer, and songwriter)

I wrote "Accidents Will Happen" in early 1978, just prior to my U.S. tour that spring. For the lyrics, I couldn't bring myself to invent an honest narrative for the life I was living at the time. As a song, "Accidents" has a romantic sound, but it also has this moral dilemma baked in. I've had to make peace with my own failings during that time as a husband and as a father. All of those years ended in a painful divorce.

The song wasn't inspired by a romantic encounter with a female cab driver in Tucson, Arizona, as I wrote in my 2015 memoir. In the book, I needed to construct a single episode in print to stand in for the truth, which was much less funny and much more embarrassing. Back in '78, I was young and newly famous, and I didn't have any sense of responsibility. Temptation came along, and I gave in to it more than I should have. That's what this song is really about. I did indeed try to run away to Mexico, as I hinted in my memoir, but that was just used as a comic way of telling the story. In truth, the song was about several dalliances gone wrong, only to realize after that I shouldn't have done that.

Several songs influenced me during the writing of "Accidents." The drama and scale of the song was swayed by Burt Bacharach and Hal David's "Anyone Who Had a Heart." Though their song doesn't resemble "Accidents" in any way, I wanted their bell-tolling sensation in the chorus that the Attractions' Steve Nieve articulated well on keyboards. The other inspiration was a lyric line—"I don't want to hear it"— from Randy Newman's "I Don't Want to Hear It Anymore." Dusty Springfield recorded it on her 1969 *Dusty in Memphis* album. I used the line in my chorus: "Accidents will happen/We only hit and run/I don't want to hear it/'Cause I know what I've done."

When writing the lyrics, I decided to add a bit of disguise by shifting the perspective throughout the song, from first to third person—he, she, him, we, they. You hear this immediately in the song's opening verse: "Oh I just don't know where to begin/Though he says he'll wait forever/It's now or never/But she keeps him hanging on."

If I had used the first person—"I"—throughout, it would have sounded too confessional. The third person distracts from the confidence the singer is sharing with the listener and makes the drama more universal and less personal. That was probably self-defense on my part. When I wrote the lyrics, I couldn't quite live with what I was saying in the first person. I also was ashamed, as I was married at the time. The first verse continues on about a guy trying to seduce some girl who has a female friend with her. The guy is trying to lose the other girl: "The silly champion/She says she can't go home/Without a chaperone."

Cast in the third person, the lyrics also became more journalistic. I'm relaying something I've witnessed. That's particularly true in the second verse: "There's so many fish in the sea/That only rise up in the sweat and smoke like mercury/But they keep you hanging on/They say you're so young/Your mind is made up but your mouth is undone."

In reality, the lyrics describe a club scene, the way the eye casts around, and everybody is looking at each other. From my career perspective, I had gone from being an outsider and not very social to being aware of people looking at me because I was on a record cover. There were girls taking an interest because I was somebody they'd heard of. There was all of that conundrum in the verse.

I think in a weird way, there's a kind of innocence in there or inexperience. I see that now. Of course, all of these things I didn't see when I was writing it. I don't know where the melody came from specifically. I think somewhere in my mind was the song "Walk Away Renée." I was a huge Levi Stubbs fan, and I knew the 1967 version by the Four Tops. Then, when I first came to America on tour in '77, I found the Left

Banke's 1966 original in a secondhand record store. I remember thinking, "I wish I could write a melody that was that airborne."

Back in London in late June '78, the Attractions and I began rehearsing "Accidents" just outside of London in a church hall next to a school. A bunch of girls came out and recognized us from TV or a pop magazine. They wanted to know what we were doing there. They came into the studio with us and became our focus group as we rehearsed. We were thrilled, since we were playing for an age group we hoped was our audience. The girls just sat there, somewhat bewildered, listening for a little while. Then they said they had to go. I remember one of them turned around and said, "You look stupid in that jacket."

In August, we went into London's Eden Studios to record. We didn't have a written musical arrangement. Everything was worked out during rehearsals and memorized. We recorded with engineer Roger Béchirian and producer Nick Lowe. The first two words of the song, "Oh, I," were always going to be sung a cappella. My influence was the Beatles' "Girl" from *Rubber Soul*. I always liked how John Lennon sang the first two words a cappella—"Is there . . . " The music kicks in and John continues: ". . . anybody going to listen to my story/All about the girl who came to stay?"

There's no guitar on the basic track of "Accidents." It's just keyboards, bass, and drums. We could have used ringing guitars, but we had Steve play these cascading keyboard arpeggios instead. In the second half, you hear Steve on an early synthesizer, which adds mystique. We had been listening a lot to ABBA's use of layered keyboards. ABBA's Benny Andersson added a very grand, almost classical style piano on their songs. Steve did that for us. Once the music was recorded, I overdubbed my vocal. Then Nick and I did all the vocal harmonies. We double-tracked our voices to make the background vocals a little wider, for a gauze effect rather than a close harmony.

With distance, I hear the song the way other people do. If there's anything in it at all, I know that there is a true story behind it. But I didn't falsify the story in my memoir. I simply romanticized it to illustrate the dilemma and tragedy I found myself in. It's the same with the song. If you relayed the details of an important life event precisely in the lyrics, they'd be crushingly boring.

You'd also be thinking of your moments of indecision and prevarication. The moment where you wanted to escape but didn't and found yourself in some compromise. Anybody can make that kind of mistake. It's also not the end of the world. That's why the song is called "Accidents Will Happen." In life, there are happy accidents as well as tragic ones.

Charlie Daniels of the Charlie Daniels Band in Nashville in 1980.

41 : The Devil Went Down to Georgia
THE CHARLIE DANIELS BAND
Released: May 1979

Southern rock came to the attention of a national audience in the early 1970s when the Allman Brothers Band, the Marshall Tucker Band, Lynyrd Skynyrd, ZZ Top, Johnny Winter, Black Oak Arkansas, and others defied Southern stereotypes by appearing with long hair and playing the blues. Many young album buyers in the North and West looked at band photos on covers and gatefolds and said to themselves, "Hey, they look just like me and my friends." To many, the South was defined by images of Black people being beaten at lunch counters and fighting off police dogs and fire hoses and other images of racial violence. Southern rock bands changed that impression in the early 1970s and showed that the region, like other parts of the country, was more diverse than many young rock fans thought.

But even before these bands emerged, there was a first wave of Southern rock musicians in the 1960s. Among them was Charlie Daniels. As far back as 1964, he cowrote "It Hurts Me," recorded by Elvis Presley. He also played bass and guitar on three Bob Dylan albums in 1969 and '70—*Nashville Skyline*, *Self Portrait*, and *New Morning*. In May

1979, the Charlie Daniels Band went back to their rural roots with the release of "The Devil Went Down to Georgia."

The song, from Daniels's *Million Mile Reflections* album, was the band's biggest pop hit and tells the story of Johnny, a kid tempted to cut a deal with the Devil to win a fiddling contest but decides he can beat the Devil on his own. The song is notable for Mr. Daniels's searing fiddle and stomping hoedown feel. The single climbed to No. 1 on *Billboard*'s country chart and peaked at No. 3 on *Billboard*'s pop chart, winning a Grammy for Best Country Vocal Performance by a Duo or Group.

Charlie Daniels
(guitarist, fiddler, lead singer, and cowriter)

In late 1978, we were pretty far along recording songs for our tenth album, *Million Mile Reflections*. We were at Nashville's Woodland Sound Studios—a good choice by our new producer, John Boylan, given how loud the six of us played. Even more important, John brought along an ingenious Los Angeles engineer named Paul Grupp. He miked us in a way that cleanly captured all our energy and sound.

John was big on the details. In November '78, just as we finished recording most of the new album, John noticed we were missing a fiddle song. We traditionally included at least one on each album. So our road crew moved our gear out of Woodland and into rehearsal space at Nashville's Studio Instrument Rentals. Fiddle songs were important to me and to our fans. They were a bridge from hard rock to our bluegrass roots. People think I came to rock in the late 1960s, but the truth is I've been playing rock since it started in the mid-1950s.

I started on the fiddle even earlier. I never took fiddle lessons as a child. In fact, I never took lessons on anything. I learned to play by ear. To learn the basics, I listened to anybody who could play three more notes than me. In high school, one of the kids said my fiddle playing sounded as if someone had stepped on a cat. So you can imagine what my parents went through while I was learning.

Despite my rough start, I was stubborn. I'd listen to records by bluegrass greats like Tommy Jackson, Dale Potter, and Benny Martin and try to imitate them. Back then, there were fiddler conventions that really were talent contests. Prizes went to the best bands and players. The first two conventions I played in, I won. Heck, I was as surprised as anyone.

When I began my career as a professional fiddler and guitarist in North Carolina in the early 1950s, I played country music, like everyone else down there. Then one day in 1955, a steel guitar player came to Gulf, North Carolina, and asked to play with the band I was in. He didn't have an amplifier, so I took him down to our local music store and cosigned one for him. A few months later, he skipped town and left me with the amp and a bunch of payments. I had nothing to play on the amp. That's when I decided to buy a Gibson electric guitar and start a rock 'n' roll band. I quit playing fiddle.

For the next thirteen years, I played in clubs all over the country. We played cover versions of hits—everything from Marty Robbins to Little Richard. For a few years in the late 1960s, I was a studio musician and producer in Nashville. By 1971, I began recording my own songs and incorporating a little bit of everything. When we began playing hard rock, I added the fiddle back in. I had laid the fiddle down because it didn't fit into the dance music we were paid to play. Ain't no fiddle in James Brown [Daniels laughs]. When I added it back, rather than write music for the fiddle, I used it where we normally had the guitar stuff.

My style of fiddle playing worked perfectly there. When I drew my bow, I tended to press down hard on the strings. That made the fiddle sound grittier. Once I saw the audience response, I wrote more songs with the fiddle in mind. In late '78, after our gear was moved out of Woodland and into our rehearsal space, we all just started jamming to come up with a song. We didn't have a title yet.

The song's inspiration had nothing to do with Vassar Clements's "Lonesome Fiddle Blues," as some people have claimed. The music for "Devil" was all stuff we came up with totally on our own. Vassar is one of my favorite fiddle players, but there was no correlation between the two songs. As soon as we knew what we wanted to do with the music, we moved back to Woodland and recorded the basic instrumental track.

That's how we often worked. The band and I would write the music for a song without ever having a title. Right down to the arrangement, the instrumental breaks, and everything—without a single word. With the basic instrumental track set for "Devil," I went home and wrote the song's words. I like to write late at night or early in the morning, when everything is quiet and I can lay there relaxed.

I've always had the ability to remember the music we recorded as if it's on a tape loop in my head. The phrase "the devil went down to Georgia" just popped into my head for the opening line. I love the way "Georgia" sounds. It's so poetic. It wouldn't be the same if it were "The Devil Went Down to New Hampshire," "New York," or "Tennessee."

The inspiration for my lyric was Stephen Vincent Benét's 1925 poem, "The Mountain Whippoorwill." I first read the poem in high school and it stuck with me. It's about a boy who grows up in Georgia's mountains playing his fiddle as free as a whippoorwill's call. He winds up in a fiddle contest and wins by playing from the heart.

Fired up by Benét's poem, I wrote a lyric about a kid named Johnny who was a great fiddler. But I needed something more exciting than an ordinary contest. The stakes had to be higher. So I had the Devil go down to Georgia to challenge Johnny. If Johnny won, he'd get the Devil's gold fiddle. But if he lost, the Devil would get his soul. Johnny accepts the challenge.

After my verse explaining all of that, I wrote a chorus lyric: "Fire on the mountain, run boys run/The Devil's in the house of the rising sun/Chicken in the bread pan pickin' out dough/'Granny does your dog bite?' 'No, child, no.'" Those are old square-dance refrains. I used to play square dances when I started out in North Carolina.

In my lyric, Johnny wins the contest, and the Devil bows his head and puts his golden fiddle on the ground at Johnny's feet. The next day, I brought in my lyric sheet to Woodland and overdubbed my vocal with the band singing the harmony parts. Then I had to record the two fiddle solos.

For the Devil's solo, I played all kinds of junk to illustrate his soul-lessness. I made the fiddle solo all fury and noise, without melody or poetry. After I finished, Paul, our engineer, had me put on headphones and overdub six more fiddle tracks to illustrate the Devil's "band of demons." On one of those tracks, I used an eight-string fiddle, which is strung like a mandolin, with two strings in place of one.

Then Paul and John brought all seven tracks together as one cohesive solo. When they mixed it, the Devil's solo had a wider, angry sound. I was amazed. I had never worked like that before in the studio. We also overdubbed an evil, devilish hiss. That was keyboardist Joel "Taz" DiGregorio's idea. He ran a guitar pick across the strings of the studio's acoustic piano. Next, I recorded Johnny's fiddle solo, which is earthier and more melodic than the Devil's—more like those hoedowns in North Carolina.

After "Devil" was released and became a big hit, someone told me that classical violinist Itzhak Perlman was trying reach me. I said, "What?" When I called him back, Mr. Perlman said, "I just want you to know that my children and myself are fans of yours." He finished by saying, "I'd like to do something with you sometime." When I got off the phone, I stood there as if someone had hit me in the face with a cold mullet. I couldn't fathom how he knew who I was. And if he did, I just assumed he would have said to himself, "My gosh, listen to this guy. He's horrible."

We run in different circles, so we never got a chance to do anything together. But the fact that he even knew who I was shocked me to the bone. As far as I'm concerned, Mr. Perlman is the best fiddle player there is.

Nile Rodgers and Bernard Edwards of Chic in Manchester, England, in 1979.

42: Good Times
CHIC
Released: June 1979

As disco softened and became formulaic in the late 1970s, a new music genre emerged in New York that didn't require instruments. Initially beat-driven to support break-dancers, hip-hop evolved as socially conscious message music that depended on improvised, rhyming lyrics delivered by gifted rappers. Often boastful, taunting, and complex in the blues-shouter tradition, rap was highly original and launched a movement that has lasted more than forty years.

One band that bridged disco and funk in the late 1970s was Chic. A sophisticated studio band whose highly produced dance music was popular at discos and roller discos, Chic dominated the last years of the disco movement thanks to original songs and deft riffs by guitarist Nile Rodgers and bassist Bernard Edwards. Chic's hit songs included "Dance, Dance, Dance (Yowsah, Yowsah, Yowsah)" (1977), "Everybody Dance" (1977), "Le Freak" (1978), and "I Want Your Love" (1978).

Then came "Good Times" in 1979. When the Sugarhill Gang copied a significant portion of the song's instrumental in "Rapper's Delight," Chic threatened legal action. A settlement was reached that included giving Rodgers and Edwards cowriter credits. Since then, the bass line to "Good Times" has inspired dozens of hit songs, including Vaughan Mason & Crew's "Bounce, Rock, Skate, Roll" (1980), Queen's "Another One Bites the Dust" (1980), Beverley Knight's "Made It Back" (1999), and Daft Punk's "Give Life Back to Music" (2013). Chic's "Good Times" reached No. 1 on *Billboard*'s pop chart in August 1979.

Nile Rodgers
(Chic guitarist and cowriter)

Back in 1970, a friend called asking for a favor. He needed me to play guitar on his gig because he had just been offered a better-paying one. I took it. When I arrived at the Fair Tree Lounge in the Bronx, the band was already playing the Meters' "Cissy Strut." I plugged in my guitar, and the bassist and I melded as if we had been playing together forever. That's how I first met Bernard Edwards. Over the next two years, we became close friends and routinely got each other gigs. In 1972, we formed the Big Apple Band and played behind the vocal group New York City. Soon our band was performing beyond New York.

In 1976, while I was in London, a girl I knew took me to see her favorite band, Roxy Music. It was quite a revelation. The band combined art, fashion, and music, and was thinking about all three as one. They had five albums out then, and all had models on the cover. When I got back to the States, I called Bernard to tell him. I said we had to do the Black version. But our band needed a new name. When I showed Bernard the Roxy Music covers, he said, "What about Chic?" We began laughing. As a name, it sounded a little obvious and high-toned, but it was in line with our vision. So in 1977, Bernard and I started Chic and we soon had big hits with songs like "Dance, Dance, Dance" and "Le Freak."

By early '79, we were working on *Risqué*, our third album. We didn't have a classic hit single on there yet. I wanted to write one that would be a Chic tribute to Kool & the Gang's hit "Hollywood Swinging." My cousin, Robert "Spike" Mickens, had helped start the band in my uncle Victor's living room. Early one evening at my Manhattan apartment, I began jamming on my guitar and came up with a 1 to 4 chord progression for a new song. It went from an E-minor 7 to an E-minor 7 with a suspended 4th to an A7 with a suspended 4th to an A13.

I dashed off an arrangement for the rhythm section. All they'd have to do is play along with me. I folded it up and put it in my pocket. Then I met up with John Deacon, Queen's bassist, and we headed out to a party. John and I partied all night and never went home. In the morning, we went straight to the Power Station studio on West 53rd Street. John hung out in the control booth with sound engineer Bob Clearmountain. Bernard wasn't there yet, so I went into the studio and took the Chic band through the four-chord arrangement I had written.

When Bernard arrived and heard what I was doing with the groove, he said, "Damn, what is that?" Bernard picked up his bass and played along with me, but it was too close to what I was doing. I screamed at him over the drums—"Walk!" He said, "What?" I said, "Walk!" We had been trying to put a walking jazz bass line on a song since we had gotten together. So Bernard started playing a walking bass line, which is what you hear on the record.

All of our Chic albums were recorded methodically, using an assembly-line process. We always gave ourselves a week to record the instrumentals for an album. During the first two days we'd cut all the songs' rhythm tracks. We'd then spend the third and fourth days adding the sweetening—horns first and then the strings. On the remaining days, Bernard and I would have conceptual sessions. Albums were like films to us, so we'd use the time to visualize the big picture, what we called DHM—or "deep hidden meaning." We'd run the cassette tapes of our tracks and let our stream-of-consciousness ideas flow.

On "Good Times," we had started by recording the lengthy instrumental groove on the back end of the song. Once we had that locked down, we turned to the front. We were recording for dance clubs, so all of our songs started with the chorus. The energy had to be high and sustained from the start. For the opening of "Good Times," I had Rob Sabino play a piano glissando. Once we had it, Bob Clearmountain used a range of techniques to make it sound bigger. What you hear is a combination of the piano glissando, reverse echo to give it heft, and phasing to give the result a sweeping sound.

I then wrote the string parts for "Good Times" by taking cassettes home from each recording session and arranging at night. I had learned to write for strings while studying at the Manhattan School of Music. As a jazz fan, I often saw Gene Orloff's name on the backs of jazz albums with strings. Gene was a top violinist, arranger, and concertmaster.

I called him for the record, and he hired a small group of strings from the New York Philharmonic. Throughout the arrangement, I wrote "falloffs"—short, dramatic figures, with bows playing sharp descending notes. These added a wow factor. Bernard and I flipped when we heard the instrumental tracks. But we still needed words, so we took a break and went to the movies. We did this often to clear our heads and get in a storytelling groove.

I had rented a selection of black-and-white VHS tapes, including Al Jolson's *Go Into Your Dance* [1935]. It got us thinking about the Great Depression, and there was this instant connection to our prior hit singles. In 1979, the country was in a recession. There were gas lines and everything felt economically depressed. We wanted to emphasize the upbeat celebratory side—like the spirit in the songs "Happy Days Are Here Again" [1929] and Al Jolson's "About a Quarter to Nine," from the film I had rented.

We worked "Happy Days" into the lyric [Rodgers sings]: "Happy days are here again/The time is right for makin' friends/Let's get together, how 'bout a quarter to ten/Come tomorrow, let's all do it again." Instead of Jolson's "about a quarter to nine," we made it a quarter to ten. It sang better. "Good Times" had to sound sophisticated, not gutbucket funk.

After "Good Times" was released as a single at the end of June 1979, it was a huge hit. That summer, Debbie Harry and Chris Stein of Blondie told me about these events in New York called hip hops—kids taking something hip and hopping on it. Debbie asked if I wanted to check out one in Queens. We drove to this high school. Two turntables were set up and they only had "Good Times" playing. There was a line of MCs waiting to rap over the long instrumental section. It was so freaky and cool. A week or so later, Debbie took me to a hip hop at an empty storefront on Jerome Avenue in the Bronx. It was the same thing.

In late September, I was at Leviticus, a disco on Manhattan's West 33rd Street. I again heard "Good Times" playing with someone rapping over it, like at the hip hops. At first I thought it was the DJ, but when I looked up at the booth, it was empty. Listening to what was playing—the Sugarhill Gang's "Rapper's Delight"—I realized it wasn't our instrumental track. The two bass lines were off by a sixteenth note, but it was obviously our song. They also had taped the strings off our record and spliced them on to theirs.

The next day I bought a copy of "Rapper's Delight," but when I looked at the record, Bernard and I weren't even credited. So we filed suit. The resolution was that going forward, Bernard's name and mine would be added to the writing credit as 50 percent stakeholders in the song. Then we had to cope with the "disco sucks" movement, which had begun in July 1979 and intensified in the fall.

Chic became a target because we were so closely identified with the disco era. As a result, Chic never had another No. 1 hit after "Good Times." Instead, Bernard and I became producers, working on albums by Madonna, Sister Sledge, Diana Ross, Duran Duran, David Bowie, Grace Jones, Pharrell Williams, and many other artists.

For better or worse, Chic was a victim of the disco backlash. Which to us was kind of funny. Bernard and I didn't think of ourselves as disco guys. We were just young jazz instrumentalists who had set out to update Kool & the Gang.

Bon Scott, top, and Angus Young of AC/DC in 1979.

43: Highway to Hell
AC/DC
Released: July 1979

New wave's rise in the late 1970s caused hard rock to mellow. The growing popularity and commercial viability of new wave bands such as Blondie, Talking Heads, Elvis Costello and the Attractions, the Cars, the Human League, the Police, and the Smiths drew a stark contrast between art rock and the soundalike tedium of hard rock and metal. The more popular new wave became, the more insistent record labels and managers were that hard rock bands had to warm up their sound and image. Many agreed to transform.

Not AC/DC. Nudged by its record label in 1978 to go with the new-wave flow for its next album, the band decided they would play their music their way—with volume, a double guitar sound, and piercing, sandpapery lead vocals—or go down trying. So instead of altering their approach, they amped it up and recorded their fifth album, *Highway to Hell*, the last to feature lead singer Bon Scott, who died in 1980.

Though the single version of the album's title track only reached No. 47 on the *Billboard* pop chart, it was nominated for a Grammy. The song also helped the album stand out on FM radio and peak at No. 17 on the *Billboard* pop chart.

Angus Young
(AC/DC lead guitarist and cowriter)

In late 1978, we were in Miami to write songs, rehearse, and record our sixth studio album. Our record label, Atlantic, wanted a big radio hit. Up until then, our albums had been produced by Harry Vanda and George Young, one of my older brothers. Both were rockers who had been with Australia's Easybeats in the '60s and had done a fantastic job with us. But we hadn't had a strong radio album or single yet in America.

We did have a following, though. After our first U.S. tour in 1977, our albums began selling worldwide. To push us over the edge, Atlantic brought in a producer who wanted us to cover Brit-pop stuff. I wasn't happy. After a few weeks in Miami with nothing to show for it, we took a Friday off. Malcolm—my late brother and the band's cofounder—and I were frustrated. He said the two of us should spend Saturday in the empty rehearsal space.

The next day, we went in. I had an idea and played it on my Gibson SG guitar for Mal. It was a two-chord intro: "Dah-dah-dah, dah-dah-dah." Mal got on the drums and laid down a basic beat. I hummed to give him direction based on what I felt in my head. I have this strange thing, especially with drums, where I hear exactly how a song should sound. It's not musical. It's intuitive. Then I came up with something on guitar for the chorus. Mal liked it and asked if I had lyrics that I could sing over that hook piece. I told him to give me five minutes.

I went into the john and thought about it. I was singing away in there and got out my little notebook where I wrote things down. Looking through the pages, I saw a line I had written when we were touring in the States months earlier: "Highway to Hell." Back when I was a kid in Australia, my big thing was midnight drive-in theaters. At that hour, you were guaranteed films with Bela Lugosi or Vincent Price. The line sounded like one of those B-movie titles.

But the title wasn't a knock on America's highways or long drives between concert venues. We were young and healthy and having fun. Rather, the line was about the destination. In those days, we played everywhere, including places I don't think U.S. bands went. When we got there, our job was to raise hell.

I returned to the rehearsal space and told Mal I had it, that the line "highway to hell" was a surefire thing. I played and sang what I had. Mal smiled and said, "That's happening." Mal and I taped what we came up with, but we almost lost it. The engineer had taken the cassette home for safekeeping. When he returned the next day, his kid had unspooled a good bunch of tape.

Bon Scott, our lead vocalist at the time, took a yellow no. 2 pencil, put it through one of the cassette's two reel holes, and wound the tape back in. Then we made a dub for safety. Bon took a copy and wrote lyrics for two verses. If you gave him guidance, he'd work out words and how he'd sing them. The first verse is a mini description of our life on the road: "Living easy, living free/Season ticket on a one-way ride/ Asking nothing, leave me be/Taking everything in my stride."

As for the second verse, a lot of people think it's about a highway in Australia that Bon drove to get to a rock bar at the end. Not true. It was all about the roads to stages where we'd get up there and raise hell: "No stop signs, speed limit/Nobody's gonna slow me down/Like a wheel, gonna spin it/Nobody's gonna mess me around."

Mal and I also agreed we needed a new producer. So we called our manager, Michael Browning. He got Mutt Lange, who earlier that year had produced the Boomtown Rats' No. 1 U.K. hit "Rat Trap."

Cliff Williams
(AC/DC bassist)

We were all in our twenties then. On tour in '78, we were just happy to have a bus. When the five of us first came to America a year earlier, we drove around in a rented station wagon. On "Highway to Hell," I used a Fender Precision bass played through an Ampeg SVT. I shadowed what Mal was playing on guitar and what Phil was doing on drums.

Phil Rudd
(AC/DC drummer)

There was nothing dark about the song title. It meant we're all in it together, riding the same horse. We worked really hard on the road to get the crowd up. I remember there was a gig in the States where the crowd was flat. Bon said in that raspy voice: "What do you want, blood?"

Young

Starting out in Australia in '73, we were a hard-rocking bar band. We weren't going to change. We didn't want our music to go above people's heads. As my brother used to say, "We get 'em before Pink Floyd gets 'em." When Mutt came in to produce, he didn't want to change our style or music. He liked us the way we sounded live. He just wanted to give the results a bit of spit and polish with better sound and better lyrics from Bon. In January '79, we flew to London to record at Roundhouse Studios, where Mutt had been recording bands.

Rudd

Listening to Angus and Mal's rehearsal tape in the studio gave me a sense of what was needed. I just stepped into the beat and whomped away. Our sound is about the feel and how we accent songs. Mutt was a maniac, leaping around and doing splits to the music. That energized us. He also showed Malcolm and Angus a lot of respect, which helped. They can be prickly. They didn't like being told what to do. "Highway" was a turning point. When the song came out in July, the album was big and the band blossomed.

Young

When we toured the album, concert crowds grew, and they con-nected with the school uniform I wore onstage. That was my older sister Margaret's idea back in Australia, as a novelty to stand out. By putting on the school uniform, I slip into character. I know who I am.

Gary Numan in Toronto in 1980.

44: Cars
GARY NUMAN
Released: August 1979

Long exposed to electronica in modern classical and avant-garde art-rock music, European new-wave artists were quick to experiment with early synthesizers. Moog had entered the market in 1970 with a portable Minimoog ideal for recording and live performances. New synthesizer companies such as ARP in the United States and EMS in the U.K. quickly followed. At first, synthesizers were monophonic and tonal, allowing you to play just one note at a time. In 1978, Sequential Circuits began making the Prophet-5, a programmable polyphonic synthesizer that used microprocessors to store packaged sounds and use them at the flip of a switch. Early electronic music bands such as Kraftwerk and Ultravox were pioneers of the mechanized synthesizer sound.

In the U.K., Gary Numan was an avid experimenter. While producing, writing songs, and singing lead for Tubeway Army in 1978, Numan penned "Down in the Park" and "Are 'Friends' Electric?," the latter of which reached No. 1 in the U.K. at the start of 1979 along with its album, *Replicas*. By then, Numan was working on an album with a new backing band and a new synthesizer sound. His distinctive android singing voice and androgynous stage persona were ideal for the electronic music he was perfecting. To complete the album, Numan wrote "Cars," a song about a road rage incident that happened to him in 1977.

"Cars" peaked at No. 9 on the *Billboard* pop chart and No. 1 in the U.K. The song's success helped send his first solo album, *The Pleasure Principle*, to No. 16 on the *Billboard* chart and No. 1 in the U.K.

Gary Numan
(lead singer, keyboardist, producer, and songwriter)

In August 1978, I discovered the synthesizer quite by accident. I was at Spaceward Studios in Cambridge, England, to record the debut album of my band Tubeway Army. We had just signed with Beggars Banquet Records. At the time, I didn't like electronic music. During the 1970s, I was aware of Kraftwerk's albums and what Brian Eno was doing. I also thought the second side of David Bowie's *Low* album was pretty cool. But I didn't enjoy electronic music enough to change my interest in the guitar. I hadn't heard anything that made me think electronic music was anything more than slightly off the wall.

At Spaceward Studios, while my drummer and bass player unloaded their gear from the car, I went in to say hello to our engineer, Mike Kemp. In the control room, I told Mike what we planned to record over the next few days. As we spoke, I looked into the studio and saw a small keyboard with wires, switches, and dials. It was a Minimoog. Mike let me have a go. Lucky for me, whoever had used the Mini last left it programmed to a specific sound. I never would have been able to set it up otherwise.

When I switched on the Mini and pressed a key, a massive roar came out. I'd never heard anything like it. The sound blew me away. Rather than record a punk album on my guitar. I was going to use the Minimoog. All of the staccato punk things I had worked out would be played on the synthesizer. It would still sound basic and crude, just more electronic.

When I took the finished album tapes to Beggars Banquet, an argument began over whether they would release it. The label had its own vision of what they wanted me to be. They seemed to view me as a punk-pop crossover. I didn't agree. I told them that electronic music was the next big thing. Finally, the label executives said, "OK, we'll put out the album and see what happens."

Once *Tubeway Army* was released in November 1978, the album failed to chart. By then, I had another album's worth of songs that I had written on my guitar and home piano, which I taught myself to play. *Replicas*, our second Tubeway Army album, came out in April 1979 and went to No. 1 in the U.K. in mid-1979. By then, the plan was for me to record my third album under my own name.

Since childhood, I've had Asperger's syndrome. It's a developmental disorder that makes social interactions difficult. If you have it, you see the world differently than most people, and you react to it differently. I never felt like I fit in, and I had no idea why. I also tended to upset people but was never quite sure what I'd done to cause that. As a result, I became cautious and reserved. From a creative perspective, I've always viewed Asperger's as a bonus. It gave me an emotional cocoon that I could hide in, and it deflected everything. I was isolated and insulated.

The idea for "Cars" first came to me in my car in 1977. I was driving my Ford Cortina in West London when traffic came to a halt. For some reason, two men in the van ahead of me got out and walked toward my car. They looked angry. As they approached, I assumed I must have done something to them. Maybe I cut them off or they thought I was someone else. Because of my Asperger's, I had no clue.

When they reached my car, they shouted, banged on the hood, and tried to open my door. They even attempted to smash my window. To get away, I drove up onto the sidewalk. Fortunately, the pavement was quite wide. I drove along, with people leaping to one side. Finally, I reached a cross street and drove off. I never did find out what the fuss was about. I've always dreaded crowds, yet I'm noticeably relaxed in a car. I come down several notches in there. A locked car is a quiet, controlled environment. I feel safe.

A few months after the road rage incident, I was in London with a friend to buy an electric bass. I bought a Shergold Modulator and brought it home. My parents lived in the Ravensbury suburbs of London. I went into a side room where our piano stood. After I plugged in everything and put the bass on my lap, the first four notes I played sounded good.

They would become the opening notes to "Cars." As I played, the road rage incident was still fresh in my mind and how fortunate I had been that day. I began to think of the car as a tank for civilians. The lyrics came in a rush: "Here in my car/I feel safest of all/I can lock all my doors/It's the only way to live/In cars... Here in my car/Where the image breaks down/Will you visit me please/If I open my door/In cars."

From the moment I opened the bass's case to writing out the lyrics on a pad, the song took me roughly thirty minutes. It was the quickest song I ever wrote. I had no grooves in mind or anything. That would come later. I was just lucky that my fingers had chosen those four notes for the melody. In mid-1979, I decided to record "Cars" for *The Pleasure Principal*, my first solo album. We recorded a demo of the song at London's Free Range Studios using synthesizers, bass, and drums.

The song's humming beehive-y opening was created with an MXR Phase Pedal hooked up to a Polymoog synthesizer. I put the device on full speed. It gave the notes a tremolo effect. I played the song's melody line on the Minimoog. It was perfect for that low-end bass sound. I wanted something that had some bite to it. The high-frequency strings were created on the Polymoog using a "Vox Humana" setting.

Chris Payne
(keyboardist)

With the synthesizers and atmosphere that Gary created, the album's demos sounded futuristic. But "Cars" was different than the other material we had recorded. It was very upbeat. Gary played the Minimoog and I played the Polymoog. We just messed around and used our ears. As I recall, Gary and I both played bass lines on the Mini and the Poly. Then bassist Paul Gardiner overdubbed his bass part by following what we had done.

Cedric Sharpley was an amazing drummer. He wasn't about being mechanical or robotic. His rhythms were firm but warm. When it was time to record his vocal, Gary doubled-tracked his voice and blasted through the song. Once we had demos of "Cars" and the rest of the album, we went into London's Marcus Music AB Studios in May 1979 to record.

Numan

When I had overdubbed the Polymoog's strings on the demo, I began by holding just one note. That wasn't planned. That one long note and the few notes that followed weren't meant to be a countermelody. Actually, I was stuck and couldn't think of anything to play. Listening back to the demo later, I liked what I heard. So I re-created it at Marcus Music, where I modified the notes slightly and recorded it properly. I was just feeling my way along. I never had music lessons or vocal lessons. I didn't know how to read or write music.

Today, my wife, Gemma, and I live in the San Fernando Valley, north of Los Angeles. Where we live, you have to get in your car just to go to a local store. But I'm happy being in traffic, just not around crowds of people. The buildings are low in L.A., and I'm always aware of the big blue sky while driving, even when stuck in traffic. There's no sense of claustrophobia. My feeling safe in a car has never gone away.

Donna Summer in 1979.

45: On the Radio
DONNA SUMMER
Released: November 1979

Disco's bouncy dance beat began in Philadelphia at Atlantic Records in 1972 and Philadelphia International Records in '73 and then was tweaked in Miami in 1974 before becoming slick in Los Angeles and New York in 1975. In the second half of the 1970s, dance music became increasingly electronic. That's when European producers fond of American bubble-gum pop and electronic music began using a range of new synthesizers.

At the forefront of the Euro-disco movement was producer Giorgio Moroder. In Berlin in the early 1960s, Moroder began as a pop singer known as Giorgio. By the early 1970s, Moroder was living in Munich, a hotbed of electronic music, where he formed Musicland Studios. In 1974, he hired Donna Summer, an American singer-actress who had come to Europe years prior with the touring show of *Hair*. Moroder recorded her singing "Lady of the Night."

Starting in 1975, Moroder began to produce a series of high-concept sighs-and-synthesizer albums with Summer that became blockbuster hits. These included *Love to Love You Baby* (1975), *A Love Trilogy* (1976), *Four Seasons of Love* (1976), *I Remember Yesterday* (1977), *Once Upon a Time* (1977), and *Bad Girls* (1979). These albums were popular at discos and in the bedroom.

In 1979, Summer recorded the Moroder-produced "On the Radio" for *Foxes*, an American teen coming-of-age film due for release in early 1980. Moroder wrote the music and Summer wrote the lyrics. Before the movie came out, the dance song was added to Summer's double album *On the Radio: Greatest Hits Volumes I & II*. In late 1979, the single reached No. 5 on *Billboard*'s pop chart, while the double album went to No. 1. Summer died in 2012.

Giorgio Moroder
(producer and cowriter)

I first met Donna Summer in Munich in 1973. I was working on a demo with Pete Bellotte, my coproducer, and we needed three backup singers who didn't have a German accent. Donna came in to audition. She had been living and working in Germany since 1967. We could hear she was a pro and that she had a lot of gospel experience. Soon after the recording session, Pete and I signed her to my Oasis record label.

In the months that followed, Donna lived in Munich and did studio work for us. I urged her to come to me anytime she had an idea for a song. Months later, she had a song title idea: "Love to Love You Baby." I thought it was great. In early 1975, after we recorded the song, Casablanca Records in the U.S. wanted to distribute a longer, seventeen-minute version. So, we rerecorded it with a much more elaborate disco production. It became a huge hit single and album.

Donna returned to the U.S. in early 1976, and I soon moved to Beverly Hills to compose for the movies and produce her disco albums. In early 1979, I wrote a song for Donna on my piano at home in Beverly Hills. The melody was great but my first languages were Italian and German, and my English was limited. So I sang along using words that didn't make much sense. When I reached the chorus, I started singing "on the radio, oh-oh oh oh oh, on the radio" just to fill it out. I recorded a demo of the song with me singing and playing piano. Then I called Donna. She came over, and I played her the tape. She didn't like the song, so we shelved it.

Six months later, Neil Bogart of Casablanca urged me to see a rough cut of the film *Foxes*. After the screening, I was asked to write a ballad score and disco vocal for a dance scene. At home, I pulled out my "On the Radio" demo and called up Donna. She came over, and I played it for her again. I told her I was considering it for the movie and wanted her to write the lyrics. This time she loved it and took my demo tape with her.

Bruce Sudano
(husband of the late Donna Summer)

At home, Donna tried to write lyrics for Giorgio's music but soon handed me the cassette. She said I should write the lyrics. I insisted that she write them. She finally said, "OK, if I can find a way in." Donna told NPR in 2003 that she was at L.A.'s Rusk Sound Studios when she became stuck writing the lyrics. Then she spotted a Stephen Bishop album on the piano. After looking at the album's lyrics, she came up with "It must have fallen out of a hole in your old brown overcoat." She wrote the rest of the song's story from that one line.

Stephen Bishop
(recording artist)

Donna and I were good friends. I think the song that inspired her was "On and On," from my 1976 album *Careless*. The song is about a breakup.

Sudano

At Rusk, she typically set up mikes and ran tape as she came up with lyrics while singing in a stream of consciousness. What emerged was a narrative about a woman who regrets dumping her boyfriend: "Don't it kinda strike you sad/When you hear our song/Things are not the same/Since we broke up last June."

But it's more complicated than that. When she hears that her boyfriend just dedicated their song to her on the radio, she has a change of heart: "Yeah, you kinda made me feel proud/when I heard him say/You couldn't find the words to say it yourself."

Ultimately, the radio became a way for the two lovers to reunite: "If you think that love isn't found on the radio/Then tune right in, you may find the love you lost/'Cause now I'm sitting here with the man I sent away long ago."

Harold Faltermeyer
(arranger)

When Donna brought me the rough demo tape of her vocal, I used it to arrange and record the basic rhythm track at Westlake Studios. For the intro, I opened playing a ballad version of the song on a grand piano. The bass line you hear throughout is me playing a Model D Minimoog. The entire ballad intro was in the key of D. When the dance section kicks in, the key ascended to E minor to give it drama.

Keith Forsey
(drummer)

It was the disco era, so the drums in the dance section were four beats on the kick drum, hitting the snare on the second and fourth beats, and using sixteenth notes on the hi-hat cymbals.

Moroder

At Rusk, I recorded Donna's master vocal. After Donna finished, she overdubbed her vocal so we could have a fuller feel in places.

Faltermeyer

Once we had Donna's master vocal, I began to overdub. On the intro, I added a Fender Rhodes electric piano on top of my grand piano notes for color. Just before Donna started to sing, I added strings. This gave the intro a reflective mood. Then Keith came in with a drum fill just before Donna's second verse, playing a solid balladesque half-time style, anticipating the beat to come. My arrangement for the disco section came pretty fast. Two bars before Donna's first chorus, I started the brass section with a crescendo chord. "Stabs" by the brass section followed, accompanied by Keith's four-on-the-floor bass drum.

Gary Herbig
(saxophonist)

I used my Selmer Mark VI alto saxophone and an AKG-C414 mike, which allowed the engineer to capture my alto's edge. I recorded my solo in one take.

Faltermeyer

On the last four bars of Gary's solo, he came up with this terrific ascending arpeggio. I overdubbed the brass section mirroring what Gary had done so they were all playing in unison leading up to Donna's reentry vocal. At the end of the final chorus, Giorgio had the song end abruptly for dramatic impact. We put an echo on Donna's voice, so you hear "On the radio, radio, radio." We did this with a Lexicon digital delay unit.

Moroder

The version we used for the *Foxes* theme and the film's incidental music was an extended version of Donna's ballad portion backed by Harold's piano. The disco section was used for the movie's dance-party scene. But we realized immediately that the song had huge potential as a hit, so I decided to include it on the greatest hits album we were preparing. I simply renamed the album *On the Radio: Greatest Hits Volumes I & II*.

Sudano

When I hear "On the Radio" now, I feel as if Donna is in the room with me. We were very much in love in late 1979 but not yet married. That would come in July 1980. She loved "On the Radio." At the song's core, she said, was a big, beautiful Italian legato melody. One day, to illustrate, she sang an operatic version of the song in fake Italian. She was so good with languages that it sounded like real Italian to me.

At home in L.A., there was a lot going on after our daughters, Brooklyn and Amanda, were born in 1981 and '82. Donna never had her awards or gold records around the house. They were in a box. She said, "I don't want you and our kids living with Donna Summer. That's over here. At home, I'm Mommy and wife."

Joan Jett in New York in 1981.

46: Bad Reputation
JOAN JETT
Released: May 1980

The Los Angeles rock scene in the mid-1970s was largely a potent mix of punk, glam, and glitter. The New Hollywood film movement had attracted many young actors, cutting-edge costume designers, and makeup artists to the city hoping for a break. In West Hollywood, a gay community evolved and thrived along with a new edgier nightlife. Punk and new-wave rock clubs sprang up on the Sunset Strip, and the area became a seedy haven for runaways and avant-garde chic. For underage teens looking to get out of the house, there was Rodney Bingenheimer's English Disco, a no-alcohol outpost of Britain's glam-rock movement.

Joan Jett's family moved to West Covina near Los Angeles in 1971. A short time later, after Jett's parents divorced, she turned to rock and took up the guitar. On weekend nights, Jett's mother drove her to Rodney Bingenheimer's teen club. In 1976, Jett cofounded the Runaways, and the all-female glam band released four studio albums and a live one. When the band folded in 1979, Jett pursued a solo career and formed the Blackhearts.

In early 1980, Jett was furious. Ignored by record labels wary about the marketability of her bad-girl image, she cowrote and recorded a song protesting the double standard female rockers faced. When her debut solo album *Bad Reputation* came out in the United States in 1981, the title song helped the album reach No. 51 on the *Billboard* album chart. The song also paved the way for Jett's single "I Love Rock 'n' Roll," which reached No. 1 in 1982.

Joan Jett
(guitarist, lead vocalist, and cowriter)

My mother told me I could be anything I wanted, so I did a lot of dreaming as a kid. Even then, while living in Rockville, Maryland, I resented being told I couldn't do something 'cause I was a girl. In 1971, when I was thirteen, we moved to West Covina, an L.A. suburb. I asked my parents for an electric guitar for Christmas. They bought me a Sears Silvertone with an amp built in to the guitar case.

I took one guitar lesson. The guy tried to teach me "On Top of Old Smokey" and said, "Girls don't play rock 'n' roll." That really set me off. Instead of going back, I bought a learn-to-play-guitar book. I listened to 45s and taught myself to play. At the time, there were no female Rolling Stones, with that in-your-face energy and sexuality. At sixteen, in 1975, I coformed the Runaways, an all-girl hard-rock band. From the start, guys in the audience felt threatened.

As we toured, especially in Europe, guys in the audience wanted to make me pay. It was more than "you suck." They wanted to humiliate me. I pushed back. I thought, "You're gonna have to kill me to get me off this stage." By late '78, a film was planned based on the Runaways called *We're All Crazee Now*. I was obligated to write six new songs. Then the Runaways broke up, but the studio still wanted my songs. My manager at the time, Toby Mamis, put me together with Kenny Laguna, a songwriter-producer. We got along right away. We had only eight days to write the songs and record them.

Kenny Laguna
(producer and cowriter)

The first song Joan and I wrote was "You Don't Know What You Got." The rest were finished by our deadline. That's when I realized

Joan needed to be positioned as the leader of a band. The next step was to record an album that we could shop around to major labels. I had connections in London. We went over there in early '79 and recorded at the Who's Ramport Studios.

Jett

We had some of the album done by March '79, when we returned to the States. Then I formed the Blackhearts in L.A. and toured California and Europe that summer. The inspiration for the band's name wasn't really deep. A black heart was easy to draw on bathroom walls, like the Stones' lips-and-tongue logo.

Laguna

I tried to get major record labels interested. Joan was breaking glass ceilings, and I guess that was a problem for some executives. Being a punk rocker also was trouble in 1979. The new-wave thing was coming in. Joan did have a bad reputation, which might have been thought of as a rock 'n' roll reputation if she had been a guy. In June '79, Joan and I were walking in Manhattan when Joan complained about not being signed to a label yet. I told Joan: "It's because labels say you have this bad reputation." Joan shot back: "I don't give a damn about my bad reputation." We said, "Whoa, that's a great line for a song." On the spot, Joan added, "You're living in the past, it's a new generation." I said it would sound great with a fast, Ramones punk tempo. Back at my home in Long Beach, New York, Joan and I wrote half of the song's lyrics.

Jett

Kenny and I had a list of every word that rhymed with "reputation"—deviation, communication, station, and so forth. Then we worked to make sure the lines fit with the song's theme: "Never said I wanted to improve my station" and "I've never been afraid of any deviation." We were tapping into real life not making up a story. The line "A girl can do what she wants to do/And that's what I'm gonna do" was a page right out of my life.

Laguna

In London, the Who's Pete Townshend let us return to Ramport. He said, "Make your record and pay us back when you can." In the studio, we recorded the music for "Bad Reputation" first. On the rhythm track, Joan played all the guitar parts, including the solo. I said to Joan, "You know what would be great? 'People try to put us down/Talkin' 'bout my reputation.' Joan says, 'That's crazy, that's a Who song!'" All of the guys who worked for the Who were standing around in the control booth and said, "That's not a Who song."

Nobody there noticed that lyrically "Bad Reputation" was influenced by "My Generation." I knew, but I thought of it as an homage, with a fast Ramones tempo.

Jett

First I recorded the basic rhythm track. The song didn't need a crazy lead guitar so I just made some noise. I played a 1968 Gibson California Melody Maker that I had bought off of Eric Carmen of the Raspberries. Then I overdubbed four more guitar parts, one at a time, to give the sound some size. For those, I used my blonde Gibson Les Paul Deluxe and my white Gibson Melody Maker.

Laguna

At some point, producer Ritchie Cordell and I discovered a synthesizer in the studio, but we didn't know how to use it. Ritchie turned it on and pressed a button. It gave off this space-age sound. We taped it for the song's intro.

Jett

When Kenny and I first discussed background vocals for the "Oh no, not me" part, I told him I wanted the "no" and "me" to echo. So Kenny sang "no, no, no" and "me, me, me" as if there was an echo.

Laguna

We recorded the song in four or five takes. The third take became the master. When we finished the song and album, we came back to

New York and sent a copy to twenty-three labels. All of them turned us down. So we started Blackheart Records and put out the album ourselves. It was initially called *Joan Jett*. Then I made a distribution deal with some guys I knew in Europe and Scandinavia. That's how we paid back the Who. The album did incredibly well over there. I called Neil Bogart, who had started Casablanca Records. He offered to rerelease the album in the States on his Boardwalk label. Then, without telling us, he changed the album's title from *Joan Jett* to *Bad Reputation*.

Jett

The new album title was a problem for me. The song was my rage against how I had been unfairly labeled and treated as a female rocker. Using *Bad Reputation* on the cover turned it around, making me seem proud to be labeled that way. It forced me to deal with that sexist stuff all over again.

Laguna

We were pissed off for a long time. But in retrospect, it was a great move. The album put Joan on the map at just the right time.

Jett

The bad reputation thing was imposed on me. It was someone else's impression of what girls and women couldn't do but guys could. It was infuriating. But if a bad reputation meant being a hard worker, always being on time, rocking hard, and not being mean, then having that reputation was a badge of honor.

Blondie's Debbie Harry and Chris Stein at New York's Mediasound in 1979.

47: Rapture
BLONDIE
Released: January 1981

Downtown New York in the mid-1970s was an epicenter of innovative art. The gritty, aggressive feel of club music, design, and painting was fed by the city's deterioration during years of financial stress. By 1977 and '78, elite stars of Broadway, film, arena rock, and fashion could be found in Midtown Manhattan partying and dancing at Studio 54. But punk and new-wave artists, cutting-edge fashion designers and models, and transformative painters were at clubs and art openings in the East Village, the Bowery, Soho, and Tribeca. Among the recording artists who shuttled between the uptown and downtown scenes was Debbie Harry, lead singer of Blondie.

Blondie was formed in 1974 by Harry and guitarist Chris Stein. Four years later, Blondie released *Parallel Lines*, their third album. Produced by Mike Chapman, the album included their first hit single, "Heart of Glass," followed by "One Way or Another." Their next album wasn't as successful, but the band's recording of "Call Me," by Harry and Giorgio Moroder, produced for the 1980 film *American Gigolo*, went to No. 1 for six straight weeks on the *Billboard* pop chart.

That same year, Blondie released *Autoamerican*, which not only featured their cover of John Holt's rock-steady hit "The Tide Is High" but also "Rapture." Recorded in 1980, a year after the Sugarhill Gang put out "Rapper's Delight," "Rapture" was the first major hip-hop hit to use original music rather than simply sampling other artists' beats and bass lines. Cowritten by Harry and Stein, the single reached No. 1 on *Billboard*'s pop and dance charts.

Debbie Harry
(Blondie lead singer and cowriter)

In the late 1970s, the art, music, and fashion scenes overlapped in New York and became an underground movement. Downtown, everyone hung out together and was inspired by each other's work. It was a natural combination of creative elements. At the time, Chris [Stein] and I lived together on 17th Street. We were friends with artists like Jean-Michel Basquiat and "Fab 5 Freddy" Brathwaite.

Freddy was a graffiti artist, DJ, and filmmaker who knew MCs in the Bronx and Brooklyn. MCs were spinning records at events and developing a new form of music called rap. One night in 1978, Freddy took Chris and me and some others up to a Police Athletic League event in the Bronx. Chris and I had heard about the hip-hop scene up there, but we hadn't seen anything up close. We wanted to experience it live.

Chris Stein
(Blondie guitarist and cowriter)

Rap was an anomaly then. It hadn't become mainstream. In the Bronx, we went to this hall with a stage, a table, two turntables, and a mixer. MCs were rhyming lyrics to the beats of spinning records. People were waiting in line to take the mike and do the same. It was competitive and improvised. In the months that followed, we went to a few more of these, including one with Nile Rodgers of Chic.

One night at our apartment in late '79, Debbie and I were watching professional wrestling on TV. I turned to her and said, "We should do a rap song and call it 'Rapture.'" It was an obvious wordplay on rap. I began fooling around on my Stratocaster guitar and multitrack recorder. I came up with a bass line doubled with the guitar that was inspired by Bernard Edwards's bass line for Chic's "Good Times."

Harry

Sometimes, when you watch TV, you're in a stupor but your brain is doing something else. I thought what Chris had come up with that night was a good idea. We always bounced stuff off each other. That was our process. Chris took what we had seen up in the Bronx and Chic's music and a lot of other stuff and came up with something else.

Stein

After I had the music, we turned to the lyrics. Debbie wrote three verses, and I came up with the chorus.

Harry

The words I had for the verses were snippets of what we had seen in the Bronx:

"Toe to toe/Dancing very close/Body breathing/Almost comatose/Wall to wall/People hypnotized/And they're stepping lightly/Hang each night in Rapture."

Up in the Bronx, we had jammed into this room with a writhing mass of humanity, dancing and pressing against each other. My verses were just trying to capture that mood: "Back to back/Sacroiliac/Spineless movement/And a wild attack/Face to face/Sightless solitude/Finger popping/Twenty-four-hour shopping in Rapture."

Mike Chapman
(producer)

I had produced Blondie's previous two albums—*Parallel Lines* and *Eat to the Beat*. When we started recording "Rapture" at Western Recorders in L.A., Debbie sang me the verses and chorus. It was beautiful, and I knew we had a monster hit. I grabbed my guitar and played riffs that

Nile would have played. Blondie's Clem Burke gave us a disco beat, and Jimmy Destri, on keyboards, filled in the holes. Debbie sang along and the band's Nigel Harrison played bass.

Clem Burke
(Blondie drummer)

My beat was influenced by David Bowie's *Station to Station* album and a dance groove that Chic drummer Tony Thompson might have put on there. I also came up with the hand clapping we did on the second and fourth beats.

At some point, Jimmy discovered a set of tubular concert bells covered in the back of the studio. By adding the bells to "Rapture," Jimmy gave the song a haunting, ethereal feel.

Tom Scott
(saxophonist)

When I arrived in the studio to overdub my sax parts, Mike [Chapman] played the basic instrumental track and told me where he wanted the saxes to come in. I layered two tenor sax lines played in unison and recorded the third saxophone part a fourth down to create a harmony line.

Frank Infante
(Blondie guitarist)

I came in later in the recording process to overdub my rock guitar solo toward the end of the song. Mike had a B. C. Rich Mockingbird guitar that he wanted me to play. We were looking for a fluid tone that sounded more metallic than woody.

Chapman

After two or three days, we had a completed instrumental track that lasted six and a half minutes with Debbie singing the verses and chorus. But her lyrics covered only the first third of the song. When I asked her what she envisioned for the remaining two-thirds, she said,

"A rap." I had no idea what she was talking about. Rap was new then. Debbie played me a few references. I said, "Great. It's crunch time. Get out there and rap." She said, "Well, we have to write it first." I was jolted. I thought Debbie already had the lyrics down. We took a break and Debbie and Chris went off to the end of the console in the control room with a pen and pad.

Harry

There weren't any rules for writing a rap at that point. On the opening, I wanted to capture the feeling we experienced in the Bronx: "Fab 5 Freddy told me everybody's fly/DJ's spinnin' I said, 'My my'/Flash is fast, Flash is cool/François sais pas, Flashé no deux."

We worked in Freddy, Flash was Grandmaster Flash who we had met in the Bronx, and François was just a stand-in name for a French rap group that didn't quite get it. Chris wrote the rest of the rap.

Stein

The reference to the Man from Mars was my affinity for B movies and sci-fi comic book imagery: "Go out to the parking lot/And get in your car and drive real far/And you drive all night and then you see a light/And it comes right down and lands on the ground/And out comes the Man from Mars."

Chapman

Ten minutes later, Chris and Debbie were done. Debbie said she was ready to record. I couldn't believe it. She went into the studio, put on the headphones. I hit "play" so she could hear the music. She stood there with the sheet of paper and rapped. I recorded her twice. On the first one, she got most of it right. The second one was perfect. I was completely blown away. I had never worked with an artist like Debbie and haven't since. She was so blasé about it and never seemed to give the lyrics or the vocal a moment's thought. The final touch was the atmosphere I added to the track in the mix. That was done with reverb using my two EMT 250s. It added a hard top to her voice and Frank's guitar.

Stein

I was gratified that "Rapture" was accepted by the rap community. I think much of that had to do with Debbie sounding like herself and being natural in the video.

Harry

I wasn't trying to be Black or a Bronx rapper. It was an homage to what I saw and to a form that was exciting for us. We treated it with respect and handled it in our own way. Looking back, we probably should have worked on it a bit more. It's a little singsong-y and child-like. But the song has evolved in performance. I feel it differently now and try to be a little more ad-lib-y.

Infante

In the video's last scene, we're all coming up the stairs from Pravda, the old Russian bar-restaurant in Soho at 281 Lafayette Street. The director, Keith McMillan, told us to turn to the camera at the top of the stairs. It was late at night, and we were all wearing these dark glasses he gave us. They had red LED lights in the middle of the lenses blinking an SOS signal. Between the red lights and the camera's lights, I was doing everything possible not to fall down the stairs.

Journey, from left, Ross Valory, Steve Perry, Neal Schon, Jonathan Cain and Steve Smith in 1981.

48. Don't Stop Believin'

JOURNEY

Released: October 1981

A power ballad, by definition, is a moderately slow, heartfelt rock or soul song with a big emotional vocal buildup and walloping crescendo. The form has its roots in movie musical songs such as Judy Garland's "Over the Rainbow" from *The Wizard of Oz* and her "The Man That Got Away" from *A Star Is Born*. Power ballads in the 1960s and 1970s include Aretha Franklin's "I Never Loved a Man the Way I Love You" (1967), Eddie Holman's "Hey There Lonely Girl" (1969), the Hollies' "He Ain't Heavy, He's My Brother" (1969), David Bowie's "Life on Mars" (1971), Elton John's "Rocket Man" (1972), Harry Nilsson's "Without You" (1972), Patti Smith's "Because the Night" (1978), and Bruce Springsteen's "Streets of Fire" (1978).

One of the first midtempo rock power ballads of the 1980s was Journey's "Don't Stop Believin'." Journey was formed in San Francisco in 1973 as a progressive rock band by former members of Santana and the Steve Miller Band. Between 1974 and 1980, Journey released six studio albums and underwent several personnel shifts as well as stylistic changes. Steve Perry, Journey's best-known vocalist, joined the band in 1977. In 1981, Journey recorded *Escape*, their seventh studio album and biggest seller. All of the album's singles— "Don't Stop Believin'," "Who's Crying Now," "Still They Ride," and "Open Arms" reached the Top 20 on *Billboard*'s pop chart, with three landing in the Top 10.

Though "Don't Stop Believin'" only reached No. 9, it became a timeless underdog anthem at sports events and karaoke bars worldwide. The song also crossed over to television, winding up as Tony Soprano's jukebox choice in the final episode of *The Sopranos* in 2007 and on *Glee* two years later. The single helped *Escape* reach the top of *Billboard*'s album chart in September 1981.

Jonathan Cain
(Journey keyboardist, guitarist, and cowriter)

Everything was caving in on me in 1977. I had my own band in Los Angeles, but our record deal fell through. I also couldn't get to first base as a singer-songwriter, my dog got hit by a car and needed surgery, and my girlfriend, who lived with me and split the rent, left. I called my dad for a loan.

On the phone, I told him nothing was working out and that maybe I should just give up on music. He wouldn't hear of it. He said, "Your blessing is right around the corner. Sit tight. Don't be discouraged. And don't come home to Chicago. Don't stop believing." He also said he'd send me the money. While on the phone, I grabbed my song idea notebook to jot down his last phrase: "Don't stop believing." I wanted a reminder. Then I closed the notebook and forgot about it.

Motivated by my father's advice, I kept at it. In San Francisco in '79, I joined the Babys, an English band, and recorded on two of their albums. In '80, I came to the attention of Journey when their keyboard player, Gregg Rolie, decided to leave.

Neal Schon
(Journey lead guitarist and cowriter)

I first met Jonathan when the Babys opened for Journey on tour. We hung out. He was a super songwriter and played both piano and rhythm guitar. Our manager, Herbie Herbert, brought him to Gush Studios in Oakland, California, our rehearsal space, where we were working on new songs for our next album, *Escape*.

Cain

On the last day of rehearsal, we needed another song. Lead vocalist Steve Perry asked if I had one that was catchy. That evening, while leafing through the pages, I came across my father's phrase. I came up with chords for a chorus and a melody that I could imagine Steve singing: "Don't stop [believin']/Hold on to that feelin'."

Schon

As Jonathan played the chords, I started messing around with a countermelody bass line that didn't stay in one place. I also came up with chords for the pre-chorus and counterbass part for the section that would become: "Strangers, waitin'/Up and down the boulevard/Their shadows/Searchin' in the night." The most unique thing about the song was its structure. We had these verses followed by a guitar solo and then the chorus, which appears at the very end.

Cain

Steve thought the chords I had were great and said we should use them for the verses, too. He had me play rolling eighth notes on the piano while he scatted the melody to the first verse to see how it would sing. Then he did the same on the second and third verses. At this point, I wondered when we were going to use the chorus. Steve wanted to save it until the end of the song.

Schon

I played my guitar solo using the chorus's melody that Jonathan had written before Steve vocalized it. At first, Steve wasn't keen on it. He was concerned I was giving away the melody before he sang it. I said, "Why not let the guitar implant the chorus melody in the listener's mind just before you sing it? When your vocal follows, it will be a bigger deal." Steve agreed.

317

Cain

Steve thought it was brilliant. It broke all the rules of songwriting. Then drummer Steve Smith added this wild and crazy beat. After Steve Perry finished scatting all the parts so he had a form for the song, I took what he did home on a cassette tape. The next afternoon, I went to Steve Perry's house in Marin County to work on lyrics.

Neal's guitar solo the day before sounded like an oncoming train. It reminded me of Gladys Knight & the Pips' "Midnight Train to Georgia," a song I loved. I said to Steve, "What if we have a midnight train going somewhere?" I told Steve I was on the Sunset Strip a few nights earlier and saw crowds of young kids waiting to get into clubs. I said, "What if we have two kids heading west by train to see if they could make it in L.A. or Las Vegas?"

It would be a song about every dreamer. Some go to Vegas to "roll the dice," while others in L.A. "were born to sing the blues." The song said everyone has a shot. The girl in the song came from a "small town," but we had to have the "city boy" come from somewhere. Journey had just come off a live album with tracks recorded at Cobo Hall in Detroit.

Steve wanted the boy to be born in Detroit. But the line needed an extra word. To see what sang best, we tried East Detroit, West, and North, but they didn't sound comfortable. South Detroit did. Of course, we learned after the song came out that there is no South Detroit. South of Detroit is Windsor, Ontario.

At Fantasy Studios in Berkeley, California, "Don't Stop Believin'" was the last song we recorded for the album. The intro's basic track is two instruments—the piano and bass. Steve [Perry] had this idea of having me play the chorus on the grand piano over and over. We did a similar thing with bassist Ross Valory, who recorded Neal's bass idea. He decided to play it in the midrange, so it sounded more like a cello.

Schon

In the studio, I overdubbed my guitar solo using my 1978 Les Paul Pro. To make the solo sound fuller, I doubled it note for note. Doubling made it sound fractionally uneven and human. At the very end of the solo, I played a harmony line against my original solo line. I then over-dubbed my high note by stretching it way up.

Cain

Steve's vocal had a lot of the same characteristics as the bass line. It's kind of swinging and dancing around a steady rhythm. So we have this steady rhythm track with a syncopated bass and Steve's playful, conversational story being sung at full force. In 1982, my parents came to Chicago to see Journey perform at the Rosemont Horizon theater. I surprised them with the song. After, when I went up to see them, my father said, "Very clever, son. Good thing you didn't stop believing."

In 2007, I knew our song was going to be used on the last episode of *The Sopranos*, but I kept it a secret for an entire year. The night of the final episode, I got my kids to watch. They weren't sure why. They said, "Dad, people get run over and shot on this show."

I said, "Wait until the end." I made them sit through it. In the final minutes, Tony Soprano puts coins in a restaurant jukebox and selects "Don't Stop Believin'." My kids went wild.

Joe Jackson in New York in 1987.

49: Steppin' Out
JOE JACKSON
Released: August 1982

In the early 1980s, a sizable chunk of the baby boomer demographic had graduated from college and was hard at work at their first job. A new phase in life had begun for many who now had discretionary income to spend on clothes, vacations, restaurants, and dating. Music also was changing. MTV had arrived in August 1981, and British and American new-wave artists crafted songs that featured pop hooks, synthesizers, and programmed drum machines—all with an eye on the videos they'd tape for the music channel.

On the cutting edge of the new U.K. pop invasion was British singer-songwriter Joe Jackson. Signed to A&M Records in the late 1970s, the Joe Jackson Band released *Look Sharp!* in 1979. The critically acclaimed album was a cocktail of rock, jazz, and new-wave pop and featured one of Jackson's best-known hit singles, "Is She Really Going Out with Him?," which reached No. 21 on the *Billboard* pop chart. Later that year, Jackson released his next album, *I'm the Man*, which peaked at No. 22. After working as a producer in 1981, Jackson released *Night and Day* in 1982.

"Steppin' Out" was the album's third single and peaked at No. 6. The song's splashy, high-glamour electronic beat and pastiche of electronic keyboards felt in sync with the upwardly mobile times. Just hearing the song's fast-paced intro takes one back to the pace and energy of the early 1980s. The song was Jackson's highest-charting hit in the United States, lifting the album, *Night and Day*, to No. 4.

Joe Jackson
(multi-instrumentalist, vocalist, coproducer, and songwriter)

December 1980 was a turning point for me. My band had just finished touring when my drummer, Dave Houghton, gave notice. I considered replacing him and carrying on. Instead, I broke up the Joe Jackson Band and took a break from pop. I wanted to try something different. I set to work arranging some of my favorite late-1940s jump blues and jazz songs. It was a bit of fun—a vacation from my own music. My album *Jumpin' Jive* came out in June 1981, and I toured until September.

That fall, I left London to live in New York. A lot was going on there, musically. I took a sublet in the East Village and went out to jazz and Latin clubs. One of the first songs I wrote for my next album, *Night and Day*, was "Steppin' Out." I was inspired by the city. I envisioned playing a diverse range of keyboards. I wanted them to conjure up the dazzle of neon lights and the feel of cabbing from club to club to take it all in. It would be a romantic ballad set to a disco beat.

As soon as I finished the music, I wrote the words. I thought of a couple who had just fought and were making up. They were telling each other "Let's forget it and take advantage of the city. Let's just throw ourselves into the night." For me, lyrics have always been the hardest part of writing a song. I sweat over words. I don't want them to sound dumb and clumsy and meaningless. So I did a lot of editing.

Except for the first verse, I started each with a different pronoun—me, we, you. I used them as cues for the narratives that followed. The lyrics were intuitive and had nothing to do with my personal life. They just felt right. The first verse set the scene: "Now, the mist across the window hides the lines/But nothing hides the color of the lights that shine/Electricity so fine/Look and dry your eyes."

The next verse urged the other person to forget the argument: "We, so tired of all the darkness in our lives/With no more angry words to say can come alive/Get into a car and drive to the other side." The rest is about heading out and the anticipation of arriving at a club: "And in a yellow taxi you turn to me and smile/We'll be there in just a while, if you follow me." Even though the song is set in late '81, I viewed it as a trip through New York of another era. I imagined the couple going to CBGB or the Village Gate but dressed up, as if in a movie set in 1940s New York.

Once I had written the music and words, I recorded a low-tech demo at a Long Island studio. For the basic rhythm track, I played a Yamaha CP-70 electric piano set to sound like an acoustic piano. It would sustain a warm, human feel after I layered on the synthesizers. For the bass, I used a Prophet-5 synthesizer. I liked Kraftwerk's electronic dance beats and bass riffs on albums such as *Computer World*. I set the synth bass so it had a completely precise and metronomic sound. I also used a Boss DR-55 drum machine. I just pressed the "club beat" button.

After the basic rhythm track was done, I overdubbed a Hammond organ and a Fender Rhodes electric piano. I also added a glockenspiel, which sounds like bells. Then I asked A&M's David Kershenbaum if he'd come to the recording sessions for an extra set of ears. David had signed me to the label in London in 1979 and worked with me on two albums.

David Kershenbaum
(coproducer)

When I first met Joe in the late '70s, his style, dress, and music were very much in sync with the surfacing new-wave movement. As we worked on his first two albums, I quickly discovered he was a superb musician who could write top-notch songs. Even more interesting was how he absorbed influences and the way they turned up in his music. By 1981, I was head of A&R at A&M. When Joe played me his demo for "Steppin' Out" that year, it ran about four minutes and fifteen seconds. That was long for a single. The song also didn't have a chorus, which listeners sing and remember. I still loved the song.

Jackson

We recorded at Blue Rock Studio on Greene Street in New York's Soho neighborhood. Soho then was a gritty area of warehouses and loft rentals. At night, it was deserted. I recorded the album in January and February of 1982, late at night. Those hours suited me. The studio was small, which was perfect, since I didn't need much room to record all the instruments.

Kershenbaum

When we recorded "Steppin' Out," Joe played the acoustic grand piano that was there. He also had a Prophet-5 synthesizer. We programmed his driving bass line on a Minimoog.

Jackson

Next, I added a Yamaha CP-80 keyboard. Later, drummer Larry Tolfree overdubbed a real snare drum on top of the electronic one to give it an authentic sound. On the Fender Rhodes, I played notes to make the acoustic piano sound shinier. The Hammond organ added texture and depth to the background. The glockenspiel came last. I didn't use a guitar on the song or the album.

Kershenbaum

The acoustic piano was Joe's signature sound. It made "Steppin' Out" richer and orchestral. When Joe finished recording the music, it was airtight. He really nailed it. The next step was to record his lead vocal.

Jackson

I recorded my vocal while listening to the instrumental track on headphones. Then I overdubbed the vocal two more times to give it dimension and for a choir effect.

Kershenbaum

I used a British Calrec mike to record Joe's vocals. The mike captured a pure sound and didn't make Joe's voice sound processed or slick. I had bought it in England years earlier and brought it to the recording session. Once we finished, I mixed the tracks. That took a day or two. Back then, I traveled with a pair of six-inch-tall German Visonik David DIN 45 500 monitor speakers. They were small—the size of paperback books. But they had the depth and dimension of much larger speakers.

Monitor speakers in the studio could be deceptive, causing you to worry only about a song's individual components. I wanted all of it to stand out. As I mixed the tape, I put my head between the Davids to hear what the finer detail sounded like. I heard the song playing for the first time in the summer of '82, in a store in L.A. It was playing softly. I remember thinking how glad I was that I mixed it on those small speakers. Every aspect of the song came through.

Jackson

After the single and album came out, I went home to the U.K. for a while, but I wasn't happy. So I returned to live in New York and went on the road for a year. Today, I often rework my original arrangement of "Steppin' Out" before we go on tour. I'm currently performing the slow version that works really well in concert. I may try a Latin version next. I don't like New York much these days. It's as if the city and I had a hot love affair and now we're just friends. But we still have to see each other to remain friends. Today I live in Berlin. The New York I knew in late '81 and '82 is long gone.

Talking Heads, from left, David Byrne, Jerry Harrison, Tina Weymouth and Chris Frantz in 1983.

50: Burning Down the House

TALKING HEADS

Released: July 1983

Despite punk's waning influence, part of its ethos lingered in the early 1980s. Shout-singing and the frantic quality of the music remained of value to new-wave bands. Disco also lingered and seeped into the music. New, affordable, and portable synthesizers hit the market, and many new-wave artists were composing with eclectic sensibilities—combining funk rhythms and Caribbean percussion with dance beats, rock overtones, thicker bass lines, and layered, programmed synthesizer keyboards.

Formed in 1975, Talking Heads was one of the new-wave movement's leading art-rock bands in New York. Three of the band's members—David Byrne, Chris Frantz, and Tina Weymouth—had attended the Rhode Island School of Design before moving to New York and joining the punk scene. The fourth member, Jerry Harrison, who joined the band in 1977, had attended Harvard. Within two years of forming, the band abandoned punk's static sound and began releasing albums that owed more to the Downtown art-rock movement. First came *Talking Heads: 77*, featuring the song "Psycho Killer," which peaked at No. 97

on *Billboard*'s album chart. Next came three albums that reached Nos. 29, 21, and 19, respectively.

Their fifth studio album, *Speaking in Tongues*, was released in May 1983, and the single "Burning Down the House" hit No. 9 on the *Billboard* pop chart, while their album *Speaking in Tongues* climbed to No. 15. The song was the Talking Heads' only Top 10 single.

David Byrne
(Talking Heads guitarist, lead vocalist, and cowriter)

"Burning Down the House" wasn't a song about arson. When I wrote the lyrics in 1982, the title phrase was a metaphor for destroying something safe that entrapped you. I envisioned the song as an expression of liberation, to break free from whatever was holding you back. As for the rest of the lyrics, there are no hidden meanings. There's no logical, linear connection. They aren't telling a story or signifying anything. I simply combined aphorisms and non sequiturs that had an emotional connection.

Chris Frantz
(Talking Heads drummer and cowriter)

The music's inspiration began when Tina and I went to Madison Square Garden in February 1979 to see Parliament, Funkadelic, Bootsy Collins, and the Brides of Funkenstein. As the Talking Heads' bassist and drummer, Tina and I were responsible for the band's groove. We loved all kinds of music, especially funk. Before Parliament came on that night, the audience chanted things like "Goddamn, get off your ass and jam" and "Burn down the house! Burn down the house!" That last one stuck with me.

Tina Weymouth
(Talking Heads bassist and cowriter)

I first met Chris in a painting class in 1971 at the Rhode Island School of Design. By 1973, we were dating. I met David Byrne that fall. The two of them came over to my place to make a three-minute soundtrack for a friend's short film. That's when they decided to form a band—the Artistics. At college, Chris introduced me to all kinds of music and took me to concerts by James Brown, Sam & Dave, Lou Reed, even early reggae, in '71. We also listened to African artists Manu Dibango and Fela Kuti.

After Chris and I graduated in '74, we moved to New York. In November, I joined him and David as a novice bassist. We called our trio Talking Heads. A friend found the phrase in a *TV Guide*. It was a film term to describe a head-and-shoulders shot of someone who delivers content, not action. That was about right, since our name wouldn't conjure any music style, which was freeing. We signed an album deal with Sire Records on November 1, 1976. That day, Chris and I became engaged. We married in '77, in the middle of touring and making our first Talking Heads album. Jerry Harrison joined the group in January '77. He had been the pianist and guitarist in the disbanded Modern Lovers.

Frantz

Between 1977 and '80, Talking Heads released four moderately successful studio albums that landed progressively higher on Billboard's album chart. In late '81, David and Jerry came over to our loft in Long Island City, Queens, to jam and write songs for our upcoming fifth album—*Speaking in Tongues*.

Weymouth

At our earliest writing session, Chris and I started this funky groove. David added rhythm guitar and Jerry bounced between rhythm guitar and keyboards. To get their creative juices going, Chris shouted enthusiastically, "Burn down the house! Burn down the house!" as he played.

Byrne

Whenever we got something going that gelled at the loft, I'd press "record" on our cassette player. At first, all we had was a loping, galloping beat and a guitar part. The music was stripped down, fractured, and very Talking Heads, not a full-on funky groove.

Jerry Harrison
(Talking Heads guitarist, keyboardist, and cowriter)

After recording the music for our previous album, *Remain in Light*, it became clear that a lack of chord changes made it challenging to write interesting melodies. There were limitations to where a melody could go. So for "Burning Down the House," we wrote out a chord structure.

Frantz

Once we nailed down our instrumental parts, we went into Blank Tapes studio in Chelsea to record the song's basic rhythm track. Then Tina and David took a cassette back to David's loft in Soho to work on a vocal melody for the song.

Weymouth

I used a four-track recorder to capture takes of David singing what initially were experimental, nonsensical vocals. As he sang, I took notes and played back the bits that I thought had the most potential for a melody.

Byrne

At home, I also identified jams on the tapes that could be A, B, and C sections of the song. Then I identified the ones that sounded interesting and would fit together. There were no lyrics or vocals yet, just a possible song structure. Once the structure was set, the band rehearsed it over and over to get it down.

Frantz

With the basic instrumental tracks for "Burning Down the House" and for the album's other songs recorded, the four of us flew down to Compass Point Studios in the Bahamas in the fall of 1982 to overdub. At Compass, Jerry and David rented a little villa a short walk from the studio. Tina and I had an apartment behind the studio.

Weymouth

While working on "Burning Down the House," I abandoned my electric bass for a Prophet-5 synthesizer. The electric bass's warm, round tone sounded muddy under added layers of guitar and keyboards. The synthesizer gave my bass line a more pronounced attack to line up with Chris's drums. It was his beat that gave the song forward momentum.

Frantz

About three weeks into recording, Parliament-Funkadelic's George Clinton and Bernie Worrell came by on a break from a music convention on nearby Paradise Island. We had become friends by then. Tina was many months pregnant. George went straight to her and said, "Ain't that child born yet? I'm gonna scare that child out of you!" George put his head down to Tina's tummy and said, "Bwhooohoooohahaha!" Unknown to Tina at the time, she was already in labor. Our son Robin was born the next morning, on November 4. Bernie was supposed to record a keyboard solo but instead, keyboardist Wally Badarou overdubbed the suspenseful, eerie sounds in the introduction, the funky eight-bar solo in the middle, and the spooky whoo-whoo lines near the end, all on the Prophet-5 synthesizer.

Weymouth

Back in New York in May '83, "Burning Down the House" still needed words to match the phrasing of the song. I suggested David rent a car and drive around to clear his mind.

Byrne

A car is a good place to write lyrics. Driving occupies one part of your brain, freeing up the other. As I drove, I scatted the melody and recorded every random phrase I could think of that fit the song's groove. Many of the phrases may have been inspired by lines in P-Funk songs. I had seen them in concert at a club and had their albums. These lines were like little verbal Zen poems. They helped me come up with aphorisms like "Time for jumpin' overboard" and "Watch out, you might get what you're after." Later, I wrote down in my tiny handwriting as many phrases from the tape that fit on one sheet. Seeing all of them at a single glance let me identify the ones that worked together. There was no logical or linear connection between them.

Weymouth

David is a great rhythm guitarist, so the words he wrote were perfect for his stabbing, lurching guitar chords: "Hold tight/Wait till the party's over/Hold tight/We're in for nasty weather/There has got to be a way/Burning down the house."

"All wet/Hey you might need a raincoat/Shakedown/Dreams walking in broad daylight/365 degrees/Burning down the house."

As a lyricist, David favored rhythm over rhyme. His lyrics had a different meaning from the words alone. Which makes sense. Lyrics are a melodic poem, not prose.

Frantz

We all went into New York's Sigma Sound Studios to record David's lead vocal and our background vocals and to mix the album. I also brought in percussionist Steve Scales to overdub concert toms—four drums on a rack. They added a big, dramatic sound. You first hear them at the end of the intro leading into David's vocal.

Byrne

When I recorded my lead vocal at Sigma, I had a sheet with optional lyrics. I often did this when recording to try out other lines. It all depended on how I felt while singing. I'd suddenly sing an alternate line here or a different one there. I can't recall which ones were replaced, but the deciding factor was how lines sounded to me mid-song, not whether they made literal sense. That was the whole point of "Burning Down the House."

Huey Lewis of Huey Lewis and the News in 1982.

51: The Power of Love
HUEY LEWIS AND THE NEWS
Released: June 1985

Three years after its launch in 1981, MTV was the country's most influential music source and its most powerful trendsetter. New groups from Europe and Australia were overnight sensations in America after just one day of music video rotation. Brands of jeans, shampoo, deodorant, and sneakers also became hot fast by advertising on the music channel during prime viewing hours. In 1984, the channel's number of subscribers jumped 37 percent in just one year, to 25.4 million households.

Visually, Huey Lewis and the News were a break from the colorful flamboyance of the British new-romantic artists whose videos dominated on MTV. Instead of makeup, feathers, and florescent-colored jackets with wide shoulders, the San Francisco band looked like six working-class guys who spent their Sundays together watching football on TV. The band formed in 1979 and released their first eponymous album in 1980. Next came *Picture This* two years later with the hit "Do You Believe in Love." The album reached No. 13 on the *Billboard* chart. Then *Sports* was released in 1983 and climbed to No. 1, with five hit singles.

The follow-up song was "The Power of Love," which the band recorded in 1984 for the film *Back to the Future*. It went to No. 1 on *Billboard*'s pop chart in 1985 and was nominated for an Oscar. The song was released before the movie came out in July 1985, while the video began airing on MTV after the movie was in theaters. The video was No. 20 on MTV's Top 100 Videos of 1985.

Huey Lewis
(News lead vocalist and cowriter)

In 1984, my manager, Bob Brown, and I met with the team at Amblin Entertainment in Los Angeles. They told us about a film they were working on called *Back to the Future*. They talked about the kid who was the lead character, Marty McFly, and said that if he had a favorite band, it would be Huey Lewis and the News. They asked if I'd write and record a song for the movie. I didn't want to write a song called "Back to the Future." The News wasn't about looking backward. I also told them I had no idea how to write for a film.

"That's OK," they said. "We don't care what you call it. We just want a Huey Lewis and the News song." By then, the News had a bunch of strong hits, including "I Want a New Drug," "The Heart of Rock & Roll," and "If This Is It." I said, "Let me have a think and I'll send you the first new song we write." They said, "Fine." When I got back to my house in Santa Venetia, California, up in Marin County, I remembered the cassette demo our guitarist Chris Hayes had given me with his chord progression for a new song.

Chris Hayes
(News guitarist and cowriter)

Whenever I had a song idea for the News, I'd sit in the study of my home in Petaluma and first try to find a good series of guitar chords. I had an Akai MG1212 mixer/multitrack recorder combo unit. It didn't create good-sounding demos, but it was good enough to get a song down on tape. On this particular day, I created a verse by strumming a rhythm guitar part. I monkeyed around and pounded on it until I came up with something that sounded cool. The melody and the rest fell together pretty quickly.

My favorite part was the bridge. I'd always been a jazz player, so I came up with a series of jazz chords. I liked the bridge so much I used it twice in the song. For the demo, I recorded two versions backed by a drum machine. The first was an instrumental, and the second was the instrumental with me scatting so Huey would have the vocal melody. Then I dropped off the tape with Huey, who lived about twenty minutes away.

Lewis

Back home from L.A., I popped Chris's tape into my Walkman and went for a run through nearby China Camp State Park on San Pablo Bay. As I ran, I listened over and over to what Chris had recorded and thought back to the '70s, when I was in the rock band Clover. Back then, I wrote songs with guitarist Alex Call. I somehow remembered him doing something with the phrase "the power of love." Then I started thinking of my family. I had married a year earlier and we had our first child, Kelly, in '84. Austin was on the way. I was no longer a bachelor. The power of love keeps you home at night.

So I used that phrase as a springboard for the lyrics I came up with during my run listening to Chris's melody: "The power of love is a curious thing/Make one man weep, make another man sing/Change a heart to a little white dove/More than a feeling, that's the power of love."

The chorus needed to be catchy: "Don't need money, don't take fame/Don't need a credit card to ride this train/It's strong and it's sudden, and it's cruel sometimes/But it might just save your life/That's the power of love."

I loved Chris's bridge on the song. It had a completely different, relaxed feel, so it needed a sweeter lyric: "They say that all in love is fair/Yeah, but you don't care/But you know what to do/When it gets hold of you/And with a little help from above/You feel the power of love."

Holding the words in my head until I got home to a pad and pen wasn't hard. As a performer, I memorize lyrics for a living. Rock 'n' roll songs are like haikus. They have certain boundaries. At my house,

I wrote out what I'd been singing over and over. I also sang the lines to get the phrasing right. Then I called Alex to ask if he had written a song called "The Power of Love." Alex said, "No song, just the title." I asked if I could use his title, and I gave him a percentage of the song. Once my lyrics were set, I overdubbed a demo vocal on top of Chris's instrumental and sent the tape down to Bob Zemeckis, the director of *Back to the Future*, for his reaction.

Johnny Colla
(News guitarist, saxophonist, and cowriter)

Bob Zemeckis felt the song wasn't peppy enough. So Huey suggested that Chris get together with me, since I was the designated "finishing" guy on News songs. I had an eight-track recorder in my extra bedroom in Novato, California. Chris came over and we listened to the demo tape, which had him playing these cool guitar chords in his riff. First, I suggested we rearrange the song and drop one of the two bridges. Mostly, though, I suggested we open the song with sharp synthesizer "stabs" on the 4 and 1 beats. I wanted them to sound like a horn section to give the song the wow effect Bob Zemeckis had wanted.

The stabs would become a signature part of the song and sort of a call-and-response to Huey's lead vocal. On the revised demo Chris and I recorded at my place, I played the stabs on a Roland D-50 synthesizer. I used them on the chorus, too, and added them on top of Chris's catchy guitar riff to widen the sound and give the song some urgency. Chris put a scat vocal on the demo—a lot of do-do do-do's and wop-bop bah-dah's—as a melody guide. We passed the tape with two versions to Huey. He added his vocal to the instrumental version and sent the cassette down to Bob. We got the green light to record the song for the film. We went into the studio at the end of May '85.

Lewis

The News rehearsed and then started to record the basic rhythm track at Fantasy Studios in Berkeley, California. We all pitched in on producing. Next, we recorded the overdubs at the Record Plant in Sausalito. Keyboardist Sean Hopper used a Roland Jupiter-8 synthesizer with a horns setting for the keyboard stabs, which drove the song along with the beat.

Hayes

I improvised my guitar solo. I used a '57 Fender Stratocaster Sunburst played through a Marshall amp. I was alone in the studio, so I cranked up the speaker. We rolled tape and I blew on the solo until we had a take Huey liked. Then I punched it up by adding that four-bar riff at the end. My inspiration was a Chuck Berry blues-scale guitar riff. But I wanted more of a Stevie Ray Vaughan bluesy feel rather than a rock 'n' roll sound.

Lewis

Once we had the instrumental parts recorded, I added my lead vocal on top in Studio C at the Record Plant. My lyrics pretty much stayed the same, but the phrasing and melody were fine-tuned. We mixed "The Power of Love" at New York's Hit Factory with Bob Clearmountain, who by then had mixed Bruce Springsteen's "Born in the U.S.A.," David Bowie's "Let's Dance," the Stones' song "Miss You," and so many other great recordings. Three additional mixes of the song were released after the single came out—a movie soundtrack version, the version in the movie video, and a twelve-inch dance version mixed by John "Jellybean" Benitez.

I never told my kids they were the song's inspiration. They're in their thirties now, so I don't think it would be too powerful a sentiment for them: "Uh, OK, Dad, thanks." But I probably should tell them.

John Mellencamp in Edmonton, Alberta, in 1985.

52: Small Town
JOHN MELLENCAMP
Released: November 1985

In the first three years of the Reagan administration, the government's farm program was grossly mismanaged. Swept up in free market euphoria, the administration halted the government payments to farmers to get them to stop growing crops. As a result, farm surpluses skyrocketed and prices fell, forcing the administration to bail out agriculture by taking 82 million acres out of production through government payments. Small family farms were hurt most by the move. As surplus production spiked, land values climbed and many farmers used their land as collateral to borrow and buy more land and equipment. When the surplus was suddenly halted through government subsidies, prices tumbled and left small farms struggling to meet their debt payments. Many were sold off to larger, corporate-owned farms that could weather the economic turmoil.

Singer-songwriter John Mellencamp was from a small town—Seymour, Indiana. When "Small Town" was released on Mellencamp's *Scarecrow* album in September 1985, the song and video were warm reminders of small-town life. While many young people had left small towns for jobs in major cities in the early 1980s, they felt anonymous there and longed for the close-knit community and friends they left behind. Mellencamp's song and video rekindled a yearning for those virtues. The song also was a stark reminder of how main streets and small farms suffered in the '80s when big business moved in with malls and greater farming efficiencies and altered the character, fabric, and economies of small towns.

"Small Town" reached No. 6 on *Billboard*'s pop chart in early 1986, while *Scarecrow*, the album on which the song appeared, climbed to No. 2 on the *Billboard* album chart.

John Mellencamp
(singer and songwriter)

I was twelve when I first picked up a guitar. My family lived in Seymour, Indiana, and my older brother, Joe, was the star of our high school musicals. In one show, he had to play some guitar chords, so my parents bought him a nylon-stringed model. Once the musical was over, the guitar sat in the corner of the bedroom we shared. One day I grabbed it. My goal was to learn enough chords to play along with the songs I was listening to on the radio.

I never had a guitar lesson in my life, and I still can't read music. But I had a good ear and a feel for it. By 1965, I was in a soul band that played parties, dances, and proms at local high schools and colleges. I was fourteen and the youngest kid in the seven-member band. The older musicians all knew American soul music inside and out. We covered obscure pop and soul songs by big stars, which exposed me to music that most people never get to hear.

I also learned about racism. Three of us in the band were white and the rest of the guys were Black. The audience loved us when we played. Offstage, the Black guys in the band were often met with racial slurs. I was offended by their treatment, not to mention that my great-great-grandmother was Black.

After junior college, I went to New York hoping to get a record deal or be admitted to the Art Students League to study painting. One day I dropped off a demo tape at MainMan, the management agency. They signed me and cut a deal with MCA Records. They also insisted I use "Cougar" as my middle name. I hated that. I had no songwriting skills, so my first few albums were awful. They featured mostly cover songs and early originals. Critics didn't like me, so I knew that to make it, I'd have to write songs and convince radio to play them.

I began carrying a pad around and jotting down lyrics for songs I was working on. By 1984, I had written and recorded quite a few Top 10 hits, including "Jack & Diane," "Hurts So Good," "Crumblin' Down," and "Pink Houses." At the time, my label, Mercury, wanted an album from me every eighteen months. In between, I was on tour, so I was rarely home. But one day in '84 when I was home in Bloomington, Indiana, Vicky, my wife then, called me down to our basement laundry room. When I got there, a big box was on our clothes-folding counter.

I'm the worst speller in the world, so Vicky had ordered an electric typewriter with a built-in spell-check system. I tried to make sense of the owner's manual, but I couldn't figure it out. I'd put a sheet of paper in and start typing, but the words I misspelled weren't being corrected. Frustrated, I said to myself, "Well, I guess I'm just a stupid hillbilly. What do I know? I was born in a small town." After a few more minutes with the typewriter, I began to realize it didn't automatically correct misspelled words. It had a dictionary on a computer chip that identified words you misspelled and beeped to alert you to fix them.

I had my Gibson Dove, so I put the guitar strap around my neck and started playing and typing lyrics: "Well, I was born in a small town/And I live in a small town." But as I typed my lyrics fast, the machine let off beeps to flag spelling errors: "All my friends—beep!— are so—beep!— small town/My parents—beep!—live in the same small—beep!—town." Upstairs, I could hear Vicky and my aunt Tootes, who was also our nanny, dying of laughter over the beeps. Finally I yelled out: "Would you guys shut up!"

Once the song started to come, it came fast. I'd sing some lyrics, type them out and play the music on my guitar. Then I'd start at the beginning to sing what I had to inspire additional lines. Eventually I went upstairs, looked at Vicky and Aunt Tootes, and said, "I'm glad you guys think this is so funny." They started laughing again. I said, "OK, now laugh at this." I played them "Small Town," and they went dead quiet. When you play what you've done for a family member and you get that kind of reaction, you know you have something.

For some time, my friends and I had been talking about how small towns and the people who lived there were getting screwed economically as America changed. Soon I realized that "Small Town" was more than a phrase of my own frustration. It was a song that felt as though Woody Guthrie had sent it to me from the grave.

That's when I started working with Willie Nelson and Neil Young to organize Farm Aid. We planned a concert like Live Aid for September '85 in Champaign, Illinois. The purpose was to raise money for families trying to save their family farms from the clutches of corporate farms. The next step for "Small Town" was to arrange and rehearse it with my band. I had a second house a few minutes outside of Bloomington that operated as an office. I had added a recording studio and turned the two-car garage into rehearsal space.

In April '85, the band and I went into the garage to arrange "Small Town." I sat there like a conductor with the band facing me. There was no writing out parts. We had it all in our heads. I just told my drummer, Kenny Aronoff, what I wanted—a pounding beat—and we went to work. The "Small Town" opener was already written in my chord progressions. That was the hook line. The trick going forward was to keep the song simple and not overarrange it. But we had a problem.

The song was verse-chorus, verse-chorus, verse-chorus. It felt too same-same-y. The solution was to add a bridge. In the garage, I took one of the verses—"No, I cannot forget where it is that I come from/I cannot forget the people who love me/Yeah, I can be myself here in this small town/And people let me be just what I want to be"—and rewrote the melody to make it a bridge. This broke up the song's sameness.

The arrangement of "Small Town" was critical. I knew there was no way I could walk out onstage and sing and play it acoustically. The audience would tune out. We also had to arrange the song in a higher key. Back then, I tended to write songs in a lower key and transpose them to a higher key later so I could belt them out onstage. When the arrangement was done, we walked into the studio inside the house to record. I only sang on the record. I didn't play. Larry Crane was on lead guitar. We finished the song in just two or three takes.

The only instrument we added later was John Cascella's organ. For some reason, he wasn't there when we had recorded. He came in later that night, and we overdubbed his part. At first, John kept trying to play complex stuff that didn't work. Finally, I said, "John, damn it, stop noodling around. Just go to those big chords." What he played next was beautiful.

Before the single was released in November '85, we needed something for MTV. In Bloomington and Seymour, we took out ads asking for snapshots and home movies. We were flooded with material. The video was good, but I always felt it ruined the song. Songs are meant for dreaming, and the video gave my lyrics a literal context. The focus was all on me instead of letting listeners imagine their own small-town experiences. I never used that typewriter again. Now I have no idea where it is—probably gathering dust in one of my storage units.

Keith Richards in New York in 1988.

53 : Take It So Hard
KEITH RICHARDS
Released: October 1988

Successful rock bands have always been more than just the sum of their musical parts. They're organic units comprised of sensitive artists who spend their creative lives together traveling, performing, writing, singing, playing, and arguing. It's a marriage built on trust, support, and fidelity. As artists, they're emotional, which is why rifts and feuds become grist for the media and part of a band's lore. Every great band has had its share of battles and betrayals, including the Beatles, the Beach Boys, Led Zeppelin, Cream, Yes, and Crosby, Stills, Nash & Young, to name a few. Together since 1963, the Rolling Stones were no exception.

The mid-1980s were a particularly brittle period for the band. In 1983, when the Stones signed with Columbia Records, their contract allowed band members to take on individual projects. Mick Jagger began working on a solo album and released *She's the Boss* in 1985. Feeling betrayed by Jagger's move, Keith Richards quickly realized that as stable as the Rolling Stones seemed, he needed to diversify to play it safe. The last thing he wanted, if the Stones collapsed, was to wind up an iterant guitarist moving from band to band. When Jagger released his second solo album, Richards decided it was time to work on his own solo project.

Recorded in 1987 with Richards's X-Pensive Winos backing band and released in 1988, *Talk Is Cheap* expressed Richards's longtime passion for early rock 'n' roll. The album's first single was "Take It So Hard," cowritten by Richards and drummer Steve Jordan. The song received heavy radio airplay, reaching No. 3 on *Billboard*'s mainstream rock songs chart.

Keith Richards
(X-Pensive Winos guitarist, lead vocalist, and cowriter)

In 1987, I was a little apprehensive about recording a solo album. I'd been with the Rolling Stones for twenty-five years. One band was enough. But it was time, you know? Back then, there was a hiatus with the Stones. Mick had recorded his first solo album [*She's the Boss*] in '84. Then the Stones recorded *Dirty Work* in '85. But Mick didn't want to tour for the album, which was frustrating. In '87, Mick released his second solo album [*Primitive Cool*] and announced he was going to tour for that one.

To be honest, I felt lost for a bit. Then, very quickly, I realized this was an opportunity to spread my wings. I first met drummer Steve Jordan in '86 when we recorded on Aretha Franklin's cover version of "Jumpin' Jack Flash" for the movie of the same name. Next, Steve and I assembled a band for *Hail! Hail! Rock 'n' Roll*, a concert documentary that I coproduced celebrating Chuck Berry, who had turned sixty. After *Hail! Hail!*, Steve and I spent more time together knocking around song ideas. Soon [bassist and drummer] Charley Drayton began hanging out. Somehow guitarist Waddy Wachtel turned up, and the next thing I knew keyboard player Ivan Neville, Aaron Neville's son, was there.

Suddenly, the band we wound up calling the X-Pensive Winos was together. We had one of those things you can't deny, man. I mean, it was time to do an album—*Talk Is Cheap*. "Take It So Hard" was the first song Steve and I worked on. It had been on my back burner for a while, since maybe '84, when I first came up with the guitar riff. After I found myself playing the riff a few times in the months that followed, I realized this thing was sticking around. Once a riff does that to you, you've got to follow it to the bitter end.

So the music came first on that song. But that's usually how it is with me. It's the riff, and then I try to find the English that floats with the music. I only had the lyric phrase "You shouldn't take it so hard." Back then, I was working on the song for the Stones. But it wasn't finished in time for *Dirty Work* in '85. So I held it for another time. Two years later, Steve and I were in New York in a rehearsal space jamming for *Talk Is Cheap*. It was just the two of us. We quickly found we could write songs together. At some point, I brought up the riff to "Take It So Hard."

Steve Jordan
(X-Pensive Winos drummer, bassist, and cowriter)

We were at Studio 900 in Manhattan. Keith had some lyric ideas for the song, so we did this thing called "vowel movements." You sing just vowel sounds to the melody—ahh, eee, eye, oh, and you—in any order you wish. No consonants. The vowels become words if the words fit the music you're playing. We already had Keith's "You shouldn't take it so hard" for the chorus, but the verses were up for grabs.

Richards

As I played the riff, it led to things. Steve on drums brought out some rhythm that was so bizarre. I had to try and follow it, and that led us to other things. I mean, songwriting is a very confusing thing. You write verses and verses, and you have to make them alliterative to follow the rhythm.

Jordan

When we finished that night, I took a tape of Keith singing using the vowel technique. Weeks later, Keith and I were down in Antigua. I deciphered the words on the tape and produced two pages of lyrics. They told a good, poetic story. When I brought the pages to Keith, he read through them. Then he took a pen and scratched out every other line. It was a fascinating process. Keith edited the lyrics based on the music he heard in his head so the words would sing better. To his ear, the lyrics on paper were too busy. By removing the lines, the story still made sense, but now the song had space to breathe.

Richards

The lyrics we settled on were a mixture of Steve and me bouncing things back and forth: "Take a look around you, tell me, what do you see?/People with little bits/Try, tryin' to smile/Most of what you've gotten is free."

The meaning behind the chorus—"You shouldn't take it so hard"—is what I call the MacGuffin. It's the unexplained mystery line that pulls the song forward.

Quite possibly, in retrospect, I was thinking about Mick when I first began working on the song in '84. But while writing with Steve, I wasn't thinking about Mick at all. The words we came up with had nothing to do with him. Steve and I wanted to make the lyrics universal. We said, "Let's get out of any sort of personal thing." Which makes it a better song. Once we had the first verse and the general feel down, the rest of it flowed.

Jordan

Up at Le Studio in Quebec in the summer of '87, "Take It So Hard" was the first song the band recorded. But the music was tricky. It's not blocky, like most songs. It's uneven in places. Only Keith and I knew the song's form. So I switched instruments with Charley Drayton. I played bass and Charley played drums. We did this because I knew where the groove was supposed to be. It's right off Keith's riff. The bass helped define the song's structure.

Richards

Steve moving to the bass and Charley moving to the drums changed everything. After the switcheroo, we recorded the song in one take. I remember there was a great congratulations on the faces of the band. We all looked at each other like, "Wow, I think we have it." Everyone agreed. "Hey, baby, that was it."

Jordan

Keith used his 1954 blonde Fender Blackguard Telecaster, the guitar he calls Micawber. The bass I used was Charley's. It was a 1962 Fender Precision.

Richards

To get that grizzly sound on my riff, we recorded my guitar coming through a small amp turned up very loud. Waddy took the guitar solo. I'm just playing rhythm. The biggest challenge for me was figuring out how to sing as a front man. With the Stones all those years, I just stepped up to the mike to sing a few words and stepped back. I wasn't singing for an extended period.

On "Take It So Hard" and the others, I had to look at these songs and think, "I'm gonna have to sing these all the way through. How do I handle it?" I learned a lot about being a lead singer. I appreciated Mick's job a whole lot more. Being a guitar player, you don't have to think about a lot of areas. But being the front man is like nonstop, man. It's constant. That's what I had to learn. I came to appreciate the pressure of being a front man. With Mick, the man knows his stuff.

Jordan

On the song's intro, if you listen carefully, you can hear a faint buzzing sound. That was the snare drum shimmering to Keith's guitar chords. We left the buzzing in. It added dimension.

Richards

Back in '85, when the Stones were recording *Dirty Work*, I never got around to playing the unfinished "Take It So Hard" for Mick. Mick could have had that song. After "Take It So Hard" was released as a single in '88, Mick never sang it. But I know he liked the song and album very much. He said to me, "Hey, with the Winos, how did you do this or that?"

351

I still like "Take It So Hard." I wonder what it might have sounded like if the Stones had recorded it. But I don't think anyone could have topped what the Winos did, not even the Stones. It was one of those moments where everything fell into place, you know? The Stones will never play "Take It So Hard" in concert or any of the others songs the Winos did. I would never mix the two groups. No, no. I wouldn't want to confuse the issue. The Stones are the Stones.

Neil Tennant and Chris Lowe of Pet Shop Boys in London in 1990.

54: Being Boring
PET SHOP BOYS
Released: November 1990

Electronic dance music, or EDM, evolved in the U.K. and Germany in the late 1980s, beginning as acid house music. The form featured drawn-out, beat-driven songs created by DJs mixing electronic instruments, sound effects, and drum machines. At first, EDM was featured in clubs, at raves in abandoned warehouses and at unoccupied houses, and at EDM festivals. The music's hard-driving, hypnotic quality was particularly favored by drug-induced crowds seeking seamless dance music. To maximize its impact, EDM was amplified with special gear to crystalize the highs, break out the midrange, and reinforce the bass and beat. EDM often was supplemented by light shows and other special effects that provided visuals to accompany and supercharge the pulsating music, delivering a full audio-visual experience.

Pet Shop Boys, an English duo that formed in London in 1981 at the start of Britain's synth-pop movement, were early developers of EDM. Influenced by "Souvenir" by Orchestral Manoeuvres in the Dark and "Bedsitter" by Soft Cell, Neil Tennant and Chris Lowe both loved electronic music and disco. They named themselves after friends who worked at a London pet shop. The duo's first big hit was "West

End Girls" in 1984, a No. 1 hit on the *Billboard* pop and dance charts in 1986. The song's success was helped in great measure by the duo's MTV video for the song. They continued to have high-charting *Billboard* hits in the 1980s.

"Being Boring" was released in November 1990 but never became a *Billboard* pop hit in the United States. Yet the song had a significant influence on EDM's evolution and today is considered a cult classic.

Neil Tennant
(Pet Shop Boys lead singer and cowriter)

My feelings weren't hurt. After [Pet Shop Boys cofounder] Chris Lowe and I performed at Tokyo's Budokan arena in early July 1989, a Japanese reviewer wrote, "The Pet Shop Boys are often accused of being boring." Reading the words "being boring" took me back to the early '70s and an invitation I had received to the Great Urban Dionysia Party in Newcastle, England, where I grew up. On the invitation was this adaptation of a 1922 Zelda Fitzgerald quote about a flapper friend who had died: "She was never bored because she was never boring."

Thinking of that invitation and quotation reminded me of a close friend who had died of AIDS four months earlier at age thirty-four. He had organized the party. I immediately began writing lyrics to a song I called "Being Boring." The theme was an autobiographical look back. My chorus came first [Tennant sings]: "'Cause we were never being boring/We had too much time to find for ourselves/And we were never being boring/We dressed up and fought, then thought: 'Make amends'/And we were never holding back or worried that/ Time would come to an end."

The first verse was about those parties and the invitation that included the Fitzgerald "being boring" quote: "From someone's wife, a famous writer/In the nineteen-twenties/When you're young you find inspiration/In anyone who's ever gone/And opened up a closing door. She said we were never feeling bored."

The second verse was about me leaving Newcastle on the train to study in London in the early 1970s. I assumed I was never going to move back: "I'd bolted through a closing door/And I would never find myself feeling bored."

By then, Chris and I had sufficient lyrics to begin writing the music in a little studio in Glasgow, Scotland, in 1989. The third verse would have to wait until we were closer to recording the song. Chris and I shared a love for songs by Stock, Aitken, and Waterman. They're a British songwriting team who wrote dozens of huge pop dance hits, including Rick Astley's "Never Gonna Give You Up" and Kylie Minogue's "I Should Be So Lucky."

When Chris and I wrote the music for our chorus, we used a variation of a satisfying chord sequence that Stock, Aitken, and Waterman sometimes used: A-flat, B-flat, G-minor 7, and C minor. We also wanted our song to be elegiac rather than a rave, but we didn't want it to be a dirge. Elegiac music is more effecting when it's uplifting, creating a happy-sad feeling. In May 1990, we began to record our album *Behaviour*. While we were at producer Harold Faltermeyer's Red Deer Studios in Munich, Germany, I wrote the last verse on a typewriter.

The lyrics were about traveling the world in the 1980s as the Pet Shop Boys, recording in Munich, and wishing my friend who had died was still here: "I never dreamt that I would get to be/The creature that I always meant to be/But I thought in spite of dreams/You'd be sitting somewhere here with me." The demo Chris and I created on our synthesizer was made during our rehearsal for the recording session. We brought the reel to Harold at his studio.

Harold Faltermeyer
(producer-arranger)

When Neil and Chris first came to me, they played me their demo. Neil was a great lyricist and Chris was highly informed about trends in cutting-edge music and fashion. They said, "We want your expertise in analog synthesizers."

To the average ear, a synthesizer is a synthesizer, especially back in the late '80s. But there are big differences. Early digital synthesizers had a simple sequence of operations to emulate various sounds. Analog synthesizers give you much more flexibility to experiment and customize what you want. The results also are much warmer. From their demo, I could hear where the musical journey was supposed to go.

The first thing I did with Chris was create a drum loop. We used classic analog drum machines—the Roland TR-909, the TR-808, and TB-303, which had great bass sounds. I started the song with a strings pad that opened faint and grew louder. I created this sound with a Roland Jupiter-8 analog synthesizer. I added five or six layers for a dense texture.

Tennant

I recorded my vocal on two separate tracks, an octave apart—one high and the other low. Then we took those and double-tracked them so there were four voices of me singing. I recorded my vocal softly, to give it a confidential and dreamy quality. My four tracks became a single ethereal vocal.

Faltermeyer

For the song's melody played throughout the song, we used a combination of FM synthesizers—an Oberheim OB-8 and a Jupiter-8. Then we used the Synclavier II for the harp glissando. It was a sample from a real harp. We used it in several places to signify when the song's narrative was moving backward or forward in time.

Tennant

Chris and I returned to London. At Sarm West Studios, we mixed the song and overdubbed additional elements with engineer and producer Julian Mendelsohn. Dominic Clarke, our programmer, began fooling around with a plastic tube he found in the studio. When he swung it around over his head, the wind caught the plastic lip and made a hypnotic sound that went up a fifth as he swung it faster.

Julian recorded Dominic swinging the tube and we added the results to the song's synth intro. I've always loved the guitar's wah-wah effect made famous on Isaac Hayes's "Theme From 'Shaft.'" At Sarm, Julian brought in J. J. Belle to play guitar. His "wakka-wakka" sound made the song sort of funky.

Faltermeyer

Once we had J. J. Belle's wah-wah guitar recorded, I took one of his licks and used it playing backward just after the drum loop starts during the introduction. I kept Belle's reverse lick subliminal throughout the song for coloration. My goal was to integrate a weird sound that was difficult for the listener to identify. Throughout the song, I had the synth texture grow denser behind each verse so that by the third verse, it feels like a full orchestra.

Tennant

When we finished the album, we asked Bruce Weber to direct our "Being Boring" video. When we met with Bruce, Chris and I had some complicated idea about Latin gangs in New York filmed in black-and-white. To his credit, Bruce listened patiently. Then he came up with the idea of renting an empty house in the Hamptons on New York's Long Island and filming fashion models preparing for a party and the party itself. It sounded about right to us.

Blimey, our record company hated the video. I don't think they were pleased with the naked guy in the beginning or flashes of the couple having sex at the end. But the video looked very beautiful and had the right atmosphere for the song. "Being Boring" was never a huge hit but somehow people either discovered the song or heard about it from people who already loved it.

During our tour in 1991, when we performed in L.A., our manager told us Axl Rose, the lead singer of Guns N' Roses, was outside our dressing room. When Axl came in, he said, "Man, why didn't you play 'Boring'?" We thought it was too gentle a song to be performed live in the States. We obviously were wrong.

I think Christopher Dowell, my friend who died of AIDS, would have liked the song and the video. Christopher was larger than life. He studied drama and dominated our group of friends. He was gay, but we weren't lovers. I admired his self-confidence. "Being Boring" is a memorial to him and our friendship.

Sheryl Crow in 1995.

55: If It Makes You Happy

SHERYL CROW

Released: September 1996

Pop's first surge of female singer-songwriters emerged in the late 1960s and 1970s as part of the folk-rock movement. Then they were largely eclipsed by disco in the 1970s and the synth-pop movement of the 1980s. By the 1990s, a new generation of female singer-songwriters surfaced who wrote about their lives, loves, anxieties, and struggles. These included Aimee Mann, Mary J. Blige, Fiona Apple, Mariah Carey, Liz Phair, Alanis Morissette, Lisa Loeb, Jewel, Anita Baker, and Tori Amos. In addition to having hits, they set the stage for the many female pop megastars who would follow in the 2000s, including Amy Winehouse, Lady Gaga, Beyoncé, Taylor Swift, Alicia Keys, Adele, Billie Eilish, Avril Lavigne, Christina Aguilera, Katy Perry, and Ashanti.

Among the female singer-songwriter standouts who came up in the 1990s was Sheryl Crow. A music major in college, she took a job after graduation teaching music at a Missouri elementary school. On the weekends, she sang in bands. After being introduced to a local musician and producer, she sang ad jingles he wrote, which provided her with a decent income. Between 1987 and 1989, Crow was a background singer on Michael Jackson "Bad" tour, performing with him on "I Just Can't

Stop Loving You." The experience led to a series of top opportunities as a background singer with headline artists. Her first attempt at a solo album was shelved, but songs she wrote were recorded by Tina Turner, Celine Dion, and Wynonna Judd. Her second shot at an album, *Tuesday Night Music Club*, in 1993, was a success, with the hit singles "All I Wanna Do" and "Strong Enough" in 1994, yielding three Grammys.

Crow produced her next, eponymous album herself and cowrote many of the songs with guitarist Jeff Trott, including "If It Makes You Happy." Released in September 1996, the single peaked at No. 10 on the *Billboard* pop chart. Crow won a Grammy for Best Female Rock Vocal Performance for "If It Makes You Happy"; her album, *Sheryl Crow*, won another.

Sheryl Crow
(lead singer, guitarist, keyboardist, producer, and cowriter)

After my first solo album, *Tuesday Night Music Club*, came out in 1993, I went out on tour, won three Grammys, and stayed out for another two years. By the time I came off the road in early '96, I was worn out and overexposed. After a brief rest, I went down to New Orleans to get away from the music industry and to record my second album. I had recorded my first album with great players. But when it became successful, many seemed disgruntled that I had a successful record. They wanted the album to be a band success. So for my second album, I dropped the band and reached out to guitarist-songwriter Jeff Trott. I had a lot to prove.

Jeff Trott
(guitarist and cowriter)

I started writing "If It Makes You Happy" right after my girlfriend, Quinn, broke up with me in January 1994—just hours before the Los Angeles earthquake. Starting the song was part of the grieving process for me. I needed to figure out how such a perfect, loving relationship could go so wrong. Over the next two years, the song became a work in progress.

I'm originally from San Francisco, but back in the early 1990s, I lived in L.A. I first met Quinn in November in 1992 while touring. We met backstage after a concert and it was love at first sight. We went out that night and spent several hours talking about music and life. I felt I had met a kindred spirit. We corresponded while I was on the road, and Quinn ended up coming down to L.A. Eventually she moved in with me in 1993.

By January 1994, Quinn was done with L.A. She couldn't take the traffic or the city's impersonal character. On the afternoon of January 16, she packed up and left. As her little car drove off to Roseville, California, near Sacramento, I was heartbroken. That evening, I opened a crappy one-dollar bottle of sherry and sat at my little Baldwin Acrosonic piano. I thought about what I could have done to keep her in L.A. I turned on my little cassette player-recorder and started ranting.

I played and sang about my past years in bands and how Quinn and I liked to go to thrift shops and find weird things. Then I went to bed. At about 4:30 a.m., a 6.7 magnitude earthquake rattled the apartment and plaster came dumping down on me. When the shaking stopped, I couldn't get out of my apartment. Fortunately, Sabrina, my next-door neighbor, was dating a big guy who took a crowbar and pried open the door. The next day, I was told to evacuate the building.

I was allowed back into the apartment briefly a few days later. I grabbed my music tapes, including the one with "If It Makes You Happy." The following month, I moved back to L.A. By then, I had the song's first verse and chorus: "I've been a long, long way from here/Put on a poncho and played for mosquitoes/And drank 'til I was thirsty again/ We went searching through thrift-store jungles/Found Geronimo's rifle/ Elvis's shampoo/And Benny Goodman's corset and pen."

The poncho was a reference to the garb we wore in the band Wire Train when we toured with Bob Dylan in 1990. The mosquitos referred to us playing on the banks of the Columbia River and me inhaling the insects while I sang.

The thrift-shop lines were about my treasure hunts with Quinn. The chorus was also about her: "If it makes you happy/It can't be that bad/ If it makes you happy/Then why the hell are you so sad?"

Then I wrote part of the second verse: "Get down, real low down/ You listen to Coltrane, derail your own train/Well, who hasn't been there before?"

363

In 1995, I got a gig playing with Pete Droge, and we opened for Sheryl Crow. During that tour, Sheryl watched our show every night. She wanted me to join her backing band after the tour and thought we should write together.

I first played "If It Makes You Happy" for Sheryl at a cabin near Yosemite National Park owned by drummer Brian MacLeod from Wire Train. He had all this recording gear up there.

Crow

When Jeff played me what he had for "If It Makes You Happy," I heard it as a message to quit complaining. By that point, my first album had sold 6 million copies, so how could everything be so bad?

Trott

Sheryl loved the song and wrote the second half of the second verse: "I come 'round, around the hard way/Bring your comics in bed/Scrape the mold off the bread/and serve you French toast again/OK, I still get stoned/I'm not the kind of girl you'd take home."

We worked on the third verse together: "We've been far, far away from here/I put on a poncho and played for mosquitoes/And everywhere in between/Well, OK, we get along/So what if right now everything's wrong?"

Sheryl also changed "Elvis's shampoo" to "Marilyn's shampoo," which sang better. She decided to record her album at Kingsway Studio in New Orleans. I was going to join her a week after she started. But she called me in L.A. right away and asked me to come down as soon as I could.

Crow

When Jeff arrived, I strapped on a bass and he took out his guitar. A buddy played drums. "If It Makes You Happy" was the first song we worked on. Singing the song was my way of shaking the blues. It was a cathartic moment. I said to myself, "If everything you want as a song-writer is to make money, you've made a lot of money so why are you so sad?" The truth is I wasn't sad at all. I just felt I needed to deliver the message: For everyone who feels bitter about something in their lives, there are so many things to be happy about. Jeff being a really positive person tapped into that experience.

Trott

Once we had the basic rhythm track for "If It Makes You Happy," Sheryl overdubbed some Wurlitzer electric piano, and I worked on the intro. We felt the song was really special and big. I played two electric guitars—a 1973 Gibson Les Paul run through a Vox AC30. I overdubbed the same lines on a 1963 Telecaster running through a Fender Concert amp.

For the solo on the bridge, I used a Silvertone electric baritone guitar, which has a sound that's between a bass and guitar. The baritone guitar also plays the lead. Then I overdubbed a mandolin playing pizzicato eighth notes. When Sheryl added her lead vocal, she gave the song musical sensibility. Her phrasing was beautiful, and her octave vocal jump on the title line in the chorus made the song a hit.

When the album came out in September 1996, we went out on a yearlong tour. After the tour, I bought a house in Portland, Oregon. I moved up there in 1998. Then I reached out to Quinn, who was still living in Roseville. It had been a while, and I asked her if she'd heard "If It Makes You Happy." She said she had. I told her that she was the inspiration. The phone line went quiet. Then she said, "Oh wow."

Today, Quinn and I live in Nashville, Tennessee. We married in 2005 and have two sons—Adrian and Griffin. Tennessee doesn't have California-size earthquakes, but we had six minor ones in July. We didn't feel anything shake at home. We worry more about hurricanes and tornadoes.

Crow

Jeff and I didn't change his original instrumental feel. His guitar tone was emblematic of the imagery that came naturally to me. His influences were in line with what I had grown up listening to—Keith Richards and a lot of English rock. Jeff was my alter ego. "If It Makes You Happy" was me saying, "Hey, I've been a musician since I was three.

I grew up with parents who were musicians. I played seven different instruments. I know how to front a band." When I hear the record now, it puts me back in that place of being the underdog. But it's empowering and tells me to be as great as I can be. I hear that in the angst of the song and the angst of my delivery.

ACKNOWLEDGMENTS

A heartfelt thanks to my *Wall Street Journal* editors over the years for giving me the opportunity to write the "Anatomy of a Song" column and to preserve music history in the words of the artists who composed and recorded the hits in this book.

I am especially grateful for the friendship and guidance of Glen Hartley, my literary agent, and Lynn Chu, my literary attorney.

I would like to thank my preeminent editor, Grove Atlantic CEO and publisher Morgan Entrekin, who shares my love of popular culture and curiosity about how musicians craft and record hit songs. I'm also grateful to assistant editor Sara Vitale for her editorial input, sound judgment, and organizational skills.

Also thanks to the Grove Atlantic team: Judy Hottensen, associate publisher; Deb Seager, publicity director; John Mark Boling, publicist; Julia Berner-Tobin, managing editor; Sal Destro, production director; Gretchen Mergenthaler, art director; Zoe Harris, publisher's assistant; Paula Cooper Hughes, copy editor; and Caroline Trefler, proofreader.

Gratitude and love for my wife, Alyse, whose support and understanding allowed me to devote long hours to the column and this book.

Hugs for my fabulous daughter, Olivia, and son-in-law, Dylan, who share my adoration of music and respect for musicians. And a special thanks to my brother, Danny, who became a musician, and his wife, Bonnie.

And finally, I'm indebted to the artists in this book who made time for me and opened their hearts and shared their recollections. I'm especially appreciative of the managers and publicists and label executives who understood the towering importance of the column and urged artists to make themselves available.